CHALLENGING
CAPITAL PUNISHMENT

SAGE CRIMINAL JUSTICE SYSTEM ANNUALS

Volumes in the **Sage Criminal Justice System Annuals** focus on and develop topics and themes that are important to the study of criminal justice. Each edited volume combines multiple perspectives to provide an interdisciplinary approach that is useful to students, researchers, and policymakers.

Recent Books in This Series:

Volume 24. **Sage** Criminal Justice System Annuals

CHALLENGING CAPITAL PUNISHMENT
Legal and Social Science Approaches

Kenneth C. Haas
James A. Inciardi
Editors

SAGE PUBLICATIONS
The International Professional Publishers
Newbury Park   London   New Delhi

For information address:

SAGE Publications, Inc.
2111 West Hillcrest Drive
Newbury Park, California 91320

SAGE Publications Ltd.
28 Banner Street
London EC1Y 8QE
England

SAGE Publications India Pvt. Ltd.
M-32 Market
Greater Kailash I
New Delhi 110 048 India

Printed in the United States of America

Library of Congress Cataloging-in-Publication Data

Challenging capital punishment : legal and social science approachs /
    edited by Kenneth C. Haas and James A. Inciardi.
        p. cm. — (Sage criminal justice systems annual ; v. 24)
        Bibliography: p.
        Includes index.
        ISBN 0-8039-2909-9 : ISBN 0-8039-2910-2 (pbk.)
        1. Capital punishment—United States. I. Haas, Kenneth C.
II. Inciardi, James A.   III. Series: Sage criminal justice systems
annuals ; v. 24.
    KF9227.C2C46 1988   87-32092
    364.6'6'0973—dc19   CIP

SECOND PRINTING, 1990

CONTENTS

PREFACE

It would appear that the death penalty should be a tiresome topic. Like terrorism, it accounts for few deaths—far less than railroad and plane crashes, and overwhelmingly fewer than the carnage seen along the highways and streets of rural and urban America. And there undoubtedly are some who wonder why so much intellectual energy and time must be devoted to discussions and analyses of capital punishment issues.

There is another point. Hasn't the death penalty "problem" been solved? There are those who have argued that some 181 years after the adoption of the Bill of Rights, the Supreme Court of the United States created a problem with its ruling in *Furman v. Georgia* (1972). Holding that all existing death penalty statutes lacked adequate standards to prevent caprice, arbitrariness, and discrimination in death sentencing, and thus were violative of the Eighth Amendment ban against cruel and unusual punishment, the Court effectively abolished capital punishment throughout the United States. But state legislatures were quick to respond, preparing new statutes that would pass constitutional muster. Within a decade or so, at a time when the overwhelming majority of the American people favored capital punishment, 37 states had death penalty laws in place, most of the constitutional objections to capital punishment had been disposed of by the High Court, state courts were routinely increasing the size of death row populations, and the pace of actual executions had begun to quicken. Given recent history, then, wherein lies the "problem"?

The death penalty problem remains a significant one, presenting a variety of legal, moral, ethical, and philosophical questions. It is easily argued that execution is a gruesome form of punishment. One need only

7

witness sudden death from any cause to understand that. From this perspective, it seems surprising that the American people have not yet declared capital punishment to be unworthy of a decent society. But then, there are the inevitable "monsters" who inflame public passions. A few of those actually put to death in recent years immediately come to mind. There was Steven Judy, convicted of the rape and murder of a mother and the deliberate drowning of her three young children. He admitted to no regrets about the murders he had committed, and he was electrocuted by the state of Indiana on March 9, 1981. And then there is Jimmy Lee Gray, who died in Mississippi's gas chamber on September 2, 1983. Gray, described by prison workers who knew him as "sensitive, shy, gentle, and bright," had nonetheless taken a three-year-old girl to a wooded area near her house, sodomized her, and then killed her by suffocating her in mud. In reflecting on these kinds of cases, it could easily be concluded that the death penalty is the only answer to truly evil crime.

But then, another recently executed offender comes to mind. John Spenkelink was electrocuted by the state of Florida on May 25, 1979 because he was found guilty of killing a traveling companion in a motel room struggle over money his fellow hitchhiker had stolen from him. The victim was bigger, stronger, had spent much of his life in prison, and was on parole at the time of his death. He had homosexually raped Spenkelink, threatened his life, and boasted of killing a fellow inmate while in prison. Spenkelink's court-appointed attorneys, inexperienced in capital cases and lacking sufficient resources to conduct the defense, had failed to object to numerous questionable procedures during the trial. And incredibly, they never made the sentencing jury aware of many mitigating factors in Spenkelink's favor—including compelling psychiatric evidence that John Spenkelink still suffered from the traumatic effects of finding his suicidal father dead on the floor of his garage when John was 11 years old.

Cases such as John Spenkelink's remind us that those condemned to die will not necessarily be those who have committed the most savage and atrocious crimes. They will instead be those from the poor and socially disadvantaged classes who are least capable of defending themselves before juries and judges. Every prison warden in the death penalty states knows of prisoners serving relatively short prison terms whose crimes were far more atrocious than those committed by Spenkelink and others now on death row. All too often, regional attitudes, community prejudices, and local idiosyncrasies play a more important role in determining who gets the death penalty than do the nature of the crime and the defendant's prior record. Moreover, in a legal system that allows capital defendants to be convicted on the basis of a jury's judgment that no *reasonable doubt* of guilt exists—as opposed to a system that demands absolute certainty on the jury's part—we know as a statistical matter that if we execute often enough, some innocent lives will be lost.

In short, reasonable men and women on both sides of the death penalty controversy must acknowledge that any criminal justice system administered by human beings will inevitably experience caprice and mistake. Whether or not the inevitable cases of class bias, racial prejudice, and factual error are frequent enough and sufficiently shocking to our sense of justice to justify the abolition of capital punishment is just one of many issues in the death penalty debate. All of these issues need to be examined not just on the basis of our justifiable anger toward the Steven Judys and Jimmy Lee Grays of the world, but on a foundation of scholarly inquiry and scientific scrutiny. We believe that the studies in this book provide excellent examples of how law and social science can contribute to our understanding of some of the major issues and questions concerning the contemporary death penalty.

Accordingly, we would like to express our thanks and appreciation to the contributing authors for their hard work and fine scholarship. Their enthusiasm for the project made the editing of this volume an enjoyable and rewarding experience. We would also like to thank Tanya Coke of the NAACP Legal Defense Fund Inc. and Patrick Minges and Tania Sapko of Amnesty International U.S.A. for sending us the latest figures on death row populations and post-*Gregg* executions. Nancy Quillen and Judy Watson provided their usual intelligence, skill, and efficiency in typing, proofreading, and other tasks that go into editing a volume like this. Finally, we would like to thank Mitch Allen of Sage Publications for his support and patience as we struggled to complete the manuscript in a reasonable amount of time.

Kenneth C. Haas
James A. Inciardi
University of Delaware

Chapter 1

LINGERING DOUBTS ABOUT
A POPULAR PUNISHMENT

KENNETH C. HAAS
JAMES A. INCIARDI

Over the past 200 years, Americans have been arguing passionately about the death penalty without reaching a moral, legal, or practical consensus. However, recent public opinion polls show that the American public favors capital punishment by better than a three-to-one margin. Whereas a 1966 Harris Survey found 47% of the public opposed to capital punishment, 38% in favor of it, and 15% unsure, the Gallup Poll of 1986 reported 70% in favor of the death penalty, 22% opposed to it, and only 8% undecided.

Yet support for the death penalty is not nearly as deep as it is broad. Most people are highly ambivalent about capital punishment. A 1986 survey of over 900 Georgians, three-fourths of whom favored the death penalty, revealed that 52% of the respondents would favor abolishing capital punishment if offenders could be sentenced to life imprisonment with no possibility of parole for 25 years, combined with a restitution program (Thomas and Hutcheson, 1986). It is also telling that juries return death penalty verdicts in less than 25% of first-degree murder cases. In one simulated jury study, less than one-third of those who said that they support the death penalty were willing to recommend the death penalty in actual cases involving such crimes as killing a police officer or beating a woman to death (Ellsworth, 1978). This great reluctance to impose the death penalty in particular cases provides strong evidence that people's willingness to endorse capital punishment in the abstract is not necessarily an accurate measure of their willingness to put it into practice.

The moral uncertainty surrounding the death penalty may explain why (as of March 22, 1988) only 96 people have been executed in the United States since the U.S. Supreme Court resurrected capital punishment on July 2, 1976 in *Gregg* v. *Georgia* and four other cases announced the same day. Now, nearly 12 years later, 37 states have death penalty laws on their books;[1] there are over 2,000 people on death rows; and more than 250 defendants are sentenced to death each year. Yet executions are hardly routine events in most states. Since *Gregg* was decided, only 12 states have executed anyone, and only four states— Texas (27), Florida (18), Louisiana (16), and Georgia (12)—have executed more than ten people. Indeed, nearly all executions occur in the South. Virginia (6), Mississippi (3), North Carolina (3), South Carolina (2), and Alabama (3) have carried out post-*Gregg* executions, but only five persons have been put to death in nonsouthern states (Indiana (2), Nevada (2), Utah (2)).[2]

Because of concerns about the inevitability of factual and legal errors in capital cases, all states with death penalty statutes provide for automatic appellate review of death sentences (Special Project, 1984: 1241-1243). Indeed, in most states, the highest state court will review a death sentence even when the capital defendant has not moved for an appeal. As a result of these reviews, direct and discretionary appeals, collateral postconviction proceedings in state and federal courts, and occasional gubernatorial commutations, nearly 100 death row inmates have their death sentences vacated each year. In a 1981 dissenting opinion, Justice (now Chief Justice) Rehnquist complained that the many levels of appellate review of death sentences were making it virtually impossible to carry out executions (*Coleman v. Balkcom,* 1981: 956-964). But the Chief Justice may have misunderstood the significance of this judicial reluctance to dispense quick, rubber-stamp verdicts of death. In all likelihood, this phenomenon is another example of the deep ambivalence judges, legislators, and ordinary Americans have about capital punishment. Their support for the death penalty is best explained as a symbolic attitude—a reflection of their anger toward violent law-breakers—rather than as a firm, deeply entrenched preference for the death penalty (see Tyler and Weber, 1982).

Moral, social, and legal attacks on the death penalty are likely to mount in the late 1980s and 1990s. In *Capital Punishment and the American Agenda,* Franklin Zimring and Gordon Hawkins (1987: 148) argue that "America has outgrown the death penalty, but is reluctant to acknowledge that fact in the 1980s." Thus in the long run it may be inevitable that the United States will do what every other western, industrialized nation has done—abolish the death penalty. However, in the short run, executions are likely to increase, perhaps dramatically. As some of the essays in this volume stress, the U.S. Supreme Court has repudiated—at least for the time being—several promising legal challenges to the administration of capital punishment. In particular, the Court's recent holding that statistical evidence of racial discrimination in capital sentencing cannot, in and of itself, establish a violation of the Eighth or Fourteenth Amendments (*McCleskey v. Kemp*, 1987) is widely viewed as a "green light" to state officials who want to quicken the pace of executions. Moreover, the Court recently expanded the range of offenses punishable by death when it held—for the first time since *Gregg*—that someone who does not intend to commit murder and who does not actually commit murder can be executed when he or she participates in a felony that leads to murder and is found to have shown "reckless indifference" for human life (*Tison v. Arizona*, 1987).[3]

It generally takes anywhere from 4 to 10 years for condemned prisoners to exhaust all their available appeals and postconviction remedies. Thus over the next decade, an increasing number of death row inmates are likely to come face to face with their executioners. If this happens, most Americans, for the first time since the 1950s (when 717 executions occurred), will have to confront capital punishment not in the abstract, but in all its stark reality—gassings, electrocutions, hangings, shootings, and lethal injections. Despite efforts by authorities to "sanitize" executions by using modern methods, Americans inevitably will read about executions in which prisoners suffer severe and prolonged pain, such as occurred in: (1) a 1983 gassing in Mississippi during which the prisoner had convulsions for eight minutes and struck his head repeatedly on the pole behind him; (2) a 1983 electrocution in Alabama during which the prisoner died after 14 minutes and three charges of 1900 volts, the second of which caused smoke and flame to erupt from his left temple and leg; and (3) a 1984 lethal injection in Texas during which the prisoner moved about and screamed in pain for at least 10 minutes (Amnesty International, 1987: 117-119). As such cases become more frequent, Americans' instinctive sense of mercy may prevail over their collective yearning for revenge.

Mercy and compassion, however, will not be enough to reverse the tide of public opinion in favor of capital punishment unless they are accompanied by facts and logic. Justice Thurgood Marshall contended in *Furman v. Georgia* (1972: 360-363) that the American public had not been given accurate information about the effects of capital punishment and how it is used in our society. He added that such information "would almost surely convince the average citizen that the death penalty was unwise." Both of these assertions have been confirmed in recent studies that show that support for the death penalty is indeed founded on myth and misinformation. Most Americans, especially those who favor capital punishment, accept as true demonstrably incorrect statements about the effects of executions on murder rates, the verifiability of cases of executions of innocent people, the legal status of the death penalty, and the average length of prison term served by inmates sentenced to life imprisonment (Ellsworth and Ross, 1983: 139-145). Similarly, research has disclosed that when people read unbiased, factual material on the pros and cons of the death penalty, a good number of them switch from a retentionist to an abolitionist position (Sarat and Vidmar, 1976).

The results of such studies, however, will not soon be duplicated on a national basis until public officials begin to enact laws founded on scholarly analysis of the relative strengths and weaknesses of the death penalty and other types of punishment. In the past several years, social scientists and legal scholars have conducted increasingly sophisticated studies of the effectiveness of the death penalty and the fairness of the new death penalty laws upheld in *Gregg v. Georgia* (1976) (see, for example, Bedau, 1987; Nakell and Hardy, 1987; White, 1984; Bowers, 1984; Bedau, 1982; Dike, 1982). In that case, it will be remembered, a deeply divided Court, citing the laudable legislative goals of retribution and deterrence, held that states may enact and carry out death penalty laws. However, unlike the laws invalidated in *Furman v. Georgia* (1972), these laws must provide for guided discretion—statutorily defined lists of aggravating (and in most states, mitigating) circumstances that are meant to ensure that juries and judges impose the death penalty in a fair and reasonably consistent manner.[4]

In the immediate aftermath of *Gregg,* many social scientists pointed out that no statistically sound study has ever demonstrated that the death penalty is superior to lengthy imprisonment as a deterrent of murder. Equally important, many legal scholars argued that (1) *Gregg*-type safeguards, however well-intentioned, will fail to prevent discrimination and arbitrariness because of unconscious, but deeply rooted biases and prejudices among jurors and judges; and (2) the new death penalty laws will do nothing to cure discrimination and other defects in the pretrial stages (i.e. prosecutors' decisions to seek the death penalty) and posttrial stages (i.e. gubernatorial clemency and commutations of sentences) of the criminal justice process.

The studies in this volume are intended to assess the validity of these and other objections to the contemporary death penalty. The contributors combine social science research with an understanding of law, and the policy implications of their research are not hard to fathom. Lingering doubts about the wisdom of capital punishment and the fairness of the new death penalty laws will not be alleviated among those who read these studies. Taken together, they represent a formidable challenge to the most ardent supporters of the death penalty.

Scholarly proponents of the death penalty increasingly have advanced philosophical arguments to defend the death penalty. In fact, some good philosophical points can be made on behalf of capital punishment. For example, the death penalty is one (although not necessarily the only) way for society to achieve the principle of retribution.[5] And this arguably is a good thing in a society that asks its citizens to rely upon the courts rather than self-help vigilantism as a remedy to violent crime. Some of the most eloquent advocates of capital punishment stress that anger, outrage, and vengeance are eminently reasonable rationales for executing those who have committed particularly heinous murders. For example, in *For Capital Punishment,* Walter Berns (1979: 128-176) urges us to reassert moral responsibility by striking out against violent predators. By carrying out our natural, understandable desire to punish the wicked, he contends, we can cleanse the community of evil, reward those who obey the law, teach law abidingness, and reestablish a true, selfless "moral community." In *Punishing Criminals,* Ernest van den Haag (1975: 213) goes even further, decrying our "loss of nerve" in hesitating to assert our need for vengeance.

A different perspective is offered by legal philosopher Jeffrey Reiman in Chapter 2 of this volume. In "The Justice of the Death Penalty in an Unjust World," Reiman observes that it is imperative to distinguish between "the question of the justice of the death penalty *in principle*" and "the question of the justice of the death penalty *in practice.*" Citing historical and social science evidence that the death penalty is applied in a discriminatory manner and that life on death row constitutes an insidious form of psychological torture, Reiman makes a powerful case against capital punishment.

It is possible that retentionists have begun to rely heavily on philosophical justifications for the death penalty because the traditional argument that capital punishment is the best available deterrent of murder has not fared well under scientific scrutiny. Nevertheless, belief in the deterrent efficacy of the death penalty remains strong. In a 1987 poll (National Law Journal: S-1–S-20), 405 state and federal judges were asked if they believed that "the death penalty serves as a deterrent to crime." In all, 49% answered "yes," 43% said "no," and 8% said they didn't know. Obviously, the wording of this question left something to be desired. Many abolitionists would agree that a certain penalty of death would probably deter murder better than a maximum penalty of a ten-dollar fine. The key question, of course, is whether there is any evidence that the death penalty deters murder better than does life imprisonment and other lengthy terms of imprisonment.

In chapter three, William J. Bowers shows that criminologists have tested the claim that the death penalty is superior to lengthy imprisonment as a deterrent of murder in many different ways. He analyzes numerous studies on both the long-term and short-term effects of executions on homicide rates and demonstrates that every statistically sound study has led to the same conclusion: the presence of the death penalty—in law and in practice—does not reduce murder rates any more effectively than does lengthy imprisonment.

Perhaps more importantly, Bowers' close examination of research on the short-term effects of executions (including his replication of a purportedly scientific study supporting the deterrence thesis) reveals a growing body of evidence that executions cause a slight, but discernible increase in the murder rate. This "brutalizing effect" occurs within the first two months following an execution and dissipates thereafter. He argues that this effect is most likely to occur among a subgroup in the population who have reached a state of "readiness to kill"—people on the fringe of sanity for whom the suggestive or imitative message of the execution is that it is proper to kill those who betray, disgrace, or dishonor them.

A major point of contention between retentionists and abolitionists concerns the possibility of executing the innocent. Supporters of the death penalty often argue that improvements in the criminal justice system and the multiple levels of appellate review available to capital defendants ensure, insofar as is humanly possible, that innocent persons will not be executed. Abolitionists counter by pointing out that important legal issues involving alleged violations of the defendant's rights cannot normally be considered on appeal in cases in which the defense attorney erred by failing to raise these issues at the time of the trial. Furthermore, nearly all of the appeals that are available to those convicted of murder focus exclusively on legal issues and are often ineffective in uncovering factual errors that may occur during a trial. Opponents of the death penalty maintain that as a result of inherent human moral and perceptual fallibility, the process of determining guilt in our courts will always be plagued by cases of perjured (and perhaps purchased) testimony, false (and perhaps coerced) confessions, withheld or missing evidence, mistaken eyewitness identification, laboratory errors, and inattentive, confused, or prejudiced jurors.

Although increasingly sophisticated research on erroneous convictions has been done in recent years (see, for example, Huff, Rattner, and Sagarin, 1986), it is difficult to study this phenomenon. It is particularly important to distinguish between those who are wrongfully convicted from a strictly legal point of view (for example, those who are convicted despite overwhelming evidence of insanity and those convicted primarily on the basis of illegally obtained but nevertheless highly probative evidence) and those who are convicted, but are subsequently found to be factually innocent. In Chapter 4, Michael Radelet and Hugo Adam Bedau discuss the most comprehensive study ever done on miscarriages of justice in capital (and potentially capital) cases. Their research focused only on cases of factual innocence, and they located and documented twentieth century cases involving 350 defendants who were either erroneously convicted of a capital crime or who were convicted of crimes that never occurred—such as seven cases in which the "murder victim" showed up alive after a conviction had been obtained. Most significantly, their research shows that the decade with the second highest number of erroneous convictions is the 1970s. Most chillingly, they discovered compelling evidence that since 1900, at least 23 unfortunate defendants have gone to their deaths knowing all too well that no system of justice is perfect.

In *Capital Punishment: The Inevitability of Caprice and Mistake* (1981), Charles L. Black contends that the criminal justice system is not only mistake-prone, but that it is so saturated with standardless and arbitrary discretion—from arrest through appeal to executive clemency—that death-sentencing discrimination against the poor and the black is inevitable. The new death penalty laws upheld in *Gregg* are intended to ensure that judges and juries are constrained by legal guidelines and are thus less likely to be influenced by racial and class prejudice. However, even if such bias on the part of judges and juries could be significantly reduced, the *Gregg*-type standards will have no effect whatsoever on prosecutorial decisions in homicide cases. Under American law, the decisions of the prosecutor as to what charge to file, how vigorously to prosecute the case, whether to accept a plea bargain, and whether to seek the death penalty are unfettered and not subject to appellate review.

Several studies indicate that legally irrelevant factors such as race, perhaps unconsciously, are taken into account by prosecutors and that prosecutors' decisions in capital cases work to the detriment of black offenders and those charged with killing whites (see, for example, Radelet and Pierce, 1985; Baldus, Pulaski, and Woodworth, 1983: 706-710). Raymond Paternoster and Annmarie Kazyaka add to this research in Chapter 5 of *Challenging Capital Punishment*. Their analysis of prosecutors' decisions to seek a death sentence in South Carolina over the 1977-1981 time period reveals that prosecutors were more likely to seek the death penalty in cases involving white victims, especially when the alleged offender was black. By contrast, black-on-black homicides were much less likely to result in a death request. The Paternoster-Kazyaka study should be of particular interest to Justice Byron White who in his concurring opinion in *Gregg* (1976: 225) observed that the claim that prosecutors might act in an arbitrary fashion in potentially capital cases was "unsupported by any facts" and that prosecutors must be assumed to exercise their charging duties properly "absent facts to the contrary."

Once the prosecutor decides that a case merits the death sentence, the defendant moves on to a bifurcated capital trial. In the guilt adjudication phase of the trial, a jury or judge (usually a jury in most states) determines whether the defendant is guilty or innocent of first-degree murder. When a jury convicts the defendant, most states provide that the same jury shall remain empaneled for the penalty phase of the trial—the choice between life imprisonment or death. When the defendant has pled guilty or has been tried without a jury, most states provide for a jury at the sentencing proceeding. However, in some states, the trial judge or a panel of three judges determines the sentence in cases in which the capital defendant was convicted without a jury, and in a few states, the defendant who pleads guilty may choose whether to have the sentencing proceeding conducted by a judge or by a jury. Only four states—Arizona, Idaho, Montana, and Nebraska—provide that the trial judge or a panel of judges must conduct the penalty hearing, regardless of whether the judge or a jury determined the defendant's guilt (Special Project, 1984). It is especially important to note that in all but a few death penalty states, a jury's verdict of life imprisonment is binding on the court. Only in Alabama, Florida, and Indiana may a judge overrule a jury's recommendation of life imprisonment—a practice held to be constitutionally permissible by the U.S. Supreme Court (*Spaziano v. Florida,* 1984).

As Valerie Hans points out in Chapter 6 of this volume, despite the jury's prominent role in deciding between life and death, surprisingly little is known about how the penalty phase jury actually goes about its emotionally charged task. Hans develops a portrait of the penalty phase jury, with special emphasis on how capital jurors are selected and how their views affect their reactions to courtroom proceedings, evidence, and instructions. Her overview of social science research on jury decision making raises troubling questions about the adequacy of the *Gregg*-type guided discretion statutes in light of the many ways by which jurors can be influenced by legally irrelevant factors, confused by the judge's instructions, or misled by the complexity and ambiguity of lists of aggravating and mitigating circumstances. She concludes that more research will have to be done before we can answer the question of whether the penalty phase jury is properly equipped to handle its awesome burden.

Even if more research—theoretically insightful and methodologically sound—is done on the behavior of capital juries and other aspects of the death penalty question, it appears doubtful that a majority of the Justices of the U.S. Supreme Court will understand it or appreciate it. This is the thesis of Phoebe Ellsworth in Chapter 7. Ellsworth, a social psychologist at the University of Michigan, contends that when the issue is the death penalty, "the majority of the Justices have been faced with empirical research that supports an outcome they do not want." She offers an assessment of the Supreme Court's response to three empirical questions that are central to the capital punishment debate—deterrence, racial discrimination, and the fairness of capital juries. She demonstrates that in all three areas, the majority of the Justices have been unwilling to acknowledge the inescapable implications of social science studies and the relevance of these studies to fundamental constitutional questions.

In particular, Ellsworth criticizes the logic of Chief Justice Rehnquist's majority opinion in *Lockhart v. McCree* (1986). At issue in *Lockhart* was the constitutionality of "death qualification" or the removal for cause, prior to the guilt adjudication phase of a capital trial, of all prospective jurors whose opposition to capital punishment is strong enough to prevent or substantially impair their willingness to impose the death penalty at the penalty phase of the trial. Because of the possibility that death-qualified juries may be more "conviction prone" than juries that include one or more opponents of the death penalty, many legal scholars have advocated the use of two different juries in capital cases. The first or guilt phase jury would not be "death qualified"; it would include opponents of the death penalty so long as they expressed a sincere willingness to decide guilt in an impartial manner based on the facts and laws of the case. The second or penalty phase jury would be "death qualified" since it is reasonable to exclude jurors who concede that they would automatically vote against imposing the death penalty regardless of the facts of the case and the requirements of law. But is such a scheme constitutionally required? Is there sufficient scientific evidence that death qualification produces juries that are uncommonly willing to convict, thereby depriving capital defendants of their Sixth and Fourteenth Amendment rights? Ellsworth argues that by any reasonable scientific standard, the evidence is overwhelming that death-qualified juries are substantially more likely to convict than are juries on which death penalty opponents are permitted to serve. Her point-by-point dissection of the majority opinion in *Lockhart* makes a persuasive case that most of the members of the contemporary Court may be unable or unwilling to understand social science research.

If the U.S. Supreme Court, as currently constituted, is determined to keep the death penalty alive, the only hope left for a good many death row inmates may rest with the nation's state courts, particularly the 50 state courts of last resort (or, as they are called in 43 states, state supreme courts). A new and much heralded development in the law is that some state supreme courts have become more vigorous than the federal courts in protecting individual liberties (Haas, 1981; Porter and Tarr, 1982; Developments in the Law, 1982). This phenomenon is known as the "new judicial federalism"—cases in which state tribunals have protected civil rights and liberties by basing their decisions on state law or the state constitution. Since the U.S. Supreme Court generally will not review state law-based decisions that expand federally guaranteed rights (see *Oregon v. Hass,* 1975), state supreme courts can use the provisions of their state constitution to give their citizens greater civil liberties protection than the U.S. Supreme Court has found to exist under similar or identical provisions of the federal Constitution.[6]

There have been a few cases—but only a few—in which state supreme courts have struck down death penalty laws as violative of the state constitution (see Bedau, 1987: 185-194). Many state constitutions have provisions like the "due process," "equal protection," and "cruel and unusual punishment" clauses of the federal Constitution. However, state supreme court justices, especially those who must run for reelection or who must periodically face the voters in judicial retention elections, are not as well insulated from the pressures of public opinion and local politics as are federal judges, all of whom enjoy lifetime tenure. State high court justices who acquire a reputation for being too lenient with criminals run the risks of social ostracism and political oblivion. Indeed, Chief Justice Rose Bird and two other justices of the California Supreme Court were defeated in the November 1986 retention elections largely because conservative, anti-Bird groups waged a highly effective and ultimately successful campaign to arouse voter hostility to the three jurists' perceived opposition to the death penalty and leniency toward criminals generally (Wold and Culver, 1987; Grodin, 1987).

Electoral rejections of state supreme court justices have been quite rare, but state justices who frequently hand down controversial decisions on capital punishment and other criminal law issues may increasingly face challenges to their retention. Perhaps an even greater challenge is to understand and make proper use of the social science research that has become central to most challenges to the constitutionality of capital punishment. In Chapter 8 of *Challenging Capital Punishment*, political scientist Dennis Dorin accuses the Massachusetts Supreme Judicial Court of misusing social science in a case involving that state's death penalty law. But, interestingly, whereas Phoebe Ellsworth condemned the U.S. Supreme Court for the same sin in *Lockhart v. McCree*—a pro-death penalty decision—Dorin focuses upon one of the few cases in which a state supreme court has struck down a capital punishment statute on state constitutional grounds.

In *District Attorney for the Suffolk District v. Watson* (1980), the Massachusetts Court held that the state's death penalty law violated the "cruel or unusual punishment" clause of the Massachusetts Constitution, in part, because implementation of the law would inevitably lead to racial discrimination in making decisions "as to who shall live and who shall die." But the court made this decision in the absence of any empirical evidence that racial discrimination had occurred or was inevitable in Massachusetts. Is it proper for a court simply to assume that findings from social science studies of racial discrimination in death sentencing in Texas, Georgia, or Florida provide compelling evidence that such discrimination will occur in all states? Dorin answers this and other important questions about the principles that should guide any court's consideration of the proper relationship between law and social science. Many opponents of the death penalty will agree that if the struggle against capital punishment is to be won anytime in the near future, it will have to be won not on the basis of misunderstood and misapplied research, but on the basis of sound scientific study, principled law, and "the evolving standards of decency that mark the progress of a maturing society."

The above reference to "evolving standards of decency" was written by the late Chief Justice Earl Warren in his plurality opinion in *Trop v. Dulles* (1958). His point was that the founding fathers did not intend the cruel and unusual punishment clause to be a static concept. Indeed, the Supreme Court recognizes that Eighth Amendment questions must be continually reexamined in light of objective evidence of changing public judgments as to whether particular punishments are "barbaric," "needlessly cruel," or "grossly out of proportion to the severity of the crime" (see especially *Coker v. Georgia,* 1977; *Solem v. Helm,* 1983). With respect to the death penalty, this means that the courts of today—and the courts of tomorrow—are not necessarily bound by the eighteenth century notion that capital punishment in no way violates the Eighth Amendment's proscription of cruel and unusual punishment (but, see Berger, 1982).

Some legal commentators have suggested that the Supreme Court should consider international as well as national indicators of contemporary society's attitude toward capital punishment (see especially Goldberg, 1978: 3-7). If the Justices were to conduct an international survey, they would discover that the worldwide trend is unmistakably in the direction of abolition. Nearly every nation in the western world has abolished the death penalty, and even where it has not been abolished— as in Turkey and Greece—it is rarely practiced. In the 1980s the only European nation to carry out an execution is Turkey, where the last execution was in 1984. Since the 1970s, France, Norway, Luxembourg, the Netherlands, Portugal, and Australia have abolished capital punishment for all offenses. In the Americas, seven countries—Argentina, Brazil, Canada, El Salvador, Mexico, Nicaragua, and Peru—have abolished the death penalty for ordinary offenses since 1975. In 1983, a proposal to restore capital punishment in England was soundly defeated in the House of Commons, leaving the United States in the embarrasing company of the Soviet Union, South Africa, Iran, and the People's Republic of China as among the very few nations that execute more than one or two people each year.

The weight of international opinion is even more overwhelmingly arrayed against the United States on the issue of the execution of juvenile offenders. More than three-fourths of the nations of the world, even most of the nations that retain death penalty laws, obey Article 6(5) of the International Covenant on Civil and Political Rights, which states that "sentence of death shall not be imposed for crimes committed by persons below eighteen years of age . . ." However, in Chapter 9 of this volume, law professor Victor Streib shows that only 10 of the 36 American states with arguably valid death penalty laws (see note 1) prohibit executions of offenders whose crimes were committed while under 18 years of age. Ten states establish no minimum age whatsoever, and the remaining 16 states have established minimum ages ranging from 10 to 17. Moreover, Streib reports that 190 juvenile offenders have been put to death in the United States since 1900. There are, however, clear signs that the American people have come to regard the execution of juvenile offenders as offensive to our "evolving standards of decency." As of March 31, 1987, only 33 persons were on death row for crimes committed under the age of 18, and 26 of these people were sentenced to death in southern states. Perhaps more telling, only six executions for crimes committed while under 18 have been carried out since 1960.[7]

Drawing upon his many years of research on the juvenile death penalty, Streib provides a detailed breakdown of past and present American practices in condemning juvenile offenders to death. He also lists some of the legal, social, and moral reasons why he believes that the U.S. Supreme Court should abolish capital punishment for crimes committed by children. His arguments are especially timely since the Supreme Court recently granted certiorari in a case that raises the question of the constitutionality of the death penalty for juvenile offenders (*Thompson v. Oklahoma,* 1987). If the Court squarely addresses the constitutionality issue, a decision on this important question could be announced sometime in 1988.

The Supreme Court has not yet decided a case involving the constitutionality of the conditions of confinement in any of America's death rows. This is particularly disappointing because litigation in the lower courts and a number of excellent studies (see, for example, Johnson, 1981; Jackson and Christian, 1980) have established that many of the nation's death row inmates endure enforced idleness, unnecessarily repressive custodial restrictions, intentionally substandard living conditions, and mind-numbing isolation from ordinary human contacts with family, friends, or other prisoners. Death row cells typically are cramped, windowless, and arranged in tiers with little or no natural light. Poor plumbing, rare cell cleanings, and inadequate ventilation aggravate the pervasive odor of feces and urine, and sharp restrictions on medical care, food portions, showers, soap, hot water, toothpaste, and clean bedding make it virtually impossible to retain any sense of human dignity. Not surprisingly, many death row inmates suffer what Robert Johnson (1981: 99-118) has termed "a living death"—a condition characterized by severe depression, overwhelming despair, chronic anger, loss of touch with reality, and both physical and psychological deterioration.

In the tenth and final chapter of *Challenging Capital Punishment*, John Carroll, formerly a law professor and currently a U.S. Magistrate in Alabama, provides an overview of recent litigation on the constitutionality of death row living conditions across the United States. He stresses that not all death rows are equally oppressive. In Texas and California, for example, conditions are reasonably humane, largely because of provisions for meaningful out-of-cell time and opportunities for contact visitation with family and friends. However, in many other states—particularly Arkansas, Louisiana, Mississippi, Tennessee, Ohio, Pennsylvania, and New Jersey—conditions can be described only as needlessly harsh and cruel. Most significantly, Carroll demonstrates that litigation has been successful in bringing about modest but important improvements in death row conditions in several states. This legal trend offers hope for the future in that it shows that the logic of mercy and the wisdom of restraint are still alive in American law.

As the editors of this volume, we have made no attempt to hide our feelings about the death penalty. Although we understand the opinions of those who support capital punishment, and we share their desire to protect innocent victims from violent criminals, we cannot embrace the punishment of death in the face of overwhelming evidence that it inevitably leads to loss of innocent human life, is applied in an arbitrary and discriminatory manner, and is not the best available deterrent of violent crime. As mentioned previously, the studies in this book, taken together, constitute a challenge to proponents of the death penalty. The editors of this volume would welcome a response in kind from scholars who believe in the effectiveness of the death penalty and the reasonableness of existing death penalty laws. Can the defenders of capital punishment produce a comparable volume of empirically sound research to support their position?

NOTES

1. It should be noted that only 36 states have arguably valid death penalty laws. Vermont retains an unused capital punishment statute of the type struck down in *Furman v. Georgia* (1972). The Vermont law gives the capital sentencing jury absolute discretion in determining a penalty, thus violating the mandate of *Furman* and *Gregg v. Georgia* (1976). The statute remains in effect only because Vermont has never used it (See Special Project, 1984: 1217-1218).

2. As of March 1, 1988 there were 2,021 inmates awaiting death in American prisons. It is noteworthy that 953 of these death row inmates were in the 25 states that have death penalty laws, but have not yet carried out a post-*Gregg* execution. For example, California had 214 death row inmates, Illinois had 107, Pennsylvania had 95, and Ohio had 78 prisoners confined to death row. Of the states that have carried out post-*Gregg* executions, Florida and Texas have by far the largest death row populations, with 278 and 260 respectively.

3. Despite setbacks during the Supreme Court's 1986-87 term, opponents of the death penalty can take some solace in the fact that the Court still has not upheld any laws that mandate the death penalty (regardless of mitigating circumstances) for particular crimes. See especially *Woodson v. North Carolina* (1976) (striking down a mandatory death penalty for first-degree murder); *Roberts v. Louisiana* (1977) (invalidating a mandatory death penalty for first-degree murder of a law enforcement officer); and *Sumner v. Shuman* (1987) (holding that a statute mandating the death penalty for a prisoner convicted of murder while serving a life sentence without possibility of parole is unconstitutional). Also, the Court consistently has invalidated statutes that provide for a death penalty for offenses that do not in any way involve murder. See especially *Coker v. Georgia* (1977) (holding that a sentence of death for the rape of an adult woman is violative of the Eighth Amendment).

4. Among the most common aggravating circumstances designated in state capital punishment statutes are felony murder; killing for pecuniary gain or for hire; killing a police officer, prosecutor, judge, correctional employee, or fire fighter; and killing more than one person. In addition, many states consider aggravating circumstances to be present when the capital offender is a prisoner, was previously convicted of a violent felony, was "lying in wait," used explosives, or had kidnapped the victim. Many states also have enacted laws making it an aggravating factor to have created a risk to more than one person, to have committed the offense while attempting to escape from custody, or to have committed the offense in a manner that a judge or jury finds to be especially "heinous," "atrocious," "cruel," "horrible," "inhuman," "exceptionally brutal," or "outrageously or wantonly vile."

Many post-*Furman* statutes consider mitigating circumstances to exist when the defendant acted under substantial duress, extreme mental or emotional disturbance, or the domination of another person; when he or she is very young or very old (most states only list "age" without specifying particular ages); when he or she lacked the capacity to appreciate the wrongfulness of the crime; or when the offense was committed while in a state of intoxication.

The capital punishment statutes of six states do not provide lists of mitigating circumstances along with the enumerated aggravating circumstances. However, the U.S.

Supreme Court's decisions in *Lockett v. Ohio* (1978), *Eddings v. Oklahoma* (1982), *Skipper v. South Carolina* (1986), and *Hitchcock v. Dugger* (1987) established that juries or judges must be allowed to consider all relevant mitigating evidence presented by capital defendants. For a listing of the statutory aggravating and mitigating factors in force in the death penalty states, see Special Project (1984: 1227-1237).

5. In *Gregg v. Georgia* (1976: 184-187), the U.S. Supreme Court cited retribution and deterrence as the two principal social goals thought to flow from capital punishment. Surprisingly, the Justices neglected another leading justification for the death penalty—incapacitation. Some criminals appear to be incorrigibly antisocial and potentially dangerous to prison guards, their fellow prisoners, and free citizens. It is irrefutable that paroled murderers and escaped murderers sometimes have committed subsequent murders. For example, one study (Heilbrun, Heilbrun, and Heilbrun, 1978) disclosed that out of a sample of 164 paroled Georgia murderers, eight committed subsequent murders within seven years of release. Such cases are statistically rare, but statistics provide no consolation to the victims of such murders or their families.

On the other hand, opponents of capital punishment argue that killings inside prisons are rarely committed by convicted murderers; inmates serving time for robbery, burglary, and theft commit the large majority of prison murders. Moreover, murderers released from prison are less likely to commit new crimes than any other category of offender, or for that matter, various statistical categories of nonoffenders (see Sellin, 1980: 103-120). Abolitionists stress that (1) no civilized society should execute people based on its questionable ability to predict future dangerousness and (2) it is hard to believe that the most scientifically advanced nation in the world cannot devise humane ways to keep habitually violent offenders in prison and keep them from harming anyone while they are there. To those who cite the expense of life imprisonment, abolitionists reply that the best available quantitative research demonstrates that because of the additional procedural safeguards that are constitutionally required in capital cases, the death penalty costs taxpayers substantially more than life imprisonment (New York State Defenders Association, 1982; Garey, 1985; Nakell, 1978).

6. However, state courts are not permitted to rely on state law or the state constitution to undermine federally guaranteed constitutional rights. The U.S. Supreme Court sets minimum standards of rights under the federal Constitution that state courts cannot infringe.

7. Nevertheless, by executing three juvenile offenders between January, 1980 and April 1987, the United States joins Iran, Pakistan, Bangladesh, Barbados, and Rwanda as the only countries that reportedly have carried out 1980s executions of people who were under 18 at the time of their alleged crime (Amnesty International, 1987: 74).

REFERENCES

Amnesty International U.S.A. (1987) The Death Penalty. New York: Amnesty International.

BALDUS, D. C., C. PULASKI, and G. WOODWORTH (1983) "Comparative review of death sentences: An empirical study of the Georgia experience." Journal of Criminal Law and Criminology 74: 661-753.

BEDAU, H. A. (1987) Death is Different: Studies in the Morality, Law, and Politics of Capital Punishment. Boston: Northeastern University Press.

BEDAU, H. A. [ed.] (1982) The Death Penalty in America (3rd ed.) New York: Oxford University Press.

BERGER, R. (1982) Death Penalties: The Supreme Court's Obstacle Course. Cambridge, MA: Harvard University Press.

BERNS, W. (1979) For Capital Punishment: Crime and the Morality of the Death Penalty. New York: Basic Books.

BLACK, C. L., Jr. (1981) Capital Punishment: The Inevitability of Caprice and Mistake (2nd ed.). New York: W. W. Norton.

BOWERS, W. J. (1984) Legal Homicide: Death as Punishment in America. Boston: Northeastern University Press.

Developments in the Law (1982) "The Interpretation of State Constitutional Rights." Harvard Law Review 95: 1324-1502.

DIKE, S. T. (1982) Capital Punishment in the United States: A Consideration of the Evidence. Hackensack, N.J.: National Council on Crime and Delinquency.

ELLSWORTH, P. C. (1978) "Attitudes towards capital punishment: From application to theory." Presented at SESP Symposium on Psychology and Law, Stanford University.

ELLSWORTH, P. C. and L. ROSS (1983) "Public opinion and capital punishment: A close examination of the views of abolitionists and retentionists." Crime and Delinquency 29: 116-169.

GAREY, M. (1985) "The cost of taking a life: Dollars and sense of the death penalty." University of California—Davis Law Review 18: 1221-1270.

GOLDBERG, A. J. (1978) "The death penalty for rape." Hastings Constitutional Law Quarterly 5: 1-13.

GRODIN, J. R. (1987) "Judicial elections: The California experience." Judicature 70: 365-369.

HAAS, K. C. (1981) "The 'new federalism' and prisoners' rights: State supreme courts in comparative perspective." Western Political Quarterly 34: 552-571.

HEILBRUN, A. B., L. C. HEILBRUN, and K. L. HEILBRUN (1978) "Impulsive and premeditated homicide: An analysis of subsequent parole risk of the murderer." Journal of Criminal Law and Criminology 69: 110-113.

HUFF, C. R., A. RATTNER, and E. SAGARIN (1986) "Guilty until proved innocent: Wrongful conviction and public policy." Crime and Delinquency 32: 518-544.

JACKSON, B. and D. CHRISTIAN (1980) Death Row: A Devastating Report on Life Inside the Texas Death House. Boston: Beacon Press.

JOHNSON, R. (1981) Condemned to Die: Life Under Sentence of Death. New York: Elsevier.

NAKELL, B. and K. A. HARDY (1987) The Arbitrariness of the Death Penalty. Philadelphia: Temple University Press.

NAKELL, B. (1978) "The cost of the death penalty." Criminal Law Bulletin 14: 69-80.

National Law Journal (1987) "The view from the bench." 9: S-1 - S-20.

New York State Defenders Association (1982) Capital Losses: The Price of the Death Penalty for New York State.

PORTER, M. C. and G. A. TARR [eds.] (1982) State Supreme Courts: Policymakers in the Federal System. Westport, CT: Greenwood Press.

RADELET, M. L. and G. L. PIERCE (1985) "Race and prosecutorial discretion in homicide cases." Law and Society Review 19: 587-621.

SARAT, A. and N. VIDMAR (1976) "Public opinion, the death penalty, and the Eighth Amendment: Testing the Marshall hypothesis." Wisconsin Law Review 1976: 171-206.

SELLIN, T. (1980) The Penalty of Death. Beverly Hills, CA: Sage.

Special Project (1984) "Capital punishment in 1984: Abandoning the pursuit of fairness and consistency." Cornell Law Review 69: 1129-1243.

THOMAS, R. H. and J. D. HUTCHESON, Jr. (1986) "Georgia residents' attitudes toward the death penalty, the disposition of juvenile offenders, and related issues." Paper Prepared for the Clearinghouse on Georgia Prisons and Jails.

TYLER, T. R. and R. WEBER (1982) "Support for the death penalty: Instrumental response to crime or symbolic attitude?" Law and Society Review 17: 21-45.

VAN DEN HAAG, E. (1975) Punishing Criminals: Concerning a Very Old and Painful Question. New York: Basic Books.

WHITE, W. S. (1984) Life in the Balance: Procedural Safeguards in Capital Cases. Ann Arbor: University of Michigan Press.

WOLD, J. T. and J. H. CULVER (1987) "The defeat of the California justices: The campaign, the electorate and the issue of judicial accountability." Judicature 70: 348-355.

ZIMRING, F. E. and G. HAWKINS (1987) Capital Punishment and the American Agenda. Cambridge: Cambridge University Press.

CASES

Coker v. Georgia (1977) 433 U.S. 584

Coleman v. Balkcom (1981) 451 U.S. 949

District Attorney for the Suffolk District v. Watson (1980) 411 N.E. 2d 1274

Eddings v. Oklahoma (1982) 455 U.S. 104

Furman v. Georgia (1972) 408 U.S. 238

Gregg v. Georgia (1976) 428 U.S. 157

Hitchcock v. Dugger (1987) 107 S. Ct. 1821

Lockett v. Ohio (1978) 438 U.S. 536

Lockhart v. McCree (1986) 106 S. Ct. 1758

McCleskey v. Kemp (1987) 107 S. Ct. 1756

Oregon v. Hass (1975) 420 U.S. 714

Roberts v. Louisiana (1977) 431 U.S. 633

Skipper v. South Carolina (1986) 106 S. Ct. 1669

Solem v. Helm (1983) 463 U.S. 277

Spaziano v. Florida (1984) 468 U.S. 447

Sumner v. Shuman (1987) 107 S. Ct. 2716

Thompson v. Oklahoma (1986) 724 P. 2d 780 (Okla. Cr. App.), certiorari granted (1987) 107 S. Ct. 1284

Tison v. Arizona (1987) 107 S. Ct. 1676

Trop v. Dulles (1958) 356 U.S. 86

Woodson v. North Carolina (1976) 428 U.S. 280

Chapter 2

THE JUSTICE OF THE DEATH PENALTY IN AN UNJUST WORLD

JEFFREY REIMAN

JUSTICE IN PRINCIPLE AND IN PRACTICE

When it is pointed out to Ernest van den Haag, perhaps America's best known intellectual defender of capital punishment, that the death penalty has been and is still likely to be administered in a discriminatory fashion, he replies that the question of the justice of the death penalty and that of its administration are two separate questions. In his book, *Punishing Criminals*, van den Haag (1975: 221) writes:

> [O]bjections to unwarranted discrimination are relevant to the discriminatory distribution of penalties, not to the penalties distributed. Penalties themselves are not inherently discriminatory; distribution, the process which selects the persons who suffer the penalty, can be. Unjust distribution—either through unjust convictions or through unjust (unequal and biased) penalization of equally guilty convicts—can occur with respect to any penalty. The vice must be corrected by correcting the distributive process that produces it.

Having said this, van den Haag believes that he has disposed of the objection concerning discrimination, since he has shown that discriminatory application, though admittedly wrong, is not something wrong with the death penalty itself. And thus he returns to the business at hand, namely, justifying the death penalty as the appropriate response to crimes like murder.

Van den Haag is correct in believing that these two questions are distinct and that distinguishing them shields the death penalty from the force of the objection. It does so, however, at a considerable price. He is correct because the justice of a penalty and the justice of a penalty's distribution are theoretically separate matters: We can consistently believe that hanging is, in principle, an excessive and thus unjust penalty for double-parking while believing that it is administered evenhandedly, and we can consistently believe that fining double-parkers in a discriminatory fashion is unjust while believing that fines are in principle a fitting and thus just penalty for double-parking. It is possible to admit that the discriminatory application of a penalty is unjust and still maintain that the penalty itself is in principle a just one. Thus van den Haag can agree with his critics that the discriminatory application of the death penalty is unjust, and still maintain that the penalty itself is in principle a just response to murder.

But this way of disposing of the objection carries a high price tag because the very separation of the questions by means of which van den Haag evades the objection dramatically limits the scope of the conclusions he can reach from that point on. *The reason for this is that the moral question of whether the death penalty is a just punishment for murder is not the same as the moral question of whether it would be just for us to adopt the policy of executing murderers.* Consequently, an affirmative answer to the former question does not imply an affirmative answer to the latter question.

Let's call the question of whether the death penalty is a just punishment for murder "the question of the justice of the death penalty *in principle*," and call the question of whether it would be just for us—here and now in the United States, under foreseeable conditions—to adopt the policy of executing murderers "the question of the justice of the death penalty *in practice*." The reason that the two questions are different is that when we choose to adopt a policy, we are not simply affirming it in a vacuum. We are choosing to initiate a course of events that includes the actual way the policy will be carried out. We normally hold people responsible for the foreseeable consequences of their choices, even those consequences that they would rather not have happen. The foreseeable consequences of adopting a policy include the foreseeable ways that the policy will actually be administered. If we have reason to expect that a just policy will be administered unjustly, then choosing to adopt the policy is choosing to do something unjust—even though the policy itself is just in principle.

Suppose, for example, that we are considering a law establishing a 20% income tax. And suppose we agree that this is just in principle, in that those who earn more pay more, and each pays a like proportion of what he earns, and so on. If the question of the justice of the policy in principle sufficed to determine the justice of the policy in practice, that would be the end of it. But, suppose we know also—as we do—that as people earn higher incomes, they are increasingly able to shelter part of it, or to receive part of it in kind, and so on, such that a decreasing proportion of what they actually earn will show up as "taxable income" under the proposed law. Consequently, adopting this law will in effect be adopting a policy of 20% for those with lower incomes and less than 20% for those with higher incomes. But, then we cannot assume that an affirmative answer to the question "Is it just to tax everyone 20%?" implies an affirmative answer to the question "Is it just for us to pass the 20% income tax law, here and now?"

Moral assessment of the way a penalty is actually going to be carried out is a necessary ingredient in any determination of the justice of adopting that penalty as our policy. By separating the question of the justice of the death penalty itself from that of the justice of the way it is likely to be carried out, van den Haag separates as well his answer to the question of the justice of the death penalty itself from any answer to the question whether the death penalty is just as an actual policy. As a result, van den Haag may prove that the death penalty is in principle a just response to murder—but at the cost of losing the right to assert that it is just for us to adopt it in practice here and now in America.

Further, if there is reason to believe that a policy will be administered unjustly, then that is reason for believing that it is *unjust* to adopt that policy here and now in America, even though the policy is just in principle. This is not to say that injustice in the administration of a policy automatically makes it wrong to adopt the policy. It might still be that all the available alternatives are worse, such that on balance we do better by adopting this policy than by adopting any of the other possible candidates. However, in the absence of a showing that all alternatives are worse, I take it that it is wrong to adopt an unjust policy, and thus that the likelihood of substantially unjust administration of a policy has the effect of making it wrong to adopt that policy. I say "substantially" here in order to make clear that I do not claim that every, even the slightest, injustice has this effect. Given the inevitability of human error, some miscarriages of justice are inevitable in implementing any policy.

Unless we are to be paralyzed by the specter of human fallibility, we have to allow that a policy may be administered justly "on the whole" even though there is some small measure of unavoidable error. But, it is not the *unavoidability* of the error that allows us to call the policy justly administered "on the whole," it is the *smallness* of the error that allows this. If we knew that some policy had a likelihood of many grave though unavoidable errors, we would have to consider these as morally relevant costs of adopting the policy though they are unavoidable—for the simple reason that *we* can prevent these errors by not adopting the policy. Thus, I shall say that in situations in which we have reason to expect that a policy will be administered with *substantial* injustice, then that policy will likely be unjust *in practice*, and in situations in which there is not reason to believe that all alternative policies will be worse, it would be wrong to adopt a policy that is likely to be unjust *in practice* even if it was just *in principle*.

In this chapter, I aim to provide an example of the relation between moral evaluation of policies in principle and moral evaluation of policies in practice. I shall do this by considering the death penalty in both of these ways. The question "Is the death penalty just in principle?" and the question "Is the death penalty just in practice in America under current and foreseeable conditions?" are different questions that can yield different answers. It is possible to believe that the death penalty is just in principle *and* that it is unjust in practice in America under current and foreseeable conditions, and thus that it would be wrong for us to adopt it. To show this, I shall first sketch an argument for the justice of the death penalty in principle as a response to murder. I believe that this argument accounts for the appeal that the death penalty continues to have for large numbers of people in civilized nations. I shall then consider a number of features of the actual conditions under which the death penalty is likely to be carried out in America that, notwithstanding the justice of the penalty in principle, imply that the penalty is not just in America now and in the foreseeable future. I believe that this second argument accounts for the resistance to the death penalty felt by large numbers of Americans, and thus that the two arguments together go some way toward explaining the seesawing, schizophrenic attitude toward capital punishment that has characterized the American body politic in recent decades.

Thus far, I have not said anything about the standards that are to be used in determining what is just, either in principle or in practice. It goes without saying that this is a thorny and controverted issue. There is, however, a possible short-cut through the thorns and controversies: Instead of trying to develop and defend a definitive answer to the question of justice, we can ask whether a policy is just in practice according to the same principles used to show it just in principle. Thus, after presenting grounds for the justice of the death penalty in principle as a punishment for murder, I shall show that the features of the actual way that the death penalty is likely to be administered make it unjust in practice *on those same grounds.*

Use of this approach may appear to suggest that the implications of my argument can be dodged by the expedient of defending the death penalty on different grounds. But I think this is not so for two reasons. First of all, the grounds upon which I shall defend the death penalty include the notions of the equal worth of human beings and of the appropriateness of exacting from people the whole cost of the harms for which they are wholly responsible. I doubt that any plausible retributivist justification of the death penalty can get very far without these notions. Indeed, I doubt that any theory of justice generally can do without them. Thus it is to be expected that defenders of the death penalty as fitting retribution for murder, and advocates of justice generally, will themselves implicitly grant the grounds upon which the death penalty is here declared unjust in practice. And, willingness to adopt a policy that in practice runs afoul of the grounds upon which one justifies the policy in principle disqualifies appeals to the justice of the policy in principle as justifying the policy in practice. One implication of this strategy is that philosophical justifications of punishment are not only statements of the conditions under which someone deserves to receive punishment—they are equally statements of the conditions under which societies (or their members) are entitled to administer punishment.

Second, recall that my argument here is presented as *an example* of the way unjust application can render unjust a policy that is just in principle. Thus although in order to present this argument I have naturally had to select a particular way of defending capital punishment I believe that the implications of this argument go beyond this particular defense. I contend that, based on the example presented here, it will be possible to trace the ways that unjust administration of the death penalty will undermine its justice in practice no matter how it is justified in principle. For instance, at the close of this chapter, I shall suggest how this case can be made against attempts to justify the death penalty on grounds of deterrence.

THE JUSTICE OF THE DEATH PENALTY. . .

Justifications of the death penalty as the appropriate punishment for murder normally come under one of two heads, namely, deterrence and retribution. Both sorts of justification have characteristic strengths and difficulties.

Consider first, deterrence. If it could be shown that capital punishment was the most effective way to deter potential murderers, then capital punishment would be justified as an extension to society of the individual's right of self-defense—surely one of the least controversial of moral rights. The greatest difficulty facing this justification is establishment of the fact that capital punishment is more effective as a deterrent to murder than less harsh penalties, such as life in prison without chance of parole, or penalties even less harsh. It is crucial that capital punishment be shown to be more effective in deterring murder than less harsh penalties, since if punishment is justified by its deterrent impact, then only so much punishment as is needed for deterrence is justified. Punishment beyond this is strictly speaking pointless suffering, and pointless suffering is cruel if not unusual, and surely unjustified.

Although I take the deterrence justification to rest on the right of self-defense, its more usual foundation is utilitarianism. But either way, only the least harsh means of achieving deterrence is justified. The right of self-defense allows us to use only that amount of force necessary to protect ourselves from attack, and no more. Utilitarianism, in maximizing net aggregate satisfaction, implies that, when several alternative punishments will produce the same level of deterrence, the punishment that produces the least suffering must be chosen. If we used a punishment harsher than this with no prospect of deterring additional criminals, then we would produce more suffering all told and thus lower net aggregate satisfaction than we could have. And that violates the utilitarian imperative. Thus, whether deterrence is understood as based on the right of self-defense or as a means to maximize aggregate utility, it is necessary to show that the death penalty deters *more* than less harsh penalties if it is to be justified on deterrence grounds.

It is sometimes argued that even if the death penalty could be shown to be the most effective deterrent, this would not justify the penalty because it would amount to killing some persons (those who have already murdered) to enhance the well-being of others (the potential victims of deterred would-be murderers). And this seems to violate the widely-respected Kantian maxim that human beings ought not to be used simply as means to the well-being of others, and that they certainly ought not to be sacrificed for that end. Writes Murphy (1979: 493):

> And thus even a guilty man is, on this view, being punished because of the instrumental value the action of punishment will have in the future. Thus those of a Kantian persuasion, who see the importance of worrying about the treatment of persons as mere means, must, it would seem, object just as strenuously to the punishment of the guilty on utilitarian grounds as to the punishment of the innocent.

As an objection to the deterrence justification, this seems to me to be misdirected. It is based on viewing the deterrence effect of punishment as resulting from each individual act of punishment, rather than from the existence of a functioning system that punishes wrongdoers. The objection would be valid if deterrence were the product of the individual acts of punishment because then each act of punishment is done in order to benefit others. But it seems at least as plausible that what deters is the existence of a functioning punishment system. Then everyone is benefited by the system including those who end up being punished by it, since they too have received the benefit of enhanced security due to the deterring of some potential murderers. Each act of punishment, rather than done for the benefit of others, is done as a necessary condition of the existence of the system that benefits all. And no one is used or sacrificed simply for the benefit of others.

There is, however, a more telling objection to justifying the death penalty on deterrence grounds. This is that research done on the effects of the death penalty by no means indicates that it is a superior deterrent than less harsh penalties, and indeed the weight of empirical research on this issue tends to the opposite conclusion, namely, that jurisdictions without the death penalty experience no greater number of homicides than comparable jurisdictions with it.

In 1970, based on a review of the findings of empirical research on the impact of the death penalty on homicide rates (including the classic study by Thorsten Sellin), Hugo Bedau (1970) concluded that the claim that the death penalty is superior to life imprisonment as a deterrent to crimes generally, and to the crime of murder particularly, "has been disconfirmed," because the evidence shows uniformly the nonoccurrence of the results that one would expect were the death penalty a superior deterrent. In 1975, Isaac Ehrlich, a University of Chicago econometrician, published the results of a statistical study purporting to prove that in the period from 1933 to 1969, each execution may have deterred as many as eight murders. This, however, did not deter the authors of a National Academy of Sciences' study of the impact of punishment from writing in 1978: "In summary, the flaws in the earlier analyses (i.e., Sellin's and others) and the sensitivity of the more recent analyses to minor variations in model specification and the serious temporal instability of the results lead the panel to conclude that the available studies provide no useful evidence on the deterrent effect of capital punishment" (Blumstein, Cohen, and Nagin, 1978: 9). Though there is much that can be said in criticism of the death penalty/deterrence research, it remains that it is all we've got. And a society that thinks the taking of life is so grave an act that it should be done only to prevent other killing should not execute anyone in the absence of reliable evidence that other killing will be prevented as a result. For this reason, I shall set aside the deterrence justification of capital punishment for the moment as unsupported in the present state of our knowledge. I shall have more to say about it at the close.

Unlike deterrence justifications, retributivist justifications of capital punishment are not hostage to empirical research. On retributivist grounds, the death of the murderer is justified not by its effects on other potential murderers, but by the murderer's own moral guilt. By choosing to end his victim's life the murderer *earns* the loss of his own as his *just deserts*. The characteristic difficulty with such a justification is to show that it is not simply a rationalization for satisfying the desire for revenge, a desire that many find unworthy of social affirmation since it seems to be a desire for nothing else but the pointless suffering of the guilty. This difficulty can be met, however, if a better face can be put on revenge by showing that the suffering it desires is not pointless. This is complicated by the fact that there is a feature of the desire for revenge that is truly unworthy of social affirmation. This is the fact that the desire for revenge, powered as it is by the anger and suffering of the victim or his kin, is or can be literally bottomless. To give in to a bottomless desire to see wrongdoers suffer is surely barbaric. In this respect, the ancient Code of Hammurabi, often blamed for legitimating revenge in affirming the maxim of "an eye for an eye," was actually an attempt to limit the desire for revenge to the measure of suffering caused by the wrongdoer.

So limited, the desire for revenge is the desire that the wrongdoer experience suffering in the amount that he has imposed it on another. And though the point of such suffering is not to prevent other suffering, neither is it pointless. Its point is very much the same point as that of the golden rule, namely, to establish a kind of equilibrium or symmetry — between persons such that each treats the other as of equal worth to himself. Doing unto others what one would want others to do unto one treats others as of equal worth to oneself because testing the acceptability of one's own actions by whether one would accept being on the receiving end of them limits one to doing only those things that a being equal to oneself in worth (namely, oneself in the other's shoes) could accept. The acts that prompt the desire for revenge are acts that the doer would not accept being on the receiving end of, acts that he does because he can avoid being on the receiving end. By doing to the other what one would not accept done to oneself, a person treats himself as, in effect, of greater worth than his victim. The desire to do back to him what he does in this case is the desire to demonstrate to him that he is not of greater worth than his victim, that since he is of equal worth with others, whatever he does to others may rightly be done to him.

The desire that the wrongdoer experience suffering in the amount he has imposed it on another is simply the desire to have the golden rule executed by force on those who refuse to comply with it voluntarily. And as long as the desire for revenge is limited to the desire to impose suffering equal to the amount that has been imposed, there is nothing shady or barbaric about this desire. If the point of the golden rule is to establish a kind of equilibrium among persons as equal in worth to one another, the point of retribution is to reestablish this equilibrium when it has been upset. This should not be taken as a metaphor. Retribution truly does reestablish equilibrium in at least two ways. First of all, by imposing suffering on the offender equal to that which he imposed on his victim, the offender is literally forced to recognize his likeness to his victim as a person vulnerable to suffering and desiring to avoid it. Second, retribution announces to the whole society that the suffering of each person is equally a calamity, and thus reaffirms the society's commitment to the equality of the victim with the offender that the offender has violated.

That retributive punishment can be thought of as having the same point as the golden rule shows, I believe, that doing to a person what he has intentionally done to another cannot be unjust. And this suffices to show that the death penalty is just on retributive grounds. But, in my view, what this argument establishes is the *right* to execute murderers, not the *duty* to do so. Thus it does not imply that it is unjust to impose a less harsh penalty than death on murderers. It may well be that other considerations, such as a desire not to ape the cruelty of the cruelest criminals, may justify our toning our punishments down. Thus, although I shall treat the argument as justifying the *lex talionis*, an eye for an eye, and thus a life for a life, it is also compatible with the view called "proportional retributivism," in which the severity of punishment is proportioned to the severity of crime (the worst crime gets the worst punishment, the next-to-worst crime gets the next-to-worst punishment, and so on) with no attempt to match the suffering of the punishment to that caused by the crime.

There is, to be sure, much else that would have to be added to this brief sketch in order to complete the argument for the retributive justification of the death penalty for murderers.[1] However, since my purpose is to offer a plausible case for the justice of the death penalty in principle in order to see how it fares in light of the actual conditions under which the penalty is likely to be applied in America, this incomplete argument should suffice. Before proceeding, two features of this argument should be noted since they will figure in what follows. First, the retributive justification of the death penalty that I have defended depends on its capacity to affirm or act out the equal worth of persons. Second, the death penalty affirms the equal worth of persons only on the assumption that the murderer is wholly responsible for his or her crime. This is a necessary condition of the legitimacy of asking him or her to pay the whole price of the harm he or she has caused, namely, a life for a life. I shall consider four conditions under which the death penalty is likely to be applied in America. Three of them are forms of discrimination (though only in the first of these is the form referred to in the quotation from van den Haag), and the fourth is the notion that life on death row awaiting execution is torture. Though I believe that all four of these conditions are not only actual but likely to be with us for the foreseeable future, I shall not present extensive evidence to this effect in this short space. Thus, the argument that follows may be taken as evaluating the justice of the death penalty in practice *if* any or all of the four conditions obtain.

. . . IN AN UNJUST WORLD

(1) *Discrimination in the application of the death penalty among convicted murderers.* A long line of researchers has found that among equally guilty murderers, the death penalty is more likely to be given to

blacks than to whites, and to poor defendants than to well-off ones. Though racial discrimination was the main ground upon which death penalty statutes were ruled unconstitutional in *Furman v. Georgia* in 1972, there is strong evidence (though not uncontested) that it remains in the sentencing procedures ruled constitutional after *Furman*: "Among killers of whites [in Florida], blacks are five times more likely than whites to be sentenced to death." This pattern of discrimination was also evidenced, though in less pronounced form, in Texas, Ohio, and Georgia (the other three states surveyed). These four states "accounted for approximately 70 percent of the nation's death sentences" between 1972 and 1977 (Bowers and Pierce, 1982: 210, 211). More recently, studies have presented evidence for discrimination among convicted murderers on the basis of the race of their victims, with killers of whites standing a considerably larger chance of being sentenced to death than killers of blacks (see *McCleskey v. Kemp*, 753 F.2d 877, 1985).

It should be clear that a society that adopts the death penalty when it is likely to be applied in this way chooses to bring injustice into existence. At the very least, any society that punishes in such a discriminatory fashion loses the right to appeal to the retributive justification of the death penalty defended earlier. This is because that justification depends on the penalty's affirmation of the equal worth of persons, and a society that reserves the death penalty for murderers coming from certain racial and socioeconomic groups clearly treats these people as of less worth than others. Likewise, a society that reserves the death penalty for the killers of whites but not of blacks, treats blacks as of less worth than whites. Since its punishing behavior is incompatible with respect for the equal worth of persons, such a society loses the right to appeal to the equal worth of persons to justify its punishments. Moreover, insofar as actions speak louder than words, such a society loses the right to justify its executions as appropriate responses to the crime of murder, since its actions indicate that it is executing people not because they are murderers but because they are black or poor, or because their victims are white, or all of the above.

(2) *Discrimination in the definition of murder.* Those acts that the law calls "murder"—and whose perpetrators are treated by the criminal justice system as "murderers"—are by no means the only ways that people kill their fellow citizens in America. There is, for example, considerable evidence that many more Americans die as a result of diseases caused by preventable conditions in the workplace (toxic chemicals, coal and textile dust, and so on) than die at the hands of the

murderers who show up in arrest and conviction records or on death row (see Reiman, 1984: 45-76). In 1985, three corporate executives were found guilty of murder and sentenced to 25 years in prison for the death of an employee that was caused by exposure to hydrogen cyanide in a film reprocessing plant (Facts on File, 1985: 495). The executives, it was held, knew fully the dangerousness of the situation and failed to warn their employees. Most interesting for our purposes is that this was recognized as *the first case of its kind*. The uniqueness of this case and its outcome testify that general practice is to ignore or treat lightly the subjection of workers to lethal hazards on the job.

It might be thought unfair to class such things as the failure to remove deadly occupational hazards as murder because this failure is not an act intentionally aimed at ending life. This objection misconceives the nature of intentions as they function in the attribution of criminal responsibility. If I shoot someone in the head and kill him although I really intended only to scare him by grazing his hair as a prank, the law holds me responsible for (at least) reckless homicide even though I intended only to have some fun and not to kill anyone. As long as his victims have not freely and knowingly consented to put themselves at risk, the law treats the individual as intending—and thus responsible for—all the foreseeable likely consequences of his acts, *regardless of the particular outcome he hopes for when he acts*. Thus, if loss of life is among the foreseeable likely consequences of failure to remove occupational hazards, as long as the victims have not freely and knowingly consented to put themselves at risk, the individual responsible for this failure ought to be held to have intended the loss of life and thus be treated as responsible for (at least) reckless homicide, regardless of the particular outcome he hoped for when he acted. It is reasonable to assume that there is some ordinary level of risk that is accepted by all members of society as an implicit condition of enjoying the benefits of progress, and of course there are some cases in which workers can be said to have freely and knowingly consented to risk the special occupational hazards that accompany their jobs—but there are as well a large number of cases in which individuals taking hazardous jobs had no realistic alternative and a large number of cases in which extraordinary hazards were known only to management, and concealed. In these cases, employees can hardly be held to have freely put themselves at risk.

There is also evidence that the number of people who die from other practices not normally treated as murder, such as performance of unnecessary surgery and prescription of unneeded drugs, is higher than the number of reported murder victims. And these examples can be multiplied. Moreover, it is arguable that the difference between the kinds of killings that are treated as murder and the kinds that are not is not an arbitrary or haphazard difference; it is a quite systematic identification of the ways that poor people kill as "murder" and the ways that well-off people kill as something else: "disasters," "social costs of progress," or "regulatory violations" at worst (Reiman, 1984: 34-45).

If it is the case that in our society murder is not the intentional taking of life but the intentional taking of life *by poor people*, this has quite the same moral effect as the first sort of discrimination. It has the effect of treating well-off killers as of greater worth than poor killers, and supports the presumption that in our society murderers are not punished because they are murderers, but because they are poor. Then, adoption of the death penalty in practice amounts to instituting this unjust discriminatory treatment of the poor. And this disqualifies the society from claiming that it is executing murderers to pay them in kind for their crimes and to affirm the equal worth of human beings.

(3) *Discrimination in the recruitment of murderers.* The first two sorts of discrimination just considered are built into the criminal justice system; the sort that I shall now take up is arguably built into the structure of the society that that criminal justice system is supposed to protect. That the death rows of our nation are populated primarily with poor people is not only the result of discriminatory sentencing. In large measure, it is the result of the fact that murder, or at least what we call murder, is done primarily by such people. For example, most defendants in capital cases cannot afford to hire their own lawyers and thus must have attorneys appointed by the state (Johnson, 1981: 138). Accordingly, if discrimination in the handing down of death sentences was completely eliminated, it is still likely that the overwhelming majority of death row inmates would come from the bottom of society. Now, unless we assume that poor people are inherently more evil than better-off people, we must recognize that there is something about poverty (and its accompanying conditions: lack of education, transient communities, and so on) that substantially increases the likelihood of a person committing murder. And this implies that, although the media as well as law-and-order politicians like to picture violent crime as the result of individual moral defect, there is considerable evidence to suggest that violent crime has social causes.

That virtually every wave of immigrant laborers to come to the United States passed through a stage of poverty and crime, and then passed out of crime as they ascended the economic ladder, strongly suggests that much crime results from conditions associated with poverty, as opposed to such things as genetic endowment, cultural traditions, and so on, which are relatively stable during the transition from poverty to a higher standard of living. Similarly, cross-national studies in crime rates show that virtually every country that undergoes the transition from an agrarian to an industrial society endures the same pattern of changes in the composition and magnitude of its criminality. All go from low crime rates, in which violent crime predominates over property crime, to high crime rates, in which property crime predominates over violent crime: "The changes in crime patterns observed first in England, Germany, and France as a result of the industrial revolution have accompanied modernization elsewhere. . . . In terms of crime the hallmark of modernization is the transition from a society dominated by violent crime to one characterized by increasing property crime" (Shelley, 1981: 138-139). The persistence of this pattern across countries different in so many other respects is strong evidence that features of the structure of society importantly affect the incidence and nature of the society's crime.

If social factors, especially poverty, are in some way a cause of crime, then it is no longer reasonable to characterize criminals, especially poor ones, as *wholly* responsible for their crimes. This is particularly the case with a factor like poverty that is not only correctable, but from which the rest of society derives certain benefits, such as the availability of cheap labor to do the jobs others find either too hard or distasteful. A society that not only allows correctable crime-producing conditions to exist, but derives benefits from those conditions, can hardly turn around and hold the criminals thereby produced *wholly* responsible for their crimes. Rather the society must share some of the blame, and that means that it cannot exact from the murderer the "full price" for his or her act, his or her life for the life taken. When such a society takes the murderer's life as the price of his or her crime, it effectively take more than it is entitled to from the murderer, and commits an injustice.

The argument I am making here should not be confused with one made by Jeffrie Murphy, who also recognizes that a punishment policy may be just in principle but unjust in practice. Murphy (1979: 509) writes: "Is it just to punish people who act out of those very motives that society encourages and reinforces? If [Willem] Bonger [a Dutch Marxist criminologist] is correct, much criminality is motivated by greed, selfishness, and indifference to one's fellows; but does not the whole society encourage motives of greed and selfishness ('making it,' 'getting ahead'), and does not the competitive nature of the society alienate men from each other and thereby encourage indifference—even, perhaps, what psychiatrists call psychopathy?" This argument assumes that the criminal is in some sense psychologically unable to conform to legal and moral prohibitions against violence, and thus, like the insane, cannot be thought responsible for his actions. This claim seems rather extreme, and dubious as a result. My argument does not claim that criminals, murderers in particular, cannot control their actions, and thus I do not claim that they are not responsible for their actions. I do, however, argue that under current and foreseeable conditions, many criminals cannot be held *wholly* responsible for their actions. But this, in my view, arises because the society shares some of that responsibility, not because the criminals can't help doing what they do.

I think we do better to understand the way poverty mitigates culpability by (rough) analogy with the *entrapment* defense, rather than by analogy with the *insanity* defense. In entrapment, without doubting that the offender could have controlled his actions, we excuse him from criminal responsibility because the state has played a role in making a criminal act a temptingly reasonable option for him when it would not have been otherwise. I use the analogy with the entrapment defense strictly to point out that we not only relieve people of culpability because they could not control their actions (as with the insanity defense), but also when the society (through its agents) is in some way complicitous in their crimes. I am aware that this is not an analogy that can be pressed much further than this. But, on the other hand, the entrapment defense is grounds for complete exculpation, whereas I am arguing only for reduction in responsibility. If society acknowledges through the entrapment defense that its own complicity is grounds for complete exculpation, this supports the weaker claim for which I am arguing (on the various legal rationales for the entrapment defense, see Altman and Lee, 1983).

In tolerating the conditions of remediable poverty, society contributes to creating a situation in which people have less to gain from obeying the law, less protection from violence, more frustrations, and fewer alternative means to cope with them—all of which are conditions that make criminal behavior, with its lure of immediate solutions to seemingly intractable problems, a more reasonable alternative. Violence

is an adaptation to bleak and often brutal lives. Violent offenders conform to the observation rendered by Vaillant that 'the sons-of-bitches in this world are neither born nor self-willed. Sons-of-bitches evolve by their . . . efforts to adapt to what for them has proven an unreasonable world.' Environments that spawn men who murder are indeed unreasonable—and unloving, unstable, and replete with occasions of verbal and physical violence. . . . Capital offenders, to be sure, are not passive victims of circumstance; they are implicated in their fates. But society, too, is at fault, for it confronts these men with challenges for which they are not equipped to cope competently, humanly, even sanely. Born and reared in what sociologists call 'subcultures of violence,' many of these men eagerly exploited violence promotive norms because few other means of ego support were open to them. (Johnson, 1981: 26, 27, 37; see also Vaillant, 1977, and Toch, 1980).

Insofar as we as a society tolerate the existence of remediable conditions that make crime a more reasonable alternative for a specific segment of society than for other segments, we are accomplices in the crimes that quite predictably result. As such, we lose the right to extract the full price from the criminal, and this means we lose the right to take the murderer's life in return for the life he has taken. Consequently, since the vast majority of murderers will come from the bottom of society, adopting the death penalty as their punishment imposes more harm on them than they have earned—and that means that adopting the death penalty in practice amounts to bringing about injustice.

(4) *Life on death row as torture.* The argument that the person condemned to be executed lives a life of torture stems from Albert Camus, who emphasized the difference between the normal murder, which happens largely by surprise, and the state's execution, which happens on a date some time in the future that the condemned must knowingly await. "As a general rule, a man is undone by waiting for capital punishment well before he dies. Two deaths are inflicted on him, the first being worse than the second, whereas he killed but once. Compared to such torture, the penalty of retaliation seems like a civilized law" (Camus, 1961: 205).

Recently this argument has been fleshed out in fuller psychological detail by Robert Johnson (1981: 129 ff.) who, in his book *Condemned to Die*, recounts the painful psychological deterioration suffered by a substantial majority of the death row prisoners he studied. Since the death row inmate faces execution, he is viewed as having nothing to lose, and thus treated as the most dangerous of criminals. As a result, his confinement and isolation are nearly total. Since he has no future to be rehabilitated for, he receives the least and the worst of the prison's facilities. Since his guards know they are essentially warehousing him until his death, they treat him as something less than human—and so he is brutalized, taunted, powerless, and constantly reminded of it. The result of this confinement, as Johnson reports it, is quite literally the breaking down of the structures of the ego—a process not unlike that caused by brainwashing. Since we do not reserve the term *torture* only for processes resulting in physical pain, but recognize processes that result in psychological pain as torture as well (consider the so-called Chinese water torture), Johnson's application of this term to the conditions of death row confinement seems reasonable.

It might be objected that some of the responsibility for the torturous life of death row inmates must be attributed to the inmates themselves, since in pressing their legal appeals they delay their executions and thus prolong their time on death row. But this is true only if one thinks of legal appeals as means to delay punishment. If we think of them as legitimate tests of the legality of the condemned person's sentence, then they are necessary ingredients in the process that determines the validity of the death penalty. To hold the inmate somehow responsible for the delays that result from his appeals, and thus for the (increased) torment he suffers as a consequence, is effectively to confront him with the choice of accepting execution before its legality is fully tested or suffering torture until it is. Since no just society can expect (or even want) a person to accept a sentence until its legal validity has been established, it is unjust to torture him until it has, and perverse to assert that he has brought the torture on himself by his insistence that the legality of his sentence be fully tested before it is carried out.

Although it is possible that the worst features of death row might be ameliorated, it is not at all clear that its torturous nature is ever likely to be eliminated, or even that it is possible to eliminate it. In order to protect themselves against natural, painful, and ambivalent feelings of sympathy for a person awaiting a humanly inflicted death, it may be psychologically necessary for the guards who oversee a condemned person to think of him as less than human and treat him as such. Johnson (personal communication) writes: "I think it can also be argued . . . that humane death rows will *not* be achieved in practice because the purpose of death row confinement is to facilitate executions by dehumanizing both the prisoners and (to a lesser degree) their executioners and thus make it easier for both to conform to the etiquette of ritual killing."

Suppose that conditions on death row are, and are likely to continue to be, a real form of psychological torture, what are the implications for the justice of the death penalty in practice? At the very least, one must admit that it is no longer merely a penalty of death—it is now a penalty of torture-until-death. And if this is so, then it can no longer be thought of as an amount of suffering equal to that imposed by the murderer— leaving aside those murderers who have tortured their victims. Thus, at least for ordinary murderers, the death penalty would exceed the suffering they had caused, and could not be justified on the retributivist basis defended above. As to whether it would be justified retribution for murderers who had tortured their victims, perhaps it would, but I suspect not. The reason is that as we move away from common instrumental murders to the pointlessly cruel ones, we move at the same time toward offenders who are more likely to be sociopaths and less likely to be fully in control of their actions in the way that legitimates retributive punishment. There may of course be torturers of whom this is not true, but its general likelihood counts against reserving the death penalty as a special punishment for torture-murderers. In any event, since current death penalty laws do not reserve the penalty only for such murderers, this argument tells against those laws and their kin, even if not against a law that would reserve the penalty for torturers.

I think it will be granted that the four conditions I have been discussing constitute substantial injustices. If, as I think is the case, any or all of the four conditions are likely to characterize the imposition of the death penalty in the United States in the foreseeable future, it follows that adopting the death penalty under current and foreseeable conditions is willfully initiating a course of events characterized by substantial injustice. Though injustices will result from imposing lesser penalties on murderers, these are likely to be lesser in the same degree as penalties are lesser. In any event, there is no reason to assume that the injustices connected with not executing murderers will be worse than those that accompany executing them. Consequently, I conclude that it would be wrong to adopt the death penalty *in practice* in the United States as punishment for murder—although the penalty itself is *in principle* a just punishment for murder.

This argument does not apply to the deterrence justification, but a related argument does apply. Since deterrence is an extension of the right of self-defense, it does not turn on notions of equal worth or personal responsibility. One is permitted to kill a homicidal maniac in self-defense, even though there is no assertion that he (or she) is responsible for his acts or that killing him affirms anything about his worth compared to anyone else's. Thus, even if the above considered four conditions obtain, our society might still avail itself of the deterrence justification—even an unjust society has the right to defend its innocent members against harm.

But if we revert to the deterrence justification, two things must be borne in mind. First, as I said above, we do not have evidence that shows that capital punishment has a greater deterrence impact than less harsh penalties. Thus if appeal to a justification means satisfying its terms, rather than just mouthing them, deterrence does not now justify the death penalty. Second, much as the retributivist justification is not only a statement of what punishment the wrongdoer deserves but also of what conditions must be met by the society in order to have the right to administer the punishment, the same can be said of the deterrence justification. Since the deterrence approach justifies a penalty as the least harsh means necessary to produce the obtainable level of deterrence, it can be invoked for any given punishment only if no less harsh means will produce the same deterrence effect. But there is no reason to limit the means under consideration to punishments. To use the deterrence approach to justify punishment, one must have exhausted all the ways of preventing crime that are less harsh than punishment, in order to show that only some form of punishment is the least harsh means to deter crime. But this means that in order to qualify to appeal to the deterrence justification for punishment, we must already have tried to eliminate crime by such nonpunitive means as eliminating the conditions like poverty that cause crime. Until we do this, our appeals to deterrence—even if valid in principle—will ring just as hollow in practice as do our appeals to retribution.

NOTE

1. For a more extensive presentation and defense of this argument for the justice of the death penalty as well as the reasons for not instituting it despite its justice, see Reiman, 1985: 115-148. A reply by Ernest van den Haag appears in the same issue of the journal.

REFERENCES

ALTMAN, A. and LEE, S. (1983) "Legal entrapment." Philosophy & Public Affairs 12, 1 (Winter): 51-69.
BEDAU, H. A. (1970) "Deterrence and the death penalty: A reconsideration." Journal of Criminal Law, Criminology and Police Science 61, 4: 539-548.

BLUMSTEIN, A., COHEN, J., and NAGIN, D. [eds.] (1978) Deterrence and Incapacitation: Estimating the Effects of Criminal Sanctions on Crime Rates. Washington, DC: National Academy of Sciences.

BOWERS, W. J. and PIERCE, G. L. (1982) "Racial discrimination and criminal homicide under post-*Furman* capital statutes," pp. 206-224 in H. A. Bedau (ed.) The Death Penalty in America (3rd ed.). New York: Oxford University Press.

CAMUS, A. (1961) "Reflections on the guillotine," pp. 173-234 in A. Camus, Resistance, Rebellion and Death. New York: Knopf.

EHRLICH, I. (1975) "The deterrent effect of capital punishment: A question of life and death." American Economic Review 65 (June): 397-417.

Facts on File (1985). New York: Facts on File.

JOHNSON, R. (1981) Condemned to Die: Life Under Sentence of Death. New York: Elsevier.

MURPHY, J. G. (1979) "Marxism and retribution," pp. 491-512 in R. Wasserstrom (ed.) Today's Moral Problems (2nd ed.). New York: Macmillan.

REIMAN, J. H. (1984) The Rich Get Richer and the Poor Get Prison: Ideology, Class and Criminal Justice (2nd ed.). New York: John Wiley.

REIMAN, J. H. (1985) "Justice, civilization, and the death penalty: Answering van den Haag." Philosophy & Public Affairs 14, 2 (Spring): 115-148.

SHELLEY, L. I. (1981) Crime and Modernization. Carbondale, IL: Southern Illinois University Press.

TOCH, H. (1980) Violent Men. New York: Schenkman.

VAILLANT, G. (1977) Adaptation to Life. Boston: Little, Brown.

VAN DEN HAAG, E. (1975) Punishing Criminals. New York: Basic Books.

Chapter 3

THE EFFECT OF EXECUTIONS IS BRUTALIZATION, NOT DETERRENCE

WILLIAM J. BOWERS

Do we really believe that the death penalty deters? If so, why did we ban executions from public view in the nineteenth century, and why do we now keep them off television? Most states removed them from public places over a century ago to avoid the troubles—drunkenness, disturbances, and violence—that often accompanied them. It was widely acknowledged that public executions brought out the worst in people. In our own times, a chief argument for keeping them off TV is that the sight of someone being intentionally and deliberately put to death is obscene, grotesque, and might provoke violence in others—evidence, some would say, that executions are cruel and unusual punishment. Indeed, for this very reason, some have argued that putting executions on television would be the surest way to hasten their abolition (Moran, 1985).

What is more, we purposely keep executions from the view of prison inmates, who are surely most in need of the deterrence message. In the prisons where they are performed, executions are often scheduled during the times when inmates are supposed to be sleeping, to minimize the possibility of disruptions and disorders. Our experience is that those who should benefit most react instead with anger, resentment, and hostility, if not overt violence, to the "lesson" of an execution. Thus,

AUTHOR'S NOTE: *I am grateful for the assistance and encouragement of Carla Bregman, William Holmes, Susan Laws, Colin Loftin, Tracy Mayors, Jack McDevitt, and Glenn Pierce. This work was supported in part by National Science Foundation Grant Number 7804603 and by a grant from the Chicago Resource Center.*

despite our deterrence rhetoric, we act as if capital punishment has the opposite effect—as if there is something very wrong, possibly dangerous, about executions, as if they have a brutalizing effect.

Opinion polls tell us that deterrence is the chief reason people give for favoring capital punishment, but they also reveal that most of those who cite deterrence as their rationale would still favor the death penalty even if it could be proved, to their satisfaction, not to have a deterrent advantage over life imprisonment (Ellsworth and Ross, 1983). Perhaps deterrence is the "safe," "acceptable" justification for what is actually supported by the desire for vengeance (Bowers, 1984: 385 ff.).

In what follows, we first try to take a realistic look at the opposing theories of deterrence and brutalization. We next examine and evaluate the empirical evidence bearing on these arguments. We then present the results of a reanalysis of a recent study that seemingly contradicts the existing body of research—one that claims to provide "the first compelling statistical evidence" that executions deter homicides (Phillips, 1980: 139). And we conclude with a discussion of the constitutional challenge posed by the mounting empirical evidence of brutalization.

DETERRENCE

Our rationalistic society looks to utilitarian justification for its public policies and institutions, typically in terms of a favorable balance of benefits over costs. The alleged power of capital punishment to save innocent human lives by dissuading would-be murderers is a most formidable justification, if true (Nathanson, 1987). Yet, the argument for the deterrent advantage of the death penalty rests on a collection of questionable assumptions: (1) that would-be murderers act rationally in deciding whether to kill, (2) that they know what constitutes a capital murder, (3) that they are sensitive to actual variations in the likelihood of execution, (4) that they view death as less acceptable than the other punishments imposed for capital murder, and finally (5) that the deterrence message is not neutralized by other confounding or contrary messages conveyed by capital punishment.

From what we know about murder, there is reason to doubt the first of these assumptions. Most murders are acts of passion between angry or frustrated people who know one another; indeed, many murders are the unintended result of assaults occurring under the influence of alcohol (Wolfgang, 1958). Many murderers are persons who have previously and repeatedly assaulted their victims (Kelling et al., 1974). Encounters that end in murder typically involve "face saving" (Luckenbill, 1977) or the maintenance of favorable "situational identities" (Felsen and Steadman, 1979) in the presence of threats, insults, and attempted intimidation.

But, it will be argued, these are not the kinds of deliberate, premeditated killings for which the death penalty is reserved and would be effective as a deterrent. Essentially, this was the position taken by the U.S. Supreme Court in *Gregg v. Georgia* (1976: 185-186) when the plurality conceded "we may . . . assume safely that . . . the threat of death has little or no deterrent effect [on murderers] who act in passion," but asserted that for "carefully contemplated murders" entailing a "cold calculus that precedes the decision to act . . . the death penalty is *undoubtedly* a significant deterrent" [emphasis added].

Yet in reality, death sentences are not exclusively, or even primarily, handed down for "carefully contemplated killings." Specifically, the two statutory aggravating circumstances most commonly used by Florida and Georgia juries to justify a death sentence under post-*Furman* capital statutes were (1) that the killing was particularly "heinous," "vile," "atrocious," or "depraved" or (2) that the killing occurred in the course of another crime, the kind of killing often prompted by alarm, desperation, or fear of apprehension (Bowers and Pierce, 1980a, reprinted in Bowers, 1984: Chap. 7). We appear to be less concerned with the deliberation and premeditation of offenders than with the brutal, cruel, mindless, even irrational or spontaneous character of their crimes—suggesting that we are more serious about retribution or vengeance[1] than about deterrence as the rationale for capital punishment. Some have argued that identification with murder victims and their families is what governs our use of the death penalty—and accounts, as well, for its disproportionate use in cases involving white victims (Gross and Mauro, 1984; Bowers, 1984). The result is that those who reach death row do not fit the mold of the calculating murderer, a point not likely to be missed by the potential offender who pays attention to how we use the death penalty.

Furthermore, it is doubtful that the calculating potential murderer will be dissuaded by the risk of execution; it is too slight, too remote, and too difficult to gauge. Official statistics since 1930 show that only a tiny fraction of homicides each year have resulted in executions—it reached 2% only once since then, in 1938 (Bowers, 1984: Table 1.4). The execution risk for first-degree or capital murders may be three times this figure, though even experts (Bailey, 1975; Savitz, 1958) have had difficulty determining the number of "definitely" or "possibly" capital murders. About the only way would-be murderers can get some rough impression of execution risk is from the number and pacing of executions reported in the press. And they are apt to notice that executions are very infrequent relative to the number of homicides reported in the same sources.

Moreover, the contingent nature of execution risk will make the slim chance of execution seem all the more remote. An execution will occur only after a long series of failures on the offender's part—the failure to avoid suspicion, apprehension, a capital charge, prosecution on that charge, a capital conviction, a death sentence, unsuccessful appeals, and a denial of clemency. Like most people who find it difficult to incorporate remote contingencies, especially those implying ineptitude or failure, into their plans, the potential offender is apt to concentrate on the critical early stages of avoiding suspicion, apprehension, or a capital charge that will drastically alter the certainty and severity of any punishment. In effect, the risk of execution is so objectively slight and subjectively remote, if at all discernible, as to be beyond the threshold of salient considerations for would-be offenders.[2]

Still further, the deterrence argument hinges on the assumption that potential murderers will regard execution as less desirable than the chief alternatives for convicted capital offenders—many years, if not life, in prison—at the time of a decision to act. Facing execution, most condemned murderers will seek appeals to avoid death and perhaps say they would prefer a life sentence (though Gary Gilmore and Jessie Bishop, who both had protracted previous prison experience, were exceptions). But when the chances of death are less immediate, indeed slight and remote, peoples' perspectives may change. In our culture, dangerous, sometimes death-risking activities are often admired as signs of courage or "machismo." In some quarters, especially among young males involved in "violent subcultures" or committed to criminal activities, manifest indifference to such risks may contribute to peer and self-regard; potential offenders may say and even come to believe that they would rather be dead than spend the rest of their lives in prison.

Beyond these misgivings about the application of the rational deterrence model to the murder decision, there is yet another reason to doubt that potential offenders will be deterred by capital punishment. An execution may have a different meaning or convey a different message to potential murderers than we suppose or intend. If a would-be murderer identifies with an executed offender, he might be persuaded that the same could, and perhaps would, happen to him were he to follow in that offender's footsteps. But the psychology of identification tells us that people identify with those they admire or envy. From what we know about murderers who are eventually executed, it seems likely that few potential murderers would identify with them. Characteristically, they are misfits who have committed cruel or cowardly acts without provocation or remorse. They may have strangled small children, killed whole families, dismembered their victims, and the like. Will calculating potential murderers identify with such persons, or will they not infer that the death penalty is reserved as punishment only for people unlike themselves?

BRUTALIZATION

The argument that executions have a brutalizing effect on society rests on a longstanding and contrasting assumption about the message that executions convey. In 1764, the first serious critic of capital punishment in modern times, Cesare di Beccaria, attacked the death penalty for the "savage example" it presents:

> Laws designed to temper human conduct should not embrace a savage example which is all the more baneful when the legally sanctioned death is inflicted deliberately and ceremoniously. To me it is an absurdity that the law which expresses the common will and detests and punishes homicide should itself commit one [in Sellin, 1967: 43].

A similar argument was advanced in 1846 by Robert Rantoul, Jr., who was among the first to compile statistical evidence of the brutalizing effect of execution:

> After every instance in which the law violates the sanctity of human life, that life is held less sacred by the community among whom the outrage is perpetrated [in Hamilton, 1854: 494].

In other words, the lesson of an execution may be that those who have gravely offended us deserve to die and should therefore be killed. If a potential offender feels betrayed, dishonored, or disgraced by another person, the example executions provide may provoke him to kill the person who has grievously offended him. The fact that such killings are to be performed only by duly appointed officials upon duly convicted offenders may be obscured by the message that such offenders deserve to die. In effect, the fundamental message of the execution may be lethal vengeance rather than deterrence.

The brutalization argument suggests an identification process different from the one implied by deterrence theory. The potential murderer may equate someone who has greatly offended him—someone he hates, fears, or both—with the executed criminal. We might call this the psychology of "villain identification." Indeed, he himself may identify with the state as avenger; the execution may justify and reinforce his resolve to exact lethal vengeance.

Granted, it is uncommon, and perhaps discomforting, to think of potential murderers as self-righteous avengers who identify with the executioner; but the assumption that they will identify with criminals who are executed may simply be wishful thinking. Perhaps we are inclined to believe that potential murderers will recognize themselves as such and be deterred because this distinguishes "them" from the rest of "us" and provides a utilitarian rationale for capital punishment that masks our own desire for lethal vengeance.

Executions may stimulate homicides in other ways. For some people the psychology of suggestion or imitation may be activated by an execution. In the era of public executions, such imitative behavior was noted in the press and commented on by prominent social critics. In the *New York Daily Tribune* of February 18, 1853, no less a critic than Karl Marx offered documentation. Citing statistics on executions, suicides, and murders for 43 days in 1849, he commented as follows:

> This table . . . shows not only suicides but also murders of the most atrocious kind following closely upon the execution of criminals [quoted in Feuer, 1959: 487].

The *Times* of London on January 25, 1864, contained the following observation:

> It has often been remarked that in this country a public execution is generally followed closely by instances of death by hanging, either suicidal or accidental, in consequence of the powerful effect which the execution of a noted criminal produces upon a morbid and unmatured mind [quoted in Feuer, 1959: 485-486].

Nor did removing executions from public view eliminate their brutalizing impact, according to later commentators:

> This morbid press publicity has a most demoralizing effect upon the community and many weak-minded persons of inadequate self-control are thus enabled to dwell on the details of horrible crimes with the real danger of repeating them [Calvert, 1973: 111-112].

Thus, publicizing executions, even without allowing people to witness them, may cause some people—perhaps those on the fringe of sanity—to become fascinated or obsessed with the condemned person's crime, even to the point of imitating it.

Moreover, the imitative impact of an execution may not be limited to the condemned person's crime. Thus, another commentator has observed that the execution itself may be imitated:

> Lynchings are the sequel of the imposition of the death penalty by the state, which, setting the example of sending criminals to the gallows, leads mobs to adopt similar methods of punishment when aroused. This is not unlike the argument . . . that the public executions of old, instead of deterring criminals from crime, led them into it by brutalizing their feelings and cheapening the value of human life [Bye, 1919: 70-71].

Notably, the fact that lynching was itself a capital offense in most states where it occurred did not deter literally thousands of otherwise "law-abiding" citizens. There have been roughly 3,500 documented lynchings since 1890 (see Bowers, 1984: 54, Table 23).

Other publicized acts of violence appear to provoke imitation. Research on the assassination of John F. Kennedy and two highly publicized mass murders found that they were followed by significantly increased rates of violent crime in the months immediately thereafter (Berkowitz and McCauley, 1971). The investigators offer the following three-point interpretation of imitative violence:

> One, aggressive ideas and images arise. Most of these thoughts are probably quite similar to the observed event, but generalization processes also lead to other kinds of violent ideas and images as well.

Two, if inhibitions against aggression are not evoked by the witnessed violence or by the observers' anticipation of negative consequences of aggressive behavior, and if the observers are ready to act violently, the event can also evoke open aggression. And again, these aggressive responses need not resemble the instigating violence too closely.

Three, these aggressive reactions probably subside fairly quickly but may reappear if the observers encounter other environmental stimuli associated with aggression—and especially stimuli associated with the depicted violence. [p. 239].

And sometimes such suggestion or stimulation may also involve identification with the victim. Thus, research on highly publicized suicides has shown that they are followed in the succeeding month by a significantly higher-than-expected number of suicides (Phillips, 1974; Wasserman, 1984). Phillips estimated, for example, that Marilyn Monroe's suicide provoked some 363 suicides in the United States and Britain.

There is also evidence that some troubled individuals seek execution in preference to suicide. Many cases of persons who have killed others for self-destructive motives have been documented (Sellin, 1959; West, 1975; Solomon, 1975; Diamond, 1975). For those burdened with self-hatred, death by execution may be escape rather than punishment. With the crime that leads to execution, the offender also strikes back at society or particular individuals. The execution will, of course, satisfy a guilt-inspired desire for punishment, and may also be seen as providing the opportunity to be seen and heard, and may also be seen as providing the opportunity to be seen and heard, an occasion to express resentment, alienation, and defiance.

Nor should we overlook the fact that death-risking behavior is sometimes a way of affirming one's commitments and winning favor in our society. It is a sign of courage and bravery in wartime, a source of recognition and admiration among sportsmen and adventurers, an affirmation of honor in the face of insults, and a demonstration of allegiance with others who share a common cause. The very existence of the death penalty may, therefore, provide some fanatical or troubled people with a unique opportunity to "prove a point" or draw attention to themselves.

THE EVIDENCE

Strictly speaking, deterrent and brutalizing effects are not mutually exclusive; the same execution could dissuade some potential murderers and provoke others to kill. The available studies do not, however, assess these two effects independently; they simply indicate whether and to what extent one or the other predominates. Furthermore, neither effect is necessarily the result of a single unitary process. Each might operate directly on the perceptions, motives, and judgments of potential offenders, and indirectly through normative processes in the broader community, including the reference groups of potential offenders.[3] Again, the existing studies provide no explicit way of distinguishing between such direct and indirect mechanisms of effect.

These studies do, however, differ in their definition of the impact period or length of time for which capital punishment is presumed to have an effect. Most have examined what we will call the death penalty's "long-term" effect for one or more years with annually reported homicide statistics. Fewer have examined the death penalty's more immediate "short-term" impact with data on homicides in the days, weeks and months following executions. Differences between the results of long-term and short-term impact studies might yield some insights about the timing and duration of any deterrent or brutalizing effects and thus suggest whether direct and/or indirect mechanisms of effects are involved.

Long-Term Effects

Well over a century ago, the effects of publicly imposed executions in the United States were being examined with homicide statistics for extended periods of time from a number of countries. Perhaps America's foremost compiler and interpreter of such data was Massachusetts legislator and man of letters, Robert Rantoul, Jr. In 1846, he presented a report in the form of six letters containing detailed tabulations and interpretations of these data to the legislature and governor of Massachusetts. Rantoul's analyses of these data were broadly comparative across jurisdictions and over time:

> In England, France, Prussia, Belgium, and Saxony, as well as many other nations that might be mentioned, where the proportion

of executions to convictions is much smaller than in Massachusetts, and much smaller than fifty years ago in the same
countries, murders have rapidly diminished in those countries in
which executions are scarcely known; slightly in France where the
change of policy was not so great; while in England, down to about
1835, murders and attempts to murder increased, since which,
under a milder administration of the law, there has been a change
for the better [Hamilton, 1854: 504].

Rantoul was also sensitive to the correlation of executions and
homicides within restricted time intervals. Thus, for the period 1796-
1833 in Belgium, he observed,

Not only does this result follow from the table taken as a whole,
but each period in which a change in the degree of severity occurs,
teaches the same lesson. The three years in which more than fifty
executions occurred in each year, were followed respectively by
the three years of most numerous murders [Hamilton, 1854: 498].

By showing that high execution levels were followed in time by
increased murder rates, and not vice yersa, he attempted to rule out the
possibility that changing murder rates or other associated factors might
have altered the public's desire for executions—as an alternative to the
brutalization hypothesis. Clearly, the deterrence argument finds no
support in these data;[4] instead, they suggest the argument that
executions, at least public executions, have a brutalizing effect on
society.
    After public executions had virtually disappeared, the focus of
research on the effects of capital punishment shifted from the actual use
to the legal availability of the death penalty. The introduction of Census
Bureau death registration standards and mortality statistics in a number
of states around the turn of the century provided a new, more reliable
measure of homicide—one more strictly comparable across states and
over time.
    In 1919 Raymond Bye used these data to compare abolitionist states
with neighboring death penalty states, and periods of abolition with
periods of retention in states that had abolished or reinstated capital
punishment. His work marked the beginning of a series of investigations
of the effects of laws providing for the death penalty. These studies were
based initially on the willful homicide data of the Census Bureau and
later on the criminal homicide statistics of the FBI (Sutherland, 1925;

Vold, 1932, 1952; Schuessler, 1952; Sellin, 1955, 1959, 1967; Reckless, 1969). Best known in this tradition of research is the work of Thorsten Sellin (1959, partially reprinted in Sellin, 1967 and Bedau, 1967; reviewed in Baldus and Cole, 1975, and Zeisel, 1976). Although each investigator in this tradition rejected the hypothesis that the *de jure* availability of executions had a deterrent effect on homicides, as a group these investigations suggest something more: the balance of evidence favors the proposition that the death penalty has a brutalizing effect, even after the removal of executions from public view.

First of all, every study comparing abolitionist and neighboring retentionist states found that the former tended to have lower homicide rates than the latter, as indicated in the following listing of findings:

- Of seven abolitionist states examined over the period 1906-1915, six were below the mean homicide rate for retentionist states in their census registration area [Bye, 1919: 42-43].
- Of eight abolitionist states examined in 1932, the 1928-1929 homicide rates of seven were below the mean for retentionist states in their more narrowly drawn (by that time) census registration areas [Vold, 1932: 6, Table 1].
- Of five abolitionist states studied for the period 1931-1946, four had lower homicide rates than retentionist states selected according to contiguity [Schuessler, 1952: 58, Table 2].
- Of three abolitionist states studied over the period 1933-1951, each had lower homicide rates than either of two contiguous death penalty states during their periods of abolition [Vold, 1952: 4, Table 3].
- Of eight abolitionist states studied over the period 1920-1955, six had lower homicide rates than the mean for their contiguous death penalty states during their periods of abolition [Sellin, 1959: 25-33, Tables 6-8].
- Of nine abolitionist states paired with retentionist states for the year 1967, lower homicide rates were found in five of the abolitionist states and in three of the retentionist states, with one tie [Reckless, 1969: 52 ff., Tables 9 and 10].

In addition, studies of the killing of policemen, prison guards, and prison inmates also found that the rates tended to be lower in abolitionist than in death penalty states.

- Sellin's study (1955) of police homicides shows that cities in abolitionist states had lower rates than those in death penalty states, and this difference holds within three of five categories of city size.

- Campion's study (1955) of state police homicides standardized by police force size shows that rates were lower in abolitionist than in death penalty states within most regions (New England, east north central, and west north central, though the results were ambiguous for east north central).
- Sellin's study (1967) of the killing of prison guards and prison inmates does not contain sufficient information to make standardized comparisons of rates within regional groupings of contiguous states, but the qualitative results certainly give no indication of a deterrent effect.

Of course, the consistently lower homicide rates of abolitionist states could be a cause rather than a consequence of abolition or both could be a result of other common causes not adequately controlled by contiguous state comparisons.[5] To deal with these causal ambiguities, investigators have employed stronger quasi-experimental designs. In particular, they have identified statutory changes (abolition and reinstatement in a given state), compared homicide rates for periods before and after the change in their state, and used homicide rates for the corresponding periods in neighboring nonchange (abolitionist or retentionist) states to control for trends in homicide owing to factors other than the statutory change. These quasi-experimental tests of the death penalty's effect yield further evidence favoring the brutalization over the deterrence hypothesis.

- In Bye's study (1919) of the period 1906-1915, Kansas, Minnesota, and Washington abolished the death penalty, but before/after homicide rates for the change states and nonchange states increased less after abolition than in Wisconsin, Michigan, Indiana, or Ohio for comparable before-after periods.
- In Sellin's study (1959) of the period 1920-1955 South Dakota and Kansas reinstated the death penalty; homicide rates decreased less in South Dakota than in its contiguous states of North Dakota and Nebraska, but homicide rates decreased more in Kansas than in its contiguous states of Colorado and Missouri.
- In Reckless's study (1969) of the period 1963-1967, Oregon, Iowa, West Virginia, and New York abolished capital punishment. Although he did not show the corresponding homicide rates for nonchange states contiguous to these four, they are readily available from the Uniform Crime Reports for the respective years.

With the UCR homicide data for the contiguous states, we found the following patterns (Bowers and Pierce, 1980b, reprinted in Bowers, 1984: Chap. 8: 462-463, note 33):

Homicide rates in Oregon increased less than in Washington, Idaho, California, or Nevada; homicide rates in West Virginia increased less than in Virginia, Maryland, Pennsylvania, Ohio, or Kentucky; homicide rates in Iowa increased less than in Minnesota, Wisconsin, Illinois, or Nebraska but more than in Missouri or South Dakota; and homicide rates in New York increased less than in Connecticut, Massachusetts, or Ohio but more than in Pennsylvania or New Jersey.

Thus, of the seven cases identified by Bye, Sellin, and Reckless in which a state abolished or reinstated the death penalty, and homicide rates were available before and after the change both for the change state and for contiguous nonchange states, the results favor brutalization over deterrence. In four cases the brutalization argument is supported in all comparisons with nonchange states; in two cases the results are mixed, with some comparisons supporting brutalization and others supporting deterrence; and in one case the result is consistent with the deterrence argument in both comparisons with nonchange states. The two cases with mixed results favor the brutalization argument if the homicide rates for the contiguous states are averaged. In the one case that is fully consistent with the deterrence argument, one of the two comparisons with contiguous nonchange states is very close (Kansas versus Missouri).[6]

Investigators (Schuessler, 1952; Sellin, 1959) also examined the experience of other nations with abolition and reinstatement without finding evidence of deterrence. But here again, when these experiences are pooled and evaluated more systematically, there is more evidence of brutalization than deterrence. Thus Archer et al. (1983) recently identified 14 locations—12 countries and two of their major cities—that experienced such a change during a period for which data on homicide and other crimes were available in the Comparative Crime Data File on some 110 nations and 44 major cities (Archer and Gartner, 1984). They found that following abolition homicide rates were more likely to fall than rise within one year and over longer periods, especially so relative to other noncapital crimes. Such a decline in homicides relative to noncapital offenses was also observed following the 1967 experimental abolition in Canada (Fattah, 1972; Bowers, 1974: Chap. 5) and after the 1972 temporary abolition in the United States (Klein et al., 1978).

After executions had altogether ceased and the Supreme Court had declared existing capital statutes unconstitutional, the focus of research shifted back to the *de facto* use of capital punishment with the appearance of a new brand of econometric modeling studies. Instead of comparing homicide rates for matched jurisdictions and time periods as Sellin and others had done, this approach attempted to estimate the effect of execution risk on homicide rates by using multiple regression techniques to adjust statistically for differences across states or over time.

The first of these studies by Isaac Ehrlich (1975) examined annual execution risk and homicide rates for the nation as a whole over the period 1933-1969. In contrast to the previous researchers, Ehrlich purported to show that such executions saved seven or eight innocent lives (Ehrlich, 1975: 414). This work is noteworthy for its role in the U.S. Supreme Court's 1976 *Gregg* decision upholding capital punishment (Bowers, 1984: Chap. 9) and for the series of further studies it stimulated, though not for the validity of its findings, since discredited by a number of critiques and reanalyses of these data (Bowers and Pierce, 1975; Passell and Taylor, 1976; Klein et al., 1978).

Ehrlich criticized earlier studies for failing to examine the risk of executions and for failing to control adequately for other determinants of homicide, including the risk of arrest and conviction. His critics responded that sociodemographic factors and the measured risk of arrest and conviction for criminal homicide were actually quite similar in the contiguous death penalty and abolitionist states examined in earlier studies (Baldus and Cole, 1975) and that Ehrlich's measure of execution risk as the probability of execution given conviction was not the policy-relevant variable in view of likely "jury nullification," or the tendency not to convict when the penalty may be death (Friedman, 1979; Lempert, 1981).

What did careful reanalyses of Ehrlich's data show? First, execution risk tended to be positively associated with homicide rates from the mid-1930s through the early 1960s, using Ehrlich's data and analytic approach (Bowers and Pierce, 1975). Second, the relationship also tended to be positive to the 1960s when this period was examined independently of the earlier years (Bowers and Pierce, 1975; Forst, 1977, 1983). Third, the relationship tended to be even more positive when less flawed homicide data were used in the analyses (Bowers, 1984: Chap. 9).

In this connection, the National Academy of Sciences' critique of Erhlich's work observed that errors in the measurement of homicides appear to introduce a negative bias owing to the "common-term" problem[7] that tends to mask counterdeterrent or brutalizing effects.

> If the homicide rate were in fact totally insensitive to changes in the execution rate, measurement errors even as small as those caused by Ehrlich's having used a homicide series rounded to the nearest 10 murders would have biased his estimate of this key relationship toward a negative unit elasticity. That Ehrlich has estimated elasticities for $P_{e/c}$ (probability of execution given conviction) considerably nearer to zero than to −1 could be regarded as evidence that the true elasticity is positive, indicating a counterdeterrent effect of capital punishment [Klein et al., 1978: 347].

Despite this negative bias owing to measurement problems, further studies have turned up at least as many positive as negative estimated effects of execution risk. Among subsequent national-level time series analyses, positive "counterdeterrent" effects have emerged when measures of gun ownership (Kleck, 1979) and noncapital violent crime (Klein et al., 1978) were included in the analysis. Among state-level cross-sectional studies, positive estimates have again outnumbered negative estimates in investigations including measures on noncapital crime and of the certainty and duration of imprisonment for homicide (Passell, 1975; Forst, 1977, 1983; Bailey, 1977, 1980a, 1980b; Black and Orsagh, 1978). The chief exception is Ehrlich's (1977) cross-sectional study that again reported "deterrent effects," but was criticized for its use of the 1940 census year when homicide statistics were relatively unreliable, for the absence of a regional control variable, and for other analytic assumptions (Forst, 1977, 1983; Hoenack and Weiler, 1980). More generally, Barnett (1981) has questioned the utility of any of these cross-sectional studies for drawing statistically reliable inferences about the effects of execution risk on homicides.

In a series of state-level time series studies also subject to the negative bias of the common-term problem, William Bailey nevertheless found more positive than negative estimates of the effect of execution risk on homicide rates with annual time series data. Positive outnumbered negative estimates in North Carolina, California, and Oregon (Bailey, 1978b, 1979a, 1979b), whereas the converse was true for Utah and Ohio (Bailey, 1978a, 1979c). Subsequent studies of the effects of differences in

execution risk between contiguous states on differences in their
homicide rates for 11 pairs of states over the period 1920 to 1955
(Lempert, 1983) and of the availability and use of capital punishment for
lethal assaults upon the police by state for the period 1961-1971 (Bailey,
1982) again turned up as many positive as negative coefficients for
execution risk, despite the negative bias of the common-term problem.
And in an analysis free of the bias introduced by the common-term
problem (where execution risk was computed by dividing the number of
persons executed in 1960 by the number of murderers imprisoned that
year), Bailey (1980a) found significant positive effects of execution risk
on homicide rates consistent with a brutalizing effect of executions.

Recently, Stephen Layson (1985) has extended Ehrlich's analysis
through 1977, substituted Census for FBI homicide data, included
additional sociodemographic variables, and claimed to show that the
effect of executions was twice that estimated by Ehrlich—18 lives saved
by each execution. But Layson's work, like Ehrlich's, is "fatally flawed"
(Fox, 1986). Thus, the UCR conviction data used by Layson (and
Ehrlich before him) for the critical measure of execution risk were
dropped by the FBI in 1978 as too unreliable to be included in the
Uniform Crime Reports. Moreover, Fox (1986: Table 1) demonstrated
that there was a significant disjuncture in the estimated effect of
execution risk at about the time of a substantial change in the number
and mix of agencies reporting these data to the FBI (as documented in
Bowers and Pierce, 1975: Figures 1 and 2) and that alternative estimates
with procedures to minimize the problem of multicolinearity actually
yield positive effects of execution risk on homicide rates for the earlier
period when about 90% of the executions were imposed.

Although it seems unreasonable for the increased *risk* of executions
to generate higher homicide rates (counterdeterrence), if execution risk
in these studies is actually serving as a proxy for the *occurrence* of
executions, this result may reflect the possibility that executions incite
homicides (brutalization). In any case, since it may be the occurrence of
executions that affects potential offenders (whether they use the number
and pacing of executions for some impressionistic "guesstimate" of risk
or as a misguided justification for the use of lethal violence against
others) and since the number (unlike the risk) of executions is free of the
common-term problem, we have substituted the number of executions
imposed annually for Ehrlich's measure of execution risk and reproduced the analysis (Bowers, 1984: Chap. 9). This yields consistently
positive and often statistically significant estimates, especially with the

more reliable census-based homicide data. Similar positive effects, though not generally strong enough to be statistically significant, were obtained by Bailey (1984) when he substituted the number for the risk of executions in an analysis of data for Washington, D.C. over the period 1890-1970, though not by Decker and Kohfield (1984) who got very slight negative estimates using the number of executions and the lag for Illinois over the period 1933-1980.

In summary: Most investigators set out to test for deterrent effects and rejected the deterrence hypothesis. A few claimed to find deterrent effects, but have since had their findings discredited, even reversed. Our review indicates that the failure to find deterrence in study after study may add up to more than the absence of deterrence.

For the effects of public executions, we have only the fragmentary evidence from historical records. Though the evidence is consistent with the brutalizing effects of executions, the measurement of homicides is dependent on court records of homicide charges or convictions and the data are selectively reported. With the development of state level mortality statistics that include homicide as a cause of death, investigators began to compare homicide rates for jurisdictions and time periods when capital punishment was in force, abolished, and reinstated. Most of these comparisons favor brutalizing over deterrent effects, and this holds for before/after matched treatment/control comparisons as well as weaker designs. And with the advent of complex statistical approaches, especially econometric modeling techniques, positive counter-deterrence or brutalization effects appear at least as often as "deterrence findings" and more commonly in the studies that attempt to avoid or adjust for known problems in the data and analyses.[8]

Finally, the failure of these long-term effect studies to show a more sizable or more consistent brutalizing effect may be owing in part to the nature of the effects and in part to the nature of the studies. Suppose, for example, that the brutalizing effect is the result not of a long-term normative process that encourages the acceptance of violence in society, but of the more immediate and direct reactions some individuals in some circumstances have to executions. Such effects should be more clearly evident in studies that (1) examine the occurrence rather than the risk of executions; (2) look at the effect of executions within a more immediate time frame; and (3) consider relatively large samples of observations. The first two of these features are typical of most, and all three are characteristic of some short-term impact studies.

Short-Term Impact

As executions in America reached a high point in the mid-1930s, the first systematic study of the more immediate impact of executions appeared. Thus, in 1935, Robert Dann identified five well-publicized executions in Philadelphia, occurring in 1927, 1929, 1930, 1931, and 1932, each isolated from any other execution by at least 60 days (Dann, 1935: 1). He then tallied the number of homicides in 60-day periods before and after each execution. There was a total of 91 homicides before and 113 homicides after these five executions—an increase of 22 homicides, or 4.4 per execution. As it happens, Dann's results are not independent of seasonal variations in homicides (Bowers and Pierce, 1980b). A crude adjustment for the seasonality of homicides in Philadelphia indicates that a total of 105 (rather than 91) homicides might have been expected in the postexecution period.[9] Hence, a more reliable estimate of the impact of these five executions would be eight additional homicides—an average of 1.6 more homicides per execution within 60 days.

Dann's work inspired a similar study of well-publicized death sentences in Philadelphia some two decades later. In 1958, Leonard Savitz examined eight-week periods before and after death sentences were handed down in four well-publicized cases, occurring in 1944, 1946 (two) and 1947 (Savitz, 1958: 338). For these periods, he tallied "definitely capital" and "possibly capital" murders (which comprised about one-quarter of all homicides). He found 43 murders in the eight-week period before, and 41 in the eight-week period after these four death sentences. Again, like Dann, Savitz overlooked the impact of seasonal variations in homicides (Bowers and Pierce, 1980b). This time the adjustment for monthly variations in homicides in Philadelphia[10] yields an expected 36 post-death sentence murders. Hence, there were five more observed than expected postexecution murders within eight weeks—an average of 1.25 more murders per death sentence. Savitz also reported more "definitely capital" and fewer "possibly capital" murders after these death sentences, clearly contrary to the deterrence argument.

Dann's work also stimulated a study of the impact of executions within days of these events. In 1956, William Graves tabulated the daily incidence of homicides in San Francisco, Los Angeles, and Alameda counties of California over the period 1946-1955. He looked at homicides in each week with an execution and in the execution-free weeks immediately before and after each execution week. A total of 74 executions were imposed during this period, all but six of which were carried out on Fridays, a routine California practice at that time. Graves reported that during execution weeks the number of homicides was slightly higher on Thursdays and Fridays (the day before and the day of execution) and slightly lower on Saturdays and Sundays (the first and second days after execution) than the average for the corresponding days of the execution-free weeks immediately before and after. He observed that the slight depression in homicides in the two days immediately after an execution "is almost exactly canceled out by its earlier 'brutalizing' effect," and speculated, "May it be that minds already burdened with conscious or subconscious homicidal intent are stimulated by the example of the state's taking of life to act sooner?" (Graves, 1956: 137)

What Graves's data (Table 1, rows 1 and 2) also show, but he failed to notice, is that homicides were more numerous after than before these executions (Bowers and Pierce, 1980b). If he had treated the weeks preceding executions as a baseline, he would have seen that on the average there were .05 more homicides in the execution week and .20 more homicides in the week following an execution, suggesting that one out of four executions stimulates a homicide by the end of the following week.

More recently, studies have evaluated the state-wide impact of executions with monthly homicide statistics. In 1978, David King identified 20 executions in South Carolina over the period 1951-1962 that were covered in South Carolina's largest circulation daily.[11] He compared the number of homicides in the month of and the month after an execution story with the average for the corresponding months in the year before and after (adjusted if there was an execution story in one of these comparison months). King found .6 fewer homicides per execution in the month after a story, for a net increase of 1.2 homicides, on the average, in the months of, and immediately after an execution story. He reported that the rise in homicides the month after an execution story was statistically reliable in his relatively small sample of 20 cases at the .10 probability level.

New York has had more homicides and more executions than any other state since the turn of the century. By examining monthly homicide figures for New York state (first available in January 1907 from the state Department of Health) and all executions in the state from January 1906 until the last one in August 1963 (in Bowers, 1974, 1984: Appendix A), Glenn Pierce and I used time series regression analysis to estimate how the number of homicides in a given month was affected by the imposition of executions in each of the 12 preceding months (Bowers and Pierce, 1980b). The time series of 57 years and eight months provided a sample of 692 monthly observations, large enough to yield a statistically sensitive test for brutalizing effects of the magnitude observed in earlier short-term impact studies.

The study showed that in New York state over this period there were, on the average, 1.7 additional homicides in the first full month following an execution and 1.3 additional homicides in the second postexecution month. The analysis incorporated controls for time trend, seasonality, and the effect of war years, and adjustments for autocorrelation in the regression disturbance term. With the full range of controls and adjustments, the 1.7-homicide increase in the first postexecution month was statistically significant beyond the .01 probability level under all adjustments for autocorrelation; the 1.3-homicide increase in the second postexecution month was statistically significant at the .05 level under half of these adjustments. Thus, we have statistical support for a brutalizing effect consistent in timing and magnitude with those found in the previous short-term impact investigations.

In a further study using monthly homicide data for the period 1915-1921 in Chicago, William Bailey (1983) also found statistically significant brutalizing effects in the month immediately following some 26 executions. During this period, the Chicago Police Department reported the number of first-degree murder cases and other homicide cases occurring monthly. Bailey's regression analysis included measures of population density, expenditures on public assistance, seasonality, and the certainty of arrest and imprisonment as controls. He estimated that there were 3.0 more first-degree murders and 3.8 more criminal homicides (including first-degree murders) than expected in the month after an execution (with adjustments for autocorrelation).

With an alternative execution variable that weights months according to the number of executions imposed, Bailey obtained reduced (non-significant) brutalization estimates. The only difference this variable introduces is additional weight for no more than a half dozen multiple execution months (evident from the means and maximum values for the two execution variable in his Table 1). Thus, a sizable drop in homicides just after one multiple execution month could obscure an otherwise consistent pattern of rises in the month following executions.

Bailey also reported what might be "delayed" brutalizing effects, but this interpretation of the regression results seems doubtful. With the large number of lagged execution variables in his analysis (lags 1 through 12), the relatively small number of time series observations (72 months remaining after the t-12 lags) and the skewed character of the number of executions variable (see Note 11), these lagged execution variables will be especially sensitive to idiosyncratic fluctuation in homicides that are actually independent of the imposition of executions. Notably, by contrast with the short-term brutalizing effect, Bailey found a deterrent effect associated with the certainty of imprisonment for both first-degree murder and the broader category of criminal homicide.

However, different findings were reported in a study by David Phillips (1980: 139) who, citing the demonstrated flaws in Ehrlich's research, published a short-term impact study providing what he described as "the first compelling statistical evidence that capital punishment does deter homicides." Moreover, Phillips claimed to show that "the more publicity devoted to the execution, the more homicides decreased thereafter" (p. 139).

Phillips reviewed historical sources for the availability of weekly homicide data in a country that imposed executions over an extended period of time. He found that such statistics were published for London from 1858 through 1921 by the Great Britain General Register Office. To identify executions likely to have been publicized over this period, he relied upon the *Encyclopedia of Murder* (Wilson and Pitman, 1962), where he found 22 "notorious murderers" who were executed between 1864 and 1921. For the publicity accorded these cases, Phillips identified all articles about each case (including coverage of the crime, the suspect's apprehension, the coroner's inquest, and the courtroom proceedings, as well as the execution) in the index to the *Times* of London, and then measured the column inches of newsprint in each article.

With these data, Phillips reported finding that: (1) execution-week homicides dropped below the average for the two surrounding weeks in 15 cases, rose above the average in four cases, and remained on a par in three cases, for a statistically significant excess of reductions over increases, according to the binomial distribution; and (2) the Spearman rank correlation between the publicity (in column inches of newsprint) devoted to the case and the size of the execution-week homicide drop (relative to the average of the two surrounding weeks) was substantially significant.

Yet, Phillips' data, spanning the period from four weeks before through six weeks after each execution, showed no net reduction in homicides following these executions. Although homicides fell below the preexecution weekly average in the week of executions (and also in the week immediately thereafter), they rebounded to a level well above this average in the second, third and fourth week following executions. In fact, relative to the preexecution level, the initial two-week drop was .96 homicides per execution, whereas the subsequent five-week rise was .98 homicides per execution. As Phillips observed, "within five or six weeks of a publicized execution, the drop in homicides is canceled by an equally large rise in homicides" (p. 146).

This study stimulated critical commentary (Kobbervig et al., 1982; Zeisel, 1982) and an attempt at replication for recent publicized executions in the United States with weekly homicide data, available since 1972 from the National Center for Health Statistics (McFarland, 1983). For each of the first four post-*Furman* executions (Gilmore in 1977, Spenkelink and Bishop in 1979, and Judy in 1981) McFarland applied ARIMA time-series modeling techniques to remove the effects of trend, seasonality, and autoregressive processes in the weekly homicide data. For each execution, he reported that there was no statistically reliable evidence of a deterrent (or brutalizing) effect. The national homicide figures did drop significantly in the first two weeks following Gilmore's execution (see Lester, 1980), but by examining the homicide pattern for various regions of the country McFarland showed that this decline was attributable to the unusually severe weather conditions brought on by the blizzard of January 1977. Notably, the wide variation in weekly homicide figures at the national level makes this case-by-case time series analysis relatively insensitive to effects as slight as those observed in earlier short-term impact studies.

Finally, of some interest for what it appears to say about the chief alternative to capital punishment is a recent study by Phillips and Hensley (1984). They examined how punishments for murders that were publicized in newspapers and on television—13 life sentences, four death sentences, and three executions—affected the daily incidence of homicides in the United States. For this sample of predominantly life sentences, they reported a statistically significant drop of 3.3 white-victim homicides on the fourth day after these punishments were publicized and a net drop of 18.5 homicides within 21 days. Notably, the executions of Gilmore and Spinkelink contribute virtually nothing to the fourth-day homicide drop (Bishop's cannot be independently evaluated in their Table 2); moreover, the weather-related reduction in homicides following Gilmore's execution demonstrated by McFarland

(1983) could alone account for much of the 21-day net reduction in homicides of the entire sample (reported in their footnote 8). See the critique of Phillips (1983) by Baron and Reiss (1985) for a more general discussion of weaknesses in the statistical approach used by Phillips and Hensley. They did not, however, find a fourth-day drop in a sample of similar punishments that were publicized in newspapers but not on television, or in a sample of equally publicized cases that resulted in acquittals. The authors note that their finding, attributable largely to well-publicized life sentences, "tends to weaken one argument in favor of capital punishment" (p. 198).

In summary: The prevailing evidence from the short-term impact studies is that executions brutalize, that this effect is slight in magnitude (though not in consequence), that it occurs within the first month or two of an execution, and that it dissipates thereafter.

In three California counties, there was a slight but discernible increase in homicides within 10 days of an execution (.25 homicides per execution). In Philadelphia, there was an increase in homicides within 60 days of an execution (1.6 homicides per execution) and within eight weeks of a death sentence (1.2 homicides per death sentence). In Chicago, there was an increase in capital murders (3.0 per execution) and all criminal homicides (3.8 per execution) in the first month following an execution. In South Carolina there was an increase in homicides the month after an execution (1.8 homicides per execution) that was slightly offset by an execution-month reduction for a net two-month homicide increase (1.2 homicides per execution). And, in New York state, there was an average of three more homicides than expected within two months of an execution (1.7 homicides in the first month and 1.3 homicides in the second month). Only the studies of executions occurring long ago in London and quite recently in the United States failed to turn up a net brutalizing (or deterrent) effect. And the only study to show a net deterrent effect examined punishments consisting primarily of life sentences for convicted murderers.

There is a hint in some of these studies that executions may deter some homicides. However, the very same studies suggest that executions provoke more homicides than they prevent. The California study found a homicide drop in the two days immediately following executions, but it was nullified by a rise in the preceding two days and outstripped by a further rise in the following week; the South Carolina study found a homicide drop in the execution month, but it was outweighed by a homicide rise in the following month; and the London study reported a homicide drop in the week of and the week after executions, but it was fully offset by the fifth week following executions. To be sure, these studies do not rule out the possibility that some homicides are deterred by executions; they simply indicate that the brutalizing effect tends to be longer in duration and stronger in impact than any deterrent effect that may occur—that the *net* effect is brutalization rather than deterrence.

A CLOSER LOOK AT PHILLIPS'S
STUDY OF 22 LONDON EXECUTIONS

Most at odds with the other short-term impact studies is Phillips's work on executions in London. First, it is the only study to report a statistically significant deterrent effect of executions. The immediate execution-week homicide drop was found to be statistically significant; the subsequent rebound was not tested for statistical significance. Second, it also reported a statistically significant association between the effect of an execution and the publicity accorded the case. This publicity finding would seem to validate the deterrence interpretation by providing the link between the event and its effect. And it further suggests that giving enough publicity to an execution might produce a deterrent effect that would outstrip any tendency for homicides to rise following executions—unless, of course, brutalizing effects are also enhanced by publicity.

Yet there are some irregularities about this study. In summarizing his deterrence results as a 35.7% homicide decline immediately following publicized executions, Phillips (1980: 145) explicitly included the week *after* as well as the week *of* executions, though his statistical test of deterrence made the week after executions a part of the "control period" and hence explicitly excluded it from the "impact period" when the deterrent effect was supposed to occur.[12] Further, Phillips's Table 1 shows that in the week immediately following executions there were three times as many homicides among the 11 most highly publicized cases as compared to the 11 less publicized ones, suggesting, as Lempert (1981: 1205) observed, that "the more publicized executions may contribute disproportionately to [a] brutalizing effect" that begins to appear the week after an execution.[13] Thus, Phillips's deterrence and publicity findings may be quite sensitive to whether the week after executions is placed in the impact or control period.

For these and additional reasons to be described below, I have undertaken a critique of Phillips's work that includes a replication and extension of his homicide data.[14] This examination of Phillips's study begins with a critique of the statistical analyses supporting his two principal conclusions, turns to a replication of his weekly homicide figures to check on certain peculiarities in the data he presented, and concludes with a further analysis including additional homicides on either side of each execution he examined. Together, these three steps drastically alter what we can say about the effects of executing notorious murderers in London over the period 1858-1921.

Problems in Phillips's Analysis

There are two serious flaws in Phillips's analysis of the data he presented: (1) his deterrence finding is based upon a biased application of the binomial test that favors his short-term deterrence hypothesis; and (2) his publicity finding is based upon an anomalous statistical pattern that is inconsistent with his publicity hypothesis.

To begin with, Phillips's measure of execution week homicide change makes drops almost twice as likely to occur by chance as rises in this particular data set for two related reasons. First, zero is the most common (modal) weekly homicide value; of the 66 values in his Table 1 (for the week before, of and after each of the 22 executions), 28 were zero. Second, by averaging homicides in the week before and after an execution to obtain the expected number for the execution week (instead of using either the week before or after alone) he greatly reduced the chances of a zero expected value. As a result, zero homicides (the modal frequency) in the execution week has an inflated chance of being paired with a nonzero (positive) expected value, thus yielding an execution week homicide drop—taken as evidence of deterrence.[15]

In addition, the rank correlation Phillips reported between execution-week homicide drop[16] and the publicity accorded a case (rho = $-.546$[17], p = .0035[18] corrected for ties[19]) does not reflect a progressively greater homicide drop as publicity increases. In fact, there is virtually no correlation between publicity and homicide drop among the 16 most highly publicized cases (receiving between 208 and 1,695 inches of newsprint): rho = $-.083$, p = .380 (in the wrong direction). What the coefficient reported by Phillips reflects, instead, is a concentration of execution week homicide rises among the six least publicized cases (receiving between 91 and 200 inches of newsprint). Thus, it is the presence of this anomalous pattern of execution week homicide increases among the cases ranked 17 through 22 in publicity that produces the significant Spearman coefficient, (mis)interpreted by Phillips as showing "the more publicity given to the execution, the more homicides drop" (p. 144).[20]

Problems in Phillips's Data

Furthermore, there are two peculiarities in Phillips's data that point to the need for verification and extension of the weekly homicide figures: (1) he reported the number of execution-week homicides as 17 in his Figure 1, but they add up to 19 in his Table 1; and (2) he showed the aggregate weekly number of homicides for unequal periods—six weeks after but only four weeks before the 22 executions in his Figure 1.

Our verification effort revealed that the correct number of execution-week homicides is neither 19 (as in Phillips's Table 1) nor 17 (as in his Figure 1), but 21. There was an error in the highly publicized case of Mueller (ranked third in publicity). In fact, Mueller had not one, but three execution-week homicides, thus converting his case from a drop to a rise in such homicides. Hence, by Phillips's definition, there were actually 14 drops, five rises, and three ties in 22 cases, even closer to what we could expect by chance for this data set.[21]

The extension of the homicide data to an interval before, equal to the one after, these executions markedly reduces the level of preexecution homicides. The addition of week 5 (with only 14 homicides) and week 6 (with 25 homicides) brings the average for preexecution weeks down from 29.5 to 26.2. There were clearly more homicides in periods of equal duration after than before these 22 executions—190 homicides in the six weeks after these executions as compared to 157 in the six weeks before—a 22% *increase* in homicides, or an average of 1.5 *more* homicides after than before each execution. Obviously, the omission of weeks 5 and 6 from Phillips's Figure 1 and the erroneous values for week 0 in his Table 1 and Figure 1 contributed to the illusion of a short-term deterrent effect and masked the evidence of brutalization.

Extension of Phillips's Data

Since our own previous research on New York State suggested that the effect of executions may be felt for two months (Bowers, 1984: Chap.

8; Bowers and Pierce, 1980b), I decided to have the homicide data collected for 10 weeks on either side of each execution—to further extend the sample period from 13 to 21 weeks. This added another 114 homicides to the preexecution period and another 134 to the postexecution period—or another .9 homicides per execution after than before these 22 executions. It brought the excess of post- over preexecution homicides up to 53. The cumulative magnitude of the apparent brutalizing effect rose from 1.5 to 2.4 homicides per execution.

Is the apparent brutalizing effect statistically reliable? We assessed the statistical significance of the postexecution rise in homicides in both the 13-week samples (weeks –6 to +6) and the 21-week sample (weeks –10 to +10) by means of regression analysis. In the respective samples, we defined the "impact period" for each execution as the weeks following its imposition and the "baseline period" as the weeks before and of the execution. The estimated weekly increase in homicides resulting from an execution (the impact value) is represented by the unstandardized regression coefficient, or "b" value, for the impact variable. The statistical significance of the estimated impact is reflected by its *t* value and the associated probability under the two-tailed distribution.[22] The adjusted R^2 shows the fit of the full regression equation, and the Durbin-Watson statistic tests for autocorrelated disturbances that might reflect a bias in the regression estimates.

For each sample, we first estimated the simple regression equation with the impact variable (postexecution weeks coded "1," others "0") alone as the predictor of weekly homicide counts. We next included a control for the seasonality of homicides (with winter weeks coded "1"; spring and fall weeks coded "2"; and summer weeks coded "3").[23] We then added an adjustment for the prevailing level of homicides at the time of the respective executions (with dummy variable for n-l of the 13-week and 21-week execution periods). The results are shown in Table 3.1.[24]

In the 13-week sample, there was a .28 average weekly increase in homicides during the impact (as compared to the baseline) period; however, this falls short of the .05 significance standard, at $p = .080$. The introduction of seasonality as a control has absolutely no effect on the estimated impact of executions or its statistical significance, and only very slightly improves the adjusted R^2 and the D-W statistic. When we also adjust for the time period in which each execution was imposed, the impact estimate remains unchanged, and its significance, though

TABLE 3.1

The Effect of Executions on Homicides in the Weeks Following
Executions Among 22 Highly Publicized Cases
in London, 1858-1921

	b value	t value	Probability of t	Adj. R^2	D-W Statistic
13-Week Sample					
impact period alone	.284	1.755	.080	.007	1.77
with control for seasonality	.283	1.755	.080	.009	1.78
with control for seasonality and time period	.283	1.809	.072	.068	2.06
21-Week Sample					
impact period alone	.266	2.049	.041	.007	1.80
with control for seasonality	.267	2.059	.040	.007	1.80
with control for seasonality and time period	.269	2.189	.029	.113	2.10

strengthened, still falls short of the .05 mark at p = .072 with a further improved R^2 and D-W statistic.

In the 21-week sample, the average weekly increase in homicide in the impact period was very slightly less, b = .27, but qualifies as statistically significant, p = .041. Clearly, the longer impact period following executions (together with the longer baseline period) more than compensates for the slightly reduced average weekly impact in the determination of statistical significance. With the control for seasonality, there is a very slight increase in the estimated effect and its statistical significance. With the additional adjustment for time period, there is another very slight increase in estimated effect, and a more substantial improvement in statistical significance (to p = .029). Hence the observed brutalizing effect in the 21-week sample goes well beyond the .05 standard of statistical reliability (two-tailed test).

Is the brutalizing effect a function of publicity? When we compare the most highly publicized of these executions with the less publicized ones for 6- and 10-week periods immediately before and after, the following differences appear.

In periods of six weeks on either side, there were:

• 22 more homicides after than before the 11 most highly publicized cases, but only
• 11 more homicides after than before the 11 less publicized ones.

In periods of 10 weeks on either side, there were:

- 36 more homicides after than before the 11 most highly publicized cases, but only
- 17 more homicides after than before the 11 less publicized cases.

After both 6 and 10 weeks, the homicide increase among the most publicized cases was at least twice that among the less publicized ones. Evidently, the publicity accorded an execution adds to its brutalizing effect.

To bring publicity into the statistical analysis, we weighted the impact variable (weeks following executions scored "1," others scored "0") by the newsprint (column inches divided by 100) accorded the case. We then substituted this weighted impact variable for the unweighted one used in Table 3.1, as the predictor of weekly homicide levels. The results of the regression analysis with this alternative impact variable are shown in Table 3.2.

Statistically, the estimated effects are highly significant in both samples. In the 13-week sample, the three t values are close to the .01 probability level; in the 21-week sample, they are close to the .001 level. In all cases, the fit of the regression equation, reflected in the adjusted R^2, is improved (relative to the corresponding values in Table 3.1) and the Durbin-Watson statistic remains satisfactory.

Substantively, these results indicate that, on the average, each 100 column inches of newsprint added approximately .05 homicides per week for up to 10 weeks following an execution. In other words, for every 200 inches of newspaper coverage in the *Times* of London, there was one additional homicide within 10 weeks.[25] The estimated weekly effects become slightly stronger when we control for seasonality,[26] or for seasonality and period. And they are very nearly comparable in the 13- and 21-week samples.

Is the brutalizing effect an artifact? Consider the possibility that publicity about murder cases, especially the news coverage in the weeks preceding the execution of a notorious offender, might deter would-be murderers by focusing public attention on the prospect of an execution. Such an "anticipatory deterrent effect" would depress the homicide level in the period before publicized cases, especially before those receiving the most preexecution publicity. If this were so, the subsequent return of homicides to normally expected levels would then create the illusion of a brutalizing effect following executions.

TABLE 3.2

The Effect (per 100 inches) of Newspaper Coverage
on Homicides in the Weeks Following Executions
Among 22 Highly Publicized Cases in London,
1858-1921

	b value	t value	Probability 1 of t	Adj. R^2	D-W Statistic
13-Week Sample					
impact period alone	.0448	2.449	.015	.017	1.77
with control for seasonality	.0504	2.716	.007	.023	1.80
with control for seasonality and time period	.0495	2.325	.021	.075	2.06
21-Week Sample					
impact period alone	.0467	3.199	.002	.020	1.82
with control for seasonality	.0529	3.546	.000	.025	1.83
with control for seasonality and time period	.0509	3.034	.003	.122	2.11

But there is, in fact, no indication of anticipatory deterrence in these data. First, there was no decline in homicides as executions approached. In the 10 weeks preceding these 22 executions, the weekly average per execution was 1.23 homicides. In the four weeks immediately preceding these executions, the weekly average per execution actually rose somewhat to 1.34. Second, there was little difference in preexecution homicides between the more publicized and less publicized of these cases. In the preceding 10 weeks, there was a weekly average per execution of 1.25 homicides before the 11 most publicized cases and 1.22 before the 11 less publicized ones. In the four weeks preceding the more publicized cases the weekly average actually rose to 1.36, and for the less publicized ones it rose to 1.32.

It was after, not before, these executions that the level of homicide changed most and that these changes were associated with publicity. Indeed, in the 10 weeks following these executions there was a 1.47 weekly average per execution: 1.58 for the most publicized and 1.36 for the less publicized cases.

In summary: These data on executions and homicides in London during the period 1858-1921 are obviously *not* the "first compelling statistical evidence" that executions deter homicides, as Phillips claimed. Quite the contrary, they show that executions encourage homicides, more so the more they are publicized.

Such a brutalizing pattern also appears (upon close scrutiny) in most previous studies of homicides in the days, weeks, or months following executions. Yet, these studies usually examined too few executions with too few homicide observations to conclude that a brutalizing effect of as few as two or three homicides per execution was statistically reliable. The first exception was our study of some 600 executions over a 57-year period in New York State. With 692 monthly homicide observations, a rise of two homicides in the first month after an execution was statistically significant. The second exception is Phillips's study as replicated and reanalyzed here. Though Phillips selected only 22 executions for study with 462 weekly homicide observations (weeks –10 through +10), an average increase of 2.7 homicides per execution (b = .27 per week over 10 weeks)[27] is significant beyond the .05 probability level (two-tailed test).[28]

What these London data show for the first time is that the rise in homicides following an execution is associated with the publicity accorded the case. Although homicides rose following the less as well as the more publicized of these cases, the rise was considerably more pronounced among the more publicized ones. This effect of publicity is consistent with the notion that the message executions convey is one of "lethal vengeance"—to strike back with deadly force against someone who has gravely offended—and that this message is more effectively conveyed the more broadly executions are publicized.

Potential offenders who learn about an execution do not appear to identify, as we wish they would, with the murderer who is executed, but may instead identify with the state as an "enforcer" and "executioner" seeking lethal vengeance. The example of an execution may release inhibitions against killing or reinforce justifications for killing, at least among those few who have reached a state of "readiness to kill" (Frazier, 1974).[29] Moreover, the evidence of brutalization is consistent with a growing body of evidence that publicized acts of lethal violence— suicide (Phillips, 1974; Wasserman, 1984), homicide (Phillips, 1983), and fatal accidents (Phillips, 1977, 1978, 1979)—are followed in kind, and with the longstanding judicial wisdom that "brutal punishment brutalizes" (Michael and Wechsler, 1937: 1266-1267, especially note 18).

A QUESTION OF CONSTITUTIONALITY

A decade ago, judicial opinion was divided on evidence of the death penalty's utility as a deterrent. In 1975, the Massachusetts Supreme

Judicial Court considered the existing deterrence research, including the Ehrlich study, and concluded "there is simply no convincing evidence that the death penalty is a deterrent superior to lesser punishments" (*Commonwealth v. O'Neal* 1975: 252). Six months later, the U.S. Supreme Court held, citing Ehrlich's work as its sole support, that the results of "statistical attempts to evaluate the worth of the death penalty as a deterrent to crime by potential offenders have . . . simply been inconclusive" (*Gregg v. Georgia*, 1976: 184-185). Nor was the *Gregg* court of one mind on the deterrence evidence. Justice Marshall, in dissent, offered an insightful critique of the flaws in Ehrlich's work and concluded that the evidence against the deterrent superiority of the death penalty "remains convincing" (*Gregg v. Georgia*, 1976: 233-236).

Since the *Gregg* decision, the scientific evidence against deterrence and for brutalization has mounted. Ehrlich's "deterrence findings" have been discredited and even reversed. Careful review of other studies using annual homicide data has revealed a balance of brutalization over deterrence results. Close examination of homicide data from earlier studies of the days and weeks surrounding executions and death sentences has shown consistent evidence of a brutalizing effect. Recent studies conducted with monthly homicide data have provided more reliable statistical evidence of brutalization. And we now know that Phillips's study, contrary to its original claims, should properly be counted among those finding statistically significant support for the brutalization hypothesis.

To be sure, the plurality in *Gregg* seemed to invoke a narrower standard of deterrent utility than simply the reduction of criminal homicide when it asserted that the death penalty is undoubtedly a significant deterrent for "carefully contemplated murders" but not necessarily so for murderers "who act in passion" (*Gregg v. Georgia*, 1976: 185-186). Of course, no net reduction in criminal homicides as a result of the death penalty implies that any drop in capital homicides is offset by a compensatory rise in noncapital homicides. To ignore this implication and further require a demonstration that "carefully contemplated" and "coldly calculated" killings were not deterred by capital punishment would severely restrict the potential for empirical evaluation of the deterrence test with presently available data.

But, the evidence of a net increase in homicides following executions poses a constitutional challenge quite apart from the test of deterrent efficacy. A punishment that sacrifices innocent human lives in excess of any gain from deterrence is surely a violation of evolving standards in our society. The High Court might continue to believe, despite the absence of empirical evidence, that some killings under some circumstances are deterred by the death penalty. But the balance of empirical evidence now indicates that however many murders may be prevented, a larger number are provoked. More innocent lives are sacrificed than saved by the use of the death penalty. The *net* result of executions is more, not fewer, killings.

NOTES

1. We distinguish between "vengeance" as the public's desire to strike back against offenders in the manner and measure that satisfies the need for revenge, and "retribution" as the application of agreed-upon rules (usually laws) that define the (legally) salient features of an offense, offender, and victim for determining the appropriateness of punishment in a given case and for assuring the fairness of punishment across cases. The disproportionate use of the death sentence in white-victim as opposed to black-victim cases, as painstakingly documented in the recent work of Baldus and his associates (Baldus et al., 1987) and recently reviewed by the U.S. Supreme Court in *McCleskey v. Kemp*, may be interpreted as the substitution of vengeance for retribution.

2. Perhaps the most sensitive test of the argument that execution risk falls below the salience threshold is provided by studies (to be discussed below) that compare abolitionist jurisdictions and periods when it is well-known that there is absolutely no risk of execution with retentionist jurisdictions and periods when it is equally well-known that there is at least some chance that a murderer will be executed.

3. In discussions of deterrence, such indirect effects have been labeled "normative reinforcement" or "normative validation" (Andenaes, 1966; Gibbs, 1978). With respect to brutalization, similar normative processes may support or reinforce a subculture of violence to the extent that the "lesson of the scaffold" is to diminish the value of human life or the "message" of an execution is the justification of lethal vengeance.

4. Since the murder statistics available at that time typically counted only persons convicted or imprisoned for murder or attempted murder, the possibility of "jury nullification," or the tendency for murder convictions to be less likely as executions became more common, would tend to bias the results in favor of the deterrence hypothesis.

5. Subsequent efforts to evaluate the adequacy of controlling by means of contiguous state comparisons have indicated that the clusters of abolitionist and retentionist states examined by Sellin were relatively homogeneous in social and demographic characteristics and in measures of the certainty of arrest and conviction for criminal homicide (Baldus and Cole, 1975); and that homicide rates remain higher in retentionist as compared with abolitionist states in the presence of social and demographic controls and with aggravated assault rates as a control for other sources of criminal violence (Bailey, 1974, 1975).

6. Moreover, to the extent that abolition is apt to follow a period of abnormally low homicide rates, and reinstatement is likely to follow a period of exceptionally high homicide rates, the tendency of these abnormal rates to return or "regress" to the mean will falsely create the appearance of deterrence and thus mask brutalizing effects (unless the preintervention period is sufficiently long to detect the abnormality of the homicide levels immediately preceding the statutory change).

7. The problem arises when the same measured variable (in this case the number of homicides occurring annually) appears in the numerator of one index (the homicide rate) and figures in the denominator of another (the execution rate). Either random or systematic errors in measuring homicides will tend to produce an artifactual negative correlation between the two rates—and hence an illusion of deterrent effects (Klein et al., 1978).

8. The matter of statistical significance, especially in recent econometric studies, may have clouded more than clarified the picture. Only effects substantially at odds with the preponderance of existing evidence are large enough to be "statistically significant" in the relatively small samples with highly intercorrelated variables under investigation. Since these statistical analyses typically depend upon a host of untested and unmet assumptions (Brier and Feinberg, 1980; Fisher and Nagin, 1978; Barnett, 1981) the significance of their findings may as often signal the inadequacy of their models or methods (e.g., Yunker, 1976, as criticized by Fox, 1977). We have, therefore, placed greater emphasis on the balance of evidence in a variety of studies than on reports of "statistically significant" findings.

9. Using Wolfgang's (1958) data on homicides in Philadelphia by month for the period 1948-1952, we have calculated an expected before/after ratio of homicides for each execution date in Dann's study. For a given execution, each day in the before/after period was weighted by the proportion of all homicides occurring in that month (according to Wolfgang's Table 8), and the sum of the weights for the postexecution days was divided by the corresponding sum for the preexecution days to obtain its before/after homicide ratio. Multiplying the observed number of homicides before each execution by its estimated before/after ratio and summing over the five executions yields the expected number of postexecution homicides.

10. The procedure was the same as that described in Note 9.

11. There were 24 different months in which executions occurred over this period. Hence, the vast majority of executions that occurred were covered in this newspaper.

12. Though he later reported a revised estimate of a 32.8% decrease in homicides that corrected for an error in his calculations, the adjusted estimate still included the week after executions as part of the impact rather than the control period (Phillips, 1981).

13. Notably, publicity was more strongly associated with high levels of homicide the week after executions (*rho* = .425, *p* =.024) than with low levels of homicides the week of executions (*rho* = .348, *p* = .056), according to the figure in Phillips's Table 1.

14. I wish to thank Elizabeth Hanoway of Amnesty International in London for obtaining and verifying the weekly homicide data.

15. To demonstrate the bias, we can obtain the expected value for each of the three weeks (before, of, and after the execution) by averaging the number of homicides in the other two. This yields 36 drops, 22 rises, and eight ties out of 66 comparisons of observed and expected values. Thus, for any 22 comparisons, Phillips's approach might be expected to yield 12 drops, seven rises, and three ties by chance—not an equal number of drops and rises, as his application of the binomial test assumed.

16. Here, Phillips's definition of the expected number of execution-week homicides creates no problem since it does not bias the rank order of cases in homicide drop/rise (used in the Spearman coefficient) but only the number of cases that will be classified as a drop, rise, or tie (used in the binomial test).

17. Phillips presents this correlation as a direct (positive) relationship between cases ranked in amount of publicity and in extent of homicide drop. To be consistent with the

deterrence literature, I have reversed the ranking of homicide differences (observed-expected values) to run from the highest above to lowest below the expected values, thus changing the sign of the Spearman coefficient.

18. According to the SPSS Version X program for Spearman rank correlations with correction for ties, the p value for the two-tailed test is .009 and for the one-tailed test is .0045. The discrepancy between either of these values and the one reported by Phillips may reflect alternative correction procedures given a large number of ties.

19. Of the 22 values for execution-week homicide drop (Phillips's Table 1, column 7), 16 were involved in ties; eight were tied at the value of $-.5$ (as noted by Kobbervig et al., 1982; 163, Note 2). This means that the rank correlation between homicide drop and publicity will be especially sensitive to extreme values on the measure of homicide change and that the significance estimate for the correlation coefficient will be questionable.

20. What is more, the significant Spearman rank correlation that this particular pattern yields is due as much to the association of publicity with higher homicide levels the week after executions as to its association with lower homicide levels the week of executions (see Note 13).

21. Notably, 11 of the 14 homicide drops occur in cases with no execution week homicides, which are subject to the averaging bias that tends to produce artifactual experimental successes in these data, as noted above.

22. The probabilities associated with Phillips's statistical analyses were based on a one-tailed test that posits the deterrence hypothesis as the alternative to the null hypothesis. In this analysis, we adopt the more conservative two-tailed test.

23. We have used the twenty-first of March, June, September, and December as the starting dates for spring, summer, fall, and winter, respectively. Weeks including a transition point between seasons were assigned the season with the most days represented. Since homicides were most numerous in the summer, least so in the winter and intermediate in the fall and spring, we collapsed the four seasons into a single variable reflecting variations in climate and temperature.

24. By adjusting for the differences in the level of homicides at the time of the various executions, we reduce the residual variance of the regression model, and hence the standard error of the variable defining the impact period. Since the dummy variables for the respective execution periods are orthogonal to the impact variable by design, the estimated effects (b values) will be unchanged.

25. The brutalizing effect appears to be a direct linear function of publicity, not the result of a few extreme cases or a publicity threshold. Thus weighting the impact period by nonlinear transformations of the publicity variable that would be especially sensitive to the extremes of publicity (square and logarithm) to a threshold in the midrange (dichotomy at the median) gives a less adequate fit.

26. This is so because their publicity (though not their occurrence) varied by season in a manner inverse to the seasonal variation in homicides. The correlations between seasonality and the publicity weighted impact period are $-.179$ in the 13-week sample and $-.225$ in the 21-week sample (as compared to correlations of .001 and $-.009$, respectively, between seasonality and the impact period unweighted by publicity). The seasonal variations in publicity may reflect regular changes in newspaper size and circulation associated with vacations in the summer months and advertising in the winter months. In any case, the failure to control for seasonality slightly depresses the brutalizing effect of publicity in this sample of executions.

27. This figure slightly exceeds the 2.4 average homicide difference between 10-week periods before and after an execution reported above because it includes the week of an execution in the baseline or preimpact period.

28. Although quite comparable in absolute magnitude to the brutalizing effect found in New York state, the impact of these highly publicized cases in London is a good bit stronger relative to the prevailing homicide level: New York state had roughly 40 homicides per month between 1907 and 1963; London had only about six homicides per month (1.33 per week) for the selected periods between 1858 and 1921.

29. In an analysis of psychiatric case records of persons who have committed homicide, Shervert Frazier has explicitly identified a state of readiness to kill. "A second phase—not always present—is the buildup state or state of readiness—often of hours' to weeks' duration and in rare instances of 1 or 2 years' duration. This state of readiness, by no means uniform, was universal in this series of preplanned and prearranged murders— both for murderers of single individuals as well as of multiple individuals . . ." (p. 306). In this state of readiness, the killer frequently identifies one or more victims by name or status group: "Delusional ideas of the need to murder a named individual or individuals with characteristic detailed planning and processing of the act was present in eight murderers, five of whom were multiple—a physician with a list of patients, an ex-convict with a list of guards, an adolescent with a family list, and a neighbor with a list of members of another family. Three murderers of one individual had named a spouse, a famous person, and an employee. In each instance reasons were stated, and the buildup was accompanied by a planned progression of organized behavior, detailed and carefully executed goal-oriented purposive behavior despite delusional reasons and active delusional thinking sustained from three days to over one year in duration" (p. 307).

REFERENCES

ANDENAES, J. (1966) "General preventive effects of punishment." University of Pennsylvania Law Review 114: 949-983.

ARCHER, D. and R. GARTNER (1984) Violence and Crime in Cross-National Perspective. New Haven: Yale University Press.

ARCHER, D., R. GARTNER and M. BEITTEL (1983) "Homicide and the death penalty: A cross-national test of a deterrence hypothesis." Journal of Criminal Law and Criminology 74 (3): 991-1013.

BAILEY, W. C. (1974) "Murder and the death penalty." Journal of Criminal Law and Criminology 65: 416-423.

BAILEY, W. C. (1975) "Murder and capital punishment: Some further evidence." American Journal of Orthopsychiatry 45: 669-688.

BAILEY, W. C. (1977) "Imprisonment vs. the death penalty as a deterrent to murder." Law and Human Behavior 1: 239-260.

BAILEY, W. C. (1978a) "Deterrence and the death penalty for murder in Utah: A time series analysis." Journal of Contemporary Law 5: 1-20.

BAILEY, W. C. (1978b) "An analysis of the deterrent effect of the death penalty in North Carolina." North Carolina Central Law Journal 10: 29-49.

BAILEY, W. C. (1979a) "The deterrent effect of the death penalty for murder in California." Southern California Law Review 52 (March): 743-764.

BAILEY, W. C. (1979b) "Deterrence and the death penalty for murder in Oregon." Willamette Law Review 16: 67-85.

BAILEY, W. C. (1979c) "The deterrent effect of the death penalty for murder in Ohio: A time series analysis. Cleveland State Law Review 28: 51-70.

BAILEY, W. C. (1980a) "A multivariate cross-sectional analysis of the deterrent effect of the death penalty." Sociology and Social Research 64: 183-207.

BAILEY, W. C. (1980b) "Deterrence and the celerity of the death penalty: A neglected question in deterrence research." Social Forces 58: 1308-1333.

BAILEY, W. C. (1982) "Capital punishment and lethal assaults against police." Criminology 19 (February): 608-625.

BAILEY, W. C. (1983) "Disaggregation in deterrence and death penalty research: The case of murder in Chicago." Journal of Criminal Law and Criminology 74: 827-859.

BAILEY, W. C. (1984) "Murder and capital punishment in the nation's capital." Justice Quarterly 1: 211-233.

BALDUS, D. C. and J.W.L. COLE (1975) "Statistical evidence on the deterrent effect of capital punishment: A comparison of the work of Thorsten Sellin and Isaac Ehrlich on the deterrent effect of capital punishment." Yale Law Journal 85: 170-186.

BALDUS, D. C., C. PULASKI and G. WOODWORTH (1987) Arbitrariness, Discrimination, and Procedure in Capital Cases: A Legal and Empirical Analysis. Unpublished manuscript.

BARNETT, A. (1981) "The deterrent effect of capital punishment: A test of some recent studies." Operations Research 29 (2): 346-370.

BARON, J. and P. REISS (1985) "Same time next year: Aggregate analysis of the mass media and violent behavior." American Sociological Review 50: 364-371.

BEDAU, H. A. (1967) The Death Penalty in America. New York: Anchor Press.

BEDAU, H. A. and C. M. PIERCE [eds.] (1976) Capital Punishment in the United States. New York: AMS Press.

BERKOWITZ, L. and J. MACAULAY (1971) "The contagion of criminal violence." Sociometry 34 (2): 238-260.

BLACK, T. and T. ORSAGH (1978) "New evidence on the efficacy of sanctions as a deterrent to homicide." Social Science Quarterly 58 (4) (March): 616-631.

BLUMSTEIN, A., J. COHEN, and D. NAGIN (eds.) (1978) Deterrence and Incapacitation: Estimating the Effects of Criminal Sanctions on Crime Rates. Washington, DC: National Academy of Sciences.

BOWERS, W. J. (1974) Executions in America. Lexington, Mass.: D. C. Heath.

BOWERS, W. J. (1984) Legal Homicide: Death as Punishment in America, 1864-1982. Boston: Northeastern University Press.

BOWERS, W. J. and G. L. PIERCE (1975) "The illusion of deterrence in Isaac Ehrlich's research on capital punishment." Yale Law Journal 85: 187-208.

BOWERS, W. J. and G. L. PIERCE (1980a) "Arbitrariness and discrimination under Post-Furman capital statutes." Crime and Delinquency 26: 563-635.

BOWERS, W. J. and G. L. PIERCE (1980b) "Deterrence or brutalization: What is the effect of executions?" Crime and Delinquency 26: 453-484.

BRIER, S. and S. FEINBERG (1980) "Recent econometric modeling of crime and punishment: Support for the deterrence hypothesis?" Evaluation Review 4 (2): 147-191.

BYE, R. T. (1919) Capital Punishment in the United States. Philadelphia: The Committee of Philanthropic Labor of Philadelphia Yearly Meeting of Friends.

CALVERT, E. R. (1973) Capital Punishment in the Twentieth Century, fifth edition revised (1936). Montclair, NJ: Patterson-Smith.

CAMPION, D. (1955) "The state police and the death penalty." Minutes of Proceedings and Evidence, app. F, part II, no. 20, pp. 729-35. Joint Committee of the Senate and House of Commons on Capital Punishment and Lotteries. Ottawa, Canada: Queen's Printer. Reprinted in Sellin (1967).

DANN, R. H. (1935) "The deterrent effect of capital punishment." Friends Social Service Series 29: 1-20.

DECKER, S. H. and C. W. KOHFIELD (1984) "A deterrence study of the death penalty in Illinois, 1933-1980." Journal of Criminal Justice 12: 367-377.

DIAMOND, B. L. (1975) "Murder and the death penalty: A case report." American Journal of Orthopsychiatry 45 (July): 712-722.

EHRLICH, I. (1975) "The deterrent effect of capital punishment: A question of life and death." American Economic Review 65: 397-417.

EHRLICH, I. (1977) "Capital punishment and deterrence: Some further thoughts and additional evidence." Journal of Political Economy 85 (4): 741-789.

ELLSWORTH, P. C. and L. ROSS (1983) "Public opinion and capital punishment: A close examination of the views of the abolitionists and retentionists." Crime and Delinquency 29 (1): 116-169.

FATTAH, E. A. (1972) A Study of the Deterrent Effects of Capital Punishment with Special Reference to the Canadian Situation. Department of the Solicitor General, Canada.

FELSEN, R. B. and H. J. STEADMAN (1979) Situations and Processes Leading to Criminal Violence. Albany: New York Department of Mental Hygiene.

FEUER, L. (1959) Marx and Engels: Basic Writings in Politics and Philosophy. New York: Doubleday.

FISHER, F. M. and D. NAGIN (1978) "On the feasibility of identifying the crime function in a simultaneous model of crime and sanctions," in A. Blumstein, J. Cohen, and D. Nagin (eds.), Deterrence and Incapacitation: Estimating the Effects of Criminal Sanctions on Crime Rates. Washington, DC: National Academy of Sciences.

FORST, B. E. (1977) "The case against capital punishment: A cross-state analysis of the 1960s." Minnesota Law Review 61 (May): 743-767.

FORST, B. E. (1983) "Capital punishment and deterrence: conflicting evidence?" Journal of Criminal Law and Criminology 74 (3): 927-942.

FOX, J. A. (1977) "The identification and estimation of deterrence: An evaluation of Yunker's model." Journal of Behavioral Economics 6: 225-242.

FOX, J. A. (1986) "Persistent flaws in econometric studies of the death penalty: A discussion of Layson's findings." Testimony to Subcommittee on Criminal Justice, Committee on the Judiciary, U.S. House of Representatives.

FRAZIER, S. H. (1974) "Murder—single and multiple." In Aggression 52 (res. pub., Association for Research in Nervous and Mental Health Disease, 1974), ch. 16.

FRIEDMAN, L. S. (1979) "The use of multiple regression analysis to test for a deterrent effect of capital punishment: prospects and problems," pp. 61-87 in S. Messinger and E. Bittner (eds.), Criminology Review Yearbook. Beverly Hills, CA: Sage.

GIBBS, J. (1978) "Preventive effects of capital punishment other than deterrence." Criminal Law Bulletin 14 (1): 34-50.

GRAVES, W. F. (1956) "A doctor looks at capital punishment." Journal of the Loma Linda University School of Medicine 10: 137-42. Reprinted in Bedau (1967).

GROSS, S. R. and R. MAURO (1984) "Patterns of death: An analysis of racial disparities in capital sentencing and homicide victimization." Stanford Law Review 37 (1): 27-153.

HAMILTON, L. [ed.] (1854) Memoirs, Speeches and Writings of Robert Rantoul, Jr. Boston: John P. Jewett.

HOENACK, S. A. and W. C. WEILER (1980) "A structural model of murder behavior and the criminal justice system." American Economic Review 70 (June): 327-341.

KELLING, G. L., T. PATE, D. DIECKMAN, and C. E. BROWN (1974) The Kansas City Preventive Patrol Experiment. Washington, DC: Police Foundation.

KING, D. R. (1978) "The brutalization effect: Execution publicity and the incidence of homicide in South Carolina." Social Forces 57: 683-87.

KLECK, G. (1979) "Capital punishment, gun ownership and homicide." American Journal of Sociology 84 (January): 882-910.

KLEIN, L. R., B. E. FORST, and V. FILATOV (1978) "The deterrent effect of capital punishment: An assessment of the estimates," in A. Blumstein, J. Cohen, and D. Nagin (eds.), Deterrence and Incapacitation: Estimating the Effects of Criminal Sanctions on Crime Rates. Washington, DC: National Academy of Sciences.

KOBBERVIG, W., J. INVARARITY, and P. LAUDERDALE (1982) "Deterrence and the death penalty: A comment on Phillips." American Journal of Sociology 88: 161-164.

LAYSON, S. K. (1985) "Homicide and deterrence: A reexamination of the United States time-series evidence." Southern Economic Journal 52: 68-89.

LEMPERT, R. O. (1981) "Desert and deterrence: An assessment of the moral bases for capital punishment." Michigan Law Review 79 (6): 1177-1231.

LEMPERT, R. O. (1983) "The effect of executions on homicides: A new look in an old light." Crime and Delinquency 29 (1): 88-115.

LESTER, D. (1980) "Effect of Gary Gilmore's execution on homicidal behavior." Psychological Reporter 47 (December, 2): 1262.

LUCKENBILL, D. (1977) "Criminal homicide as a situational transaction." Social Problems 1977 (December): 176-186.

McFARLAND, S. G. (1983) "Is capital punishment a short-term deterrent to homicide? A study of the effect of four recent American executions." Journal of Criminal Law and Criminology 74 (3): 1014-1031.

MICHAEL, J. and H. WECHSLER (1937) "Rationale on the law of homicide." Columbia Law Review 37: 701-761, 1261-1325.

MORAN, R. (1985) The abolitionist case for public executions. San Diego: American Society of Criminology Meetings.

NATHANSON, S. (1987) An Eye for an Eye? The Morality of Punishing by Death. Totowa, NJ: Rowman and Littlefield.

Notable British Trials Series. (Various editors and publication dates) London: Hodge.

PASSELL, P. (1975) "The deterrent effect of the death penalty: A statistical test." Stanford Law Review 28: 61.

PASSELL, P. and J. B. TAYLOR (1976) "The deterrence controversy: A reconsideration of the time series evidence," pp. 359-371 in Bedau and Pierce (1976).

PHILLIPS, D. P. (1974) "The influence of suggestion on suicide: Substantive and theoretical implications of the Werther effect." American Sociological Review 39: 340-354.

PHILLIPS, D. P. (1977) "Motor vehicle fatalities increase just after publicized suicide stories." Science 196: 1464-65.

PHILLIPS, D. P. (1978) "Airplane accident fatalities increase just after stories about murder and suicide." Science 201: 748-50.

PHILLIPS, D. P. (1979) "Suicide, motor vehicle fatalities, and the mass media: Evidence toward a theory of suggestion." American Journal of Sociology 84: 1150-74.

PHILLIPS, D. P. (1980) "The deterrent effect of capital punishment: New evidence on an old controversy. American Journal of Sociology 86: 139-147.

PHILLIPS, D. P. (1981) Errata to 1980 article. American Journal of Sociology (March): unnumbered page.

PHILLIPS, D. P. (1983) "The impact of mass media violence on U.S. homicides." American Sociological Review 48 (August): 560-568.

PHILLIPS, D. P. and J. E. HENSLEY (1984) "When violence is rewarded or punished: The impact of mass media stories on homicide." Journal of Communications (Summer): 101-116.

RECKLESS, W. C. (1969) "The use of the death penalty." Crime and Delinquency 15 (1): 43-56.

SAVITZ, L. (1958) "A study in capital punishment." Journal of Criminal Law, Criminology and Police Science 49: 338-341.

SCHUESSLER, K. F. (1952) "The deterrent effect of the death penalty." Annals 284: 54-62.

SELLIN, T. (1955) "The death penalty and police safety." Minutes of Proceedings and Evidence, app. F, part I, no. 20, pp. 718-28. Joint Committee of the Senate and the House of Commons on Capital Punishment and Lotteries. Ottawa, Canada: Queens's Printer. Reprinted in Sellin (1967).

SELLIN, T. (1967) Capital Punishment. New York: Harper and Row.

SELLIN, T. [ed.] (1959) The Death Penalty. Philadelphia: American Law Institute.

SOLOMON, G. F. (1975) "Capital punishment as suicide and as murder." American Journal of Orthopsychiatry 45 (July): 701-711.

SUTHERLAND, E. H. (1925) "Murder and the death penalty." Journal of Criminal Law and Criminology 15: 522-529.

VAN DEN HAAG, E. and J. P. CONRAD (1983) The Death Penalty: A Debate. New York: Plenum.

VOLD, G. B. (1932) "Can the death penalty prevent crime?" Prison Journal 12: 3-8.

VOLD, G. B. (1952) "Extent and trend of capital crimes in the United States." Annals 284: 1-7.

WASSERMAN, I. M. (1984) "Imitation and suicide: A reexamination of the Werther effect." American Sociological Review 49 (June): 427-436.

WEST, L. J. (1975) "Psychiatric reflections on the death penalty." American Journal of Orthopsychiatry 45 (July): 689-701.

WILSON, C. and P. PITMAN (1962) Encyclopedia of Murder. New York: Putnam's.

WOLFGANG, M. E. (1958) Patterns in Criminal Homicide. Philadelphia: University of Pennsylvania Press.

YUNKER, J. (1976) "Is the death penalty a deterrent to homicide? Some time series evidence." Journal of Behavioral Economics 5: 45-81.

ZEISEL, H. (1976) "Deterrent effect of the death penalty: Facts v. faiths." 1976 Supreme Court Review: 317-343.

ZEISEL, H. (1982) "A comment on 'The deterrent effect of capital punishment' by Phillips." American Journal of Sociology 88: 166-169.

CASES

Commonwealth v. O'Neal (1975) 339 N.E. 2d 676.
Gregg v. Georgia (1976) 428 U.S. 153, 96 Sup. Ct. 2909
McCleskey v. Kemp (1987) 84-6811, 55 LW 4537.

Chapter 4

FALLIBILITY AND FINALITY
Type II Errors and Capital Punishment

MICHAEL L. RADELET
HUGO ADAM BEDAU

Statisticians refer to a Type I error as the rejection of a hypothesis even though it is true. A Type II error, on the other hand, occurs when a hypothesis is not rejected even though it is false. Like statisticians, juries make probabilistic judgments. Very few, if any, criminal cases allow the jury to be 100% certain of the defendant's guilt or innocence. A defendant may be judged to be innocent if he or she produces a dozen alibi witnesses, but if each of these witnesses is, in reality, mistaken, a Type I error will have been committed. On the other hand, even if the alleged crime is captured on film, it is theoretically possible that it was actually perpetrated by a look-alike. When an innocent defendant is found guilty, the criminal justice system commits a Type II error.

In this essay we will consider Type II errors in criminal homicide cases and their implications for contemporary death penalty debates. In American criminal trials, jurors are instructed to vote for guilt only if they are certain "beyond a reasonable doubt." This is not the same as "absolute certainty." Somewhere along the continuum ranging from certainty about guilt to certainty about innocence, jurors must draw a firm line to distinguish those defendants they judge to be guilty from the rest. Although jurors are not given any probabilistic instructions, let us assume that, on the average, they are 95% convinced of guilt before they label their judgments as "beyond a reasonable doubt" and vote for convictions. Let us further assume that such estimates are correct. These assumptions mean that jurors are willing to make erroneous judgments of guilt in 5% of the cases they see, and they indeed do make such Type II errors in 5% of the cases. If true, this results in a 5% Type II error rate in convicting the innocent. Since very few convictions can rest on the jury's absolute certainty, the risk of Type II errors is always present.

How, then, may one investigate the extent of Type II errors in criminal homicide cases? One strategy might be to conduct exit polls of jurors, asking each to assign exact probabilistic figures to the certainty of his or her judgment on the guilt of the accused. One would expect, however, at least three problems here. (1) An individual's judgment might be altered by the views of others during deliberation in the direction of weighting the probabilities toward the group's mean. (2) After a decision is made, jurors might deny any uncertainties and instead look for ways to justify it. This would be particularly true if the consequences of the decision were severe, as they are when the decision results in death or in long prison sentences. (3) This strategy investigates only the willingness to accept error, not the probability of error itself. In any event, we know of no research of this sort.

A second research strategy would be to collect and examine cases in which defendants were convicted and later found to be innocent. The problems here are twofold: (1) difficulty in identifying such cases, and (2) adequacy of evidence to judge in each case that an error has occurred. This chapter describes a research project of this type that we began in 1983. To date, we have identified some 350 relevant cases (Bedau and Radelet, 1987). Before summarizing the findings of this project, we first turn attention to previous work in this area.

PREVIOUS RESEARCH

The problem of Type II errors in the criminal justice system has attracted very little scholarly investigation in the United States. The first systematic research devoted to the issue was published by Professor Edwin Borchard of Yale Law School in 1932. Borchard described 62 American and 3 British cases in which innocent defendants had been convicted of felonies; 29 of these cases involved a homicide conviction (Borchard, 1932: vi). His approach was to present chapters on 50 of the more important cases and brief summaries of the remaining 15. Eight years later, German attorney Max Hirschberg (1940) illustrated the range of errors that could occur with 23 case examples, selected primarily from Europe. In 1952, Professor Richard Donnelly of Yale Law School published a paper with case illustrations detailing the legal avenues that erroneously convicted defendants could pursue for relief.

Only two major articles on this issue have been written by American criminologists (Pollak, 1952; MacNamara, 1969). Each is quite brief, but well-documented illustrative cases are presented in which defendants convicted of felonies were later found to be innocent. More thorough attention was directed at the problem by author-attorney Erle Stanley Gardner (1952), Judge Jerome Frank and his daughter, Barbara (1957), and by writer Edward Radin (1964). Their monographs each present detailed case summaries; Gardner's work (and of the "Court of Last Resort," which he founded) is particularly notable. He actually reinvestigated questionable convictions; in many cases this resulted in the release of defendants who had been erroneously convicted. His experiences were conveyed to an even wider audience in two television series during the 1950s and 1960s, *Perry Mason* and *The Court of Last Resort*. An important lesson still to be learned from Gardner's experience is that given the commitment and resources, investigators can indeed uncover miscarriages of justice. The extent to which Gardner demonstrated this point stands unique in American history. No similar organization exists today that systematically reexamines cases in which miscarriages have been alleged.

Other television series have also examined this problem. *The Fugitive*, a fictional account of a man erroneously convicted of homicide, became a popular TV series in the 1960s. More recently, British television viewers have seen depictions of miscarriages of justice in their country through the series titled *Rough Justice* (Young and Hill, 1983; Hill et al., 1985), and in the book by journalist Ruth Brandon and sociologist Christie Davies (1973).

Other cases involving a miscarriage of justice have been noted in scattered publications throughout the century. In 1962, the attention of one of the authors of the present chapter was drawn to the issue when he assisted Sara Ehrmann in her work on the subject (Ehrmann, 1962). Then, in 1964, he compiled a list of 85 cases since 1893 in which innocent defendants had been arrested, convicted, or condemned for homicide in American jurisdictions (Bedau, 1964).

THE BEDAU-RADELET STUDY

Methodology

In 1983, we began our collaborative effort to compile information in one central location on all well-publicized relevant cases and to search for other cases in a systematic manner. The procedures used to locate and document cases are elaborated elsewhere (Bedau and Radelet, 1987). We (somewhat arbitrarily) defined the universe of relevant cases as twentieth-century convictions (plus those occurring in the year 1900) in which innocent people were convicted of homicide or sentenced to death for rape in American jurisdictions.

Our limited resources forced us to exclude from our catalogue many important cases that also have relevance for contemporary death penalty debates, such as those in which innocent defendants narrowly and fortuitously escaped conviction for homicide, or were convicted of nonhomicidal crimes that in another jurisdiction or at another time could have led to a death sentence, or were convicted of a crime other than homicide after first being indicted for a homicide. By the end of 1986, we had documented 236 episodes involving 350 defendants. Of these, 326 defendants were convicted of homicide (117 of whom were sentenced to death), and an additional 22 defendants were condemned to death for rape (two other men sentenced to life imprisonment for rape are also included because their codefendants were sentenced to death).

Our definition of the concept of *innocence* is not without problems; some will say it is too liberal and others will see it as too conservative. We used the term to refer to those cases in which *either* the crime itself never actually occurred *or* the convicted defendant was legally and physically uninvolved in the crime. Hence, we exclude cases in which A was convicted of murdering B, but in which reinvestigation established that although A did cause the death of B, A was insane, or acted in self-defense, or killed by accident, and so on. In such cases the reinvestigation has showed that the criminal intent (*mens rea*) necessary for guilt was indeed absent, but not that the convicted defendant was uninvolved in the crime. Our research concentrates exclusively on innocent men, not innocent *mens*, so the many, many cases involving error in the evaluation of criminal intent are excluded. This does not mean that all of the 350 cases involve the conviction of the wrong person in the sense that someone else should have been convicted; in some of our cases a person was convicted for a crime that never occurred. In seven of the homicide cases, the victim showed up alive after the conviction (this happened most recently in 1974 to two California defendants convicted of murdering their daughter). There are also four cases we have found in which a defendant was convicted and sentenced to death for rape, but later reinvestigation showed the sexual relationship was consensual. No cases are included of defendants who are still serving prison terms for a conviction they allege is mistaken.

Results

After settling these methodological and conceptual issues, the next problem we faced was how to determine whether a given defendant was indeed innocent under the above criteria. Unfortunately, there is rarely a formal finding of "innocence" to which we can point in order to firmly settle the question. Even if there were, a judgment of innocence is, like a judgment of guilt, a probabilistic decision. Aside from those few cases in which a homicide victim shows up alive (and even in some of those cases in which the state argues it misidentified the real victim), there is little evidence that can be produced that would *conclusively* prove innocence. Thus, the probability of innocence in a given case varies from 0% to 100%, with very few decisions at either extreme. Further, we cannot simply use a state's admission of error as our criterion, as officials often are extremely reluctant to admit their blunders, and one official's admission of error in a given case is often inconclusive because another official refuses to agree. Furthermore, the state's admission of error is rarely direct; usually it is only indirect on grounds of violation of due process. This is insufficient reason for us to conclude that the accused is indeed innocent.

Instead, we use our perception of responsible/authoritative consensus as the criterion, and include in our catalogue only those defendants we believe that a majority of neutral observers, given the evidence at our disposal, would judge to be innocent. If a defendant could plausibly be innocent, or claims to be innocent, or is said to be innocent by his family or friends, but there is no convincing evidence, we do not include the case. Consequently, our cases range from the "probably innocent" to the "certainly innocent." Some critics will pick out the cases under our criteria where the evidence is weakest and generalize that our whole set of cases is dubious. Others will criticize our refusal to include this or that case in which they regard the evidence of innocence as very strong. There is in principle no way to avoid such criticisms, and we can only repeat that we include all and only those cases that we believe most unbiased judges, given our evidence, would also include.

What is the evidence we look for to support the claim of innocence? There are several types of evidence, which we present roughly in descending order of persuasiveness in Table 4.1. In 309 of the cases (each case being a distinct defendant), the state itself implicitly or explicitly admitted error. In 20 of the cases, this admission of error took the form of the state's voluntary award of indemnity to the defendant. For example, in 1979 Cornell Avery Estes was convicted of murder (at age

TABLE 4.1

Primary Evidence for Judgment of Error (N = 350)

			Number of Cases
I.	State action indicating error		309
	A.	Legislative indemnity	20
	B.	Executive	129
		1. Pardon	64
		2. Other executive action	65
	C.	Judicial	160
		1. Indemnity	9
		2. Reversal (by trial or appellate court)	151
		a. no retrial; conviction set aside or indictment nol prossed	113
		b. acquitted by retrial or directed verdict	38
II.	Other (unofficial) actions indicating error		41
	A.	Another person confesses	13
	B.	Another person implicated	7
	C.	Opinion of state official	6
	D.	Subsequent scholarly judgment	15

NOTE: Each case is counted only once even though in many cases, there is more than one type of evidence.

15) in Maryland and sentenced to life imprisonment. A year later he was released when the true culprit confessed and this confession was verified. In 1983 the governor pardoned Estes, and in 1984 the Maryland Board of Public Works awarded the wrongly convicted man $16,500.

In other cases, the defendant may be awarded a pardon but not compensated. A classic example involves the 1963 Florida convictions of Freddie Pitts and Wilbert Lee, who were sentenced to death after coerced guilty pleas. In all likelihood they would have been executed if the death penalty had not been suspended in Florida between 1964 and 1979. Later, the true killer confessed and a key eyewitness against Pitts and Lee recanted her testimony. Finally, in 1975, after a journalist took an interest in the case (Miller, 1975), they were awarded a full pardon and released. They were never compensated for their harrowing experiences. A pardon with no compensation is found in 64 of our cases.

A third source of evidence of innocence is a statement or other action by a governor or other state official close to the case; we have relied on such evidence in 65 cases. For example, in 1973 in California, Aaron Lee Owens was sentenced to two life terms for first-degree murder. In 1980, the original prosecutor reinvestigated the case and determined that a look-alike had committed the crimes. The following year Owens was released.

A fourth category of cases involves a judicial award of indemnity. Nine of our 350 cases involve such awards. For example, in a 1975 Georgia case, Earl Charles was convicted of murder and sentenced to death. In 1978 he was released after reinvestigation verified his alibi. In 1983 a federal judge awarded him $417,000 in damages. In another 1975 Georgia case, another innocent black man, Jerry Banks, was also sentenced to death. Banks eventually won a new trial and was released in 1980 because of newly discovered evidence. Three years later, after Banks had died, the county agreed to pay his children $150,000 for mishandling the case. In 1937 in New York, Isidore Zimmerman was two hours away from execution when the governor commuted his sentence to life imprisonment. He served 24 years before a new trial was ordered and he was released. Zimmerman spent the next 20 years trying to prove his innocence, arguing that the original prosecutor had suppressed exculpatory evidence. In 1983 he was awarded $1 million by the state, but four months later he died.

In 113 cases, the conviction was reversed on appeal and the charges were dropped; in 38 other cases evidence of innocence introduced at retrial led to an acquittal. To be sure, a reversal or acquittal at retrial (or even a pardon) is not proof of innocence; for example, an acquittal may occur because a key prosecution witness has died. Official decisions to acquit or to drop charges at retrial can be in error exactly as are decisions to convict. Consequently, each case has to be carefully examined on its own merits, and a judgment of the probable guilt or innocence of the defendant reached in light of all the available evidence. In some cases, however, a reversal followed by acquittal or formal dropping of charges clearly occurs because the defendant was innocent. For example, in 1982, Nathaniel Carter was convicted of a New York murder and sentenced to life imprisonment. In 1984, charges were dropped and he was freed when his former wife (the chief witness against him) admitted both perjury and the murder. As his lawyer said, "If New York state had the death penalty, God knows what would have happened to this man." Similarly, in 1974, Antonio Rivera and Merla Walpole were convicted of murdering their daughter in California. They were released some 20 months later when their daughter was found alive and well in San Francisco. Finally, Thomas Gladish, Richard Greer, Ronald Kleine, and Clarence Smith were sentenced to death in New Mexico in 1974. After an expensive investigation by the *Detroit News*, another person confessed to the crime, a new trial was ordered, and the original indictments against the four were dismissed. The men did not seek or receive a formal pardon, but their innocence is uncontested. Other cases reversed on appeal were found to be miscarriages when the evidence used to secure the original conviction was shown to be fraudulent. In 1983, Anthony Brown was convicted and condemned to death in Florida; on appeal, his conviction was reversed on a technicality. At retrial, a codefendant, who had been the only person to supply evidence against him at the original trial, admitted perjury and sole responsibility for the murder. Brown was promptly acquitted.

In the remaining 41 cases, despite the absence of any official admission of error by the state, other evidence no less conclusive is available. In 13 cases the evidence of innocence surfaced when the truly guilty person eventually confessed. For example, in 1980, Walter McIntosh was sentenced to life in a mental hospital after conviction for a double murder in Georgia. In 1984, the county sheriff, convinced of McIntosh's innocence, led a reinvestigation that culminated in the confession and arrest of two other people for the crimes. McIntosh, however, had died while in custody. In seven of the remaining cases, there is strong evidence (though not a confession) that implicates another suspect, though for various reasons the state did not officially admit that the original defendant was wrongly convicted. A good example comes from Ohio, where Julius Krause was sentenced to life imprisonment in 1930. Five years later, his codefendant gave a deathbed confession that another man, and not Krause, was his actual partner. When nothing was done to locate this man, Krause escaped from prison and found him. The man was duly tried and convicted. Krause voluntarily returned to prison, but despite the fact that "No one doubt(ed) his complete innocence," he was kept in prison until paroled in 1951 (Radin, 1964: 16).

In six other cases, we base our belief that the defendant was innocent on the considered judgment of a state official in a position to know. In 1956, Robert Williams confessed to first-degree murder in California (apparently to rekindle the affection of a former girlfriend); he was convicted and sentenced to life imprisonment. In 1975 he was released on parole and began to gather information to clear his name. In 1978, after testimony on his behalf from the former prosecuting attorney and the production of evidence showing that Williams had a perfect alibi (he had been in prison at the time of the crime), he was released from parole. Interestingly, two years after his first erroneous conviction, Williams confessed to a second murder—just to show that an innocent person could be convicted on a false confession. For the second time, he was right—he was again convicted of murder! It was not until the 1978 reinvestigation showed he had been in prison at the time of this murder, too, that the record was set straight.

Finally, there are 15 cases in which we rely on the preponderance of informed opinion. The most famous example of this sort in our catalogue is the 1935 case of Bruno Richard Hauptmann, executed in 1936 for the felony-murder of the baby of aviator Charles Lindbergh. Only recently has the complete story of this case—and what most will see as proof of Hauptmann's innocence—begun to emerge (Scaduto, 1976; Kennedy, 1985). A much more obscure case comes from Alabama in 1937. There, Roosevelt Collins (a.k.a. Roosevelt Wilson), on trial for rape, caused a near riot in the courtroom when he (a black) testified that the "victim" (a white) had consented to having sexual relations with him. He was executed in 1937. Interviews after the trial with several jurors and the judge by novelist William Bradford Huie revealed that although they all believed Collins, they also felt he deserved to die simply for "messin' around" with a white woman (Huie, 1964).

The cases included in our catalogue are spread throughout the country, with no region underrepresented. They are also spread throughout the century. The decade 1910-1919 includes the most cases (N = 80), but the majority of these were from a single event in Elaine, Arkansas, when, in the aftermath of a 1919 race rebellion, 51 innocent black defendants were rounded up and convicted of murder (Kluger, 1975: 112-114). For those who believe that our criminal justice system has improved to the extent that convicting the innocent is no longer possible, it will be disturbing to note that the decade with the second highest number of erroneous convictions is the 1970s. During this decade there were 55 erroneous convictions in 44 separate incidents; 14 involved a death sentence. This relatively high number may be attributable to the increase in the number of criminal homicides (and thus to the likelihood of more erroneous convictions) or to the greater likelihood that more recent miscarriages will be publicized and discovered. Whatever the explanation, the number of such cases will undoubtedly increase still further because in the years ahead additional defendants convicted in the 1970s will have their innocence established. Our catalogue includes 61 cases in which the defendant was not exonerated until 11 or more years after the conviction.

The causes of wrongful conviction in capital cases range widely.

TABLE 4.2

Causes of Erroneous Conviction

Type of Error		Number of Cases
I. Police error		82
Coerced or other false confession	49	
Negligence	11	
Other overzealous police work	22	
II. Prosecutor error		50
Suppression of exculpatory evidence	35	
Other overzealous prosecution	15	
III. Witness error		193
Mistaken eyewitness identification	56	
Perjury by prosecution witness	117	
Unreliable or erroneous prosecution testimony	20	
IV. Other error		209
Misleading circumstantial evidence	30	
Incompetence of defense counsel	10	
Judicial denial of admissibility of exculpatory evidence	7	
Inadequate consideration of alibi evidence	45	
Erroneous judgment on cause of death	16	
Defendant makes fraudulent alibi or false guilty plea	17	
Community outrage demands conviction	70	
Unknown	14	

NOTE: Number of cases counted once: 198 (including all unknown cases); number of cases counted twice: 120; number of cases counted three times: 32.

Often two or three factors are equally involved, and it is therefore impossible to identify a single primary cause. Table 4.2 displays this information, grouping the causes into categories of police error, prosecutorial error, witness error, and other errors. Of the 350 cases, one causal factor is identified in 198 cases, two causes in 120 cases, and 32 cases had three primary sources of error. Unlike other observers (see Gross, 1987, for review), we did not find erroneous eyewitness identification to be the most frequent cause of error. Perhaps this is because a lower proportion of homicide convictions than convictions for other crimes are based solely or primarily on such evidence. Or, perhaps erroneous homicide convictions based on eyewitness evidence are less likely than erroneous convictions based on other mistakes to be successfully corrected at a later date. Instead, we find another type of witness error—perjury by prosecution witnesses—to be the most common cause of erroneous convictions; it is a factor in one-third of all the cases in our catalogue. The other causes of error listed in Table 4.2 require little elaboration.

Does the existence of documented miscarriages prove that "the system works"—that it can be counted on to catch its own errors? We do not think so. The system is not designed to scrutinize guilty verdicts for possible errors. With rare exceptions, the innocent defendants in our catalogue were exonerated only because they were extremely lucky. Sometimes the real culprit confesses or is found; sometimes a defense attorney, after conviction of his or her client, persists with the investigation of the case and uncovers evidence exonerating the defendant. Occasionally a journalist or other writer takes a special interest in the case and his or her detective work is rewarded with proof that the wrong person was convicted. These are three of the major ways that innocent defendants in our catalogue were eventually exonerated. Our files show few instances in which a prisoner acting alone was able to clear his or her name. The fact that so many of the defendants in our catalogue owe their vindications to fortuitous circumstances is a clear indicator that only a fraction of the wrongly convicted in this country are lucky enough to eventually clear their names.

Our catalogue contains 23 cases of what we believe were erroneous executions, and 21 other cases in which a defendant, later exonerated, came to within 72 hours of execution. These latter, all "close calls," again focus attention on the disturbing yet unanswerable question of how many innocent defendants were not so lucky. Inclusion and verification of cases in which innocent defendants were executed is difficult and inevitably controversial. We believe that if all the evidence now available in our 23 cases had been (or could have been) examined in a neutral forum prior to the execution, the execution would not have occurred and the defendant would have been eventually exonerated and released. However, once the execution has occurred, the establishment of a neutral forum for review of the case is all but impossible; we know of no instance in this century in which one was created. The last case in American history that we are aware of in which a state officially admitted the innocence of an executed defendant occurred in Illinois in 1893, when Governor Altgeld pardoned three of the Haymarket defendants six years after four of their codefendants were hanged (Avrich, 1984).

There are two other reasons why few executed prisoners are exonerated. Once the defendant has been executed, he or she is no longer able to assist or motivate efforts to reinvestigate the case. And, once an innocent defendant has been executed, the persons actually involved in the crime, the officials involved in the erroneous arrest and prosecution and others who might know of some exculpatory evidence, are all less likely to step forward and contest the convictions. We are confident that if the true stories could be found, the number of wrongful executions in our catalogue would be much greater. Our inclusion of less than two dozen such cases is an indicator not of the reliability or fairness of the system, but of its power and finality.

What is the frequency and the associated risk of a wrongful conviction in a capital or potentially capital case in the United States? Our data do not provide the basis for an answer because we have no way of estimating what fraction of the total number of such miscarriages is represented by our 350 cases. The accidents and sheer luck involved in our ability to identify the cases we included in our catalogue parallels the accidents and sheer luck involved in clearing an erroneously convicted defendant. Many of the cases included in our catalogue were discovered by us only because we stumbled on a lead in a newspaper or in some obscure source, or because friends who had heard about our research project supplied a valuable lead. How many other miscarriages exist but have yet to be discovered, admitted, and brought to our attention we do not know; indeed the risk cannot be known or estimated.

IMPLICATIONS FOR THE ABOLITION
OF THE DEATH PENALTY

In History

Concern about executing the innocent has been expressed for over 200 years whenever the merits of capital punishment have been debated. In no jurisdiction has such concern been solely responsible for abolition, and it is of course impossible to determine the precise strength it has had in those jurisdictions in which the death penalty has been successfully abolished. We do know that in some of these jurisdictions, however, it has played a powerful role.

In 1846, Michigan became the first English-speaking jurisdiction in the world to abolish capital punishment. The law took effect on March 1, 1847. A decade earlier, a man named Patrick Fitzpatrick was hanged in Sandwich, Ontario, just across the Detroit River from Michigan's largest city. In 1840, Michigan citizens familiar with the case were shaken when a man named Maurice Sellers gave a deathbed confession to the crime (Burbey, 1938: 452; Bennett, 1978: 49; Detroit News, May

23, 1985: 1). How much their outrage contributed to the anti-death penalty sentiment in the state is unknown, but apparently it did have some significance in strengthening the sentiment for abolition.

Rhode Island abolished the death penalty in 1852. Among the factors that influenced the passage of this legislation was the 1844 trial of John and William Gordon, who were accused of killing Amasa Sprague, the brother of a U.S. Senator. Though the evidence against the Gordons was "flimsy and circumstantial" and many believed them to be victims of anti-Irish prejudice, John was convicted and hanged in 1845. On identical evidence, William was acquitted. No proof ever surfaced that conclusively established John's innocence, but doubts about his guilt flourished and helped to strengthen the case for abolition (*Providence Evening Bulletin,* May 17-22, 1933; Teeters, 1967: 442; Mackey, 1974; Sellin, 1980: 145).

In Maine, too, the recognition of the possibility of erroneous convictions influenced the movement to abolish the death penalty. MacNamara (1969: 61) quotes Edmund Muskie, governor at the time, as stating in 1968 "that the hanging of an innocent man had induced Maine to abolish the death penalty." However, this explanation is apparently overstated. In 1837, two years after the hanging of Joseph Sager "aroused great controversy," Maine severely limited the use of the death penalty. Sager had asserted his innocence to all who would listen, including the crowd of thousands who watched him die on the gallows (North, 1870: 559). Some 30 years later, in 1869, Clifton Harris was hanged for murder in a case involving "deep mystery . . . that has not yet been unraveled" (Sellin, 1980: 153). Several different innocent men had been suspected in the crime. Finally, Harris confessed his guilt, but at trial he implicated Luther Verrill as an accomplice. On this testimony, Verrill, too, was convicted. Verrill's case, however, was reversed on appeal and the charges were dropped after Harris admitted that Verrill had nothing to do with the crime (Lewiston, Maine, *Evening Journal,* March 12, 1869). Seven years later, in 1876, the legislature abolished the death penalty entirely (except for its brief reenactment from 1883 to 1887).

Tennessee abolished the death penalty for murder (but not for rape) during the years 1915 to 1917. The abolition effort was led by a wealthy Memphis merchant, Duke Bowers; a copy of the 97-page memorandum he wrote in support of this legislation can be found in the New York Public Library. In it, Bowers reports (1915: 73) that the bill passed through the House Committee because of a powerful argument made by Nashville attorney K. T. McConnico. Much of McConnico's argument, according to Bowers, was based on a 550-page document prepared by McConnico and filled with cases in which innocent defendants had been executed prior to 1901. Unfortunately, neither the Library of Congress nor the Tennessee State Archives has McConnico's document, so we have no idea of its contents or the number of cases it contained. Bowers, however, asserted that this was a "tremendous argument" for the passage of the bill. Bowers himself had a cousin who was sentenced to be hanged in Texas, but the sentence was commuted to life imprisonment, and the defendant released 12 years later when the true culprit confessed (Bowers, 1915: 16).

In 1966, England's Queen Elizabeth granted a full pardon to Timothy John Evans, who had been hanged in 1950 for the murder of his infant daughter. Concern that Evans had been wrongly executed played a large part in the successful attempt to abolish the death penalty in England, where the last man was executed in 1964 (*New York Times,* October 19, 1966: 19:3). Three years after Evans was hanged, bodies of several additional murder victims were found in his home, and his landlord, John Reginald Christie, confessed not only to them, but to the murder for which Evans had been condemned. Christie, too, was hanged (Kennedy, 1961).

In Canada in the 1960s, widespread belief in the innocence of an adolescent boy who had been sentenced to death played a role in securing public support for the abolition of the death penalty. In 1959, 14-year-old Steven Truscott was convicted of the rape and murder of a 12-year-old girl. Only rather vague circumstantial evidence implicated Truscott. He was widely believed to be innocent. Truscott's death sentence was eventually commuted to life imprisonment, and in 1961 the Canadian Parliament enacted a prohibition against a death sentence for anyone under age 18 at the time of the crime (Chandler, 1976: 31; LeBourdais, 1966). Canada temporarily abolished the death penalty in 1967, and in 1976 the abolition was made permanent.

In Theory

Evaluating the precise strength of the anti-death penalty argument that innocent defendants have been and will be executed is extremely difficult. Yet, it is *certain* that there are and will be such cases, and death penalty proponents are forced to acknowledge the problem. Ernest van den Haag, one of this country's most vocal death penalty proponents, does so. He writes:

One of the most persuasive arguments used against the death penalty is that innocent people may suffer it, owing to some mistake. This is an argument squarely based on justice—it objects to a possible injustice. However, rare, such miscarriages of justice are likely to occur. They weaken the argument of retentionists who favor the death penalty for the guilty because it is just. They have to admit that the execution of the guilty necessarily implies the unintended execution of some innocents, which is unjust (van den Haag and Conrad, 1983: 55).

For some, the moral burden of the certainty of executing the innocent is a sufficient reason in and of itself to oppose capital punishment. As Marquis de Lafayette said in 1830, "Till the infallibility of human judgments shall have been proved to me, I shall demand the abolition of the death penalty" (cited in Mackey, 1976: 98).

For others, the important factor is not the simple existence of this certainty, but the extent of its occurrence. Commenting in 1985 on the Bedau-Radelet research and on its inclusion of two dozen cases of wrongful execution, van den Haag said the total was:

> If true, a very acceptable number. All human activities—building houses, driving a car, playing golf or football—cause innocent people to suffer wrongful death, but we don't give them up because on the whole we feel there's a net gain. Here, a net gain in justice is being done (*New York Times*, November 14, 1985: 13:1).

This rationale requires that the alleged benefits of capital punishment be accurately assessed (e.g., retribution and incapacitation), and then shown to outweigh its known liabilities (e.g., cost, arbitrariness, and the risk of errors). But since there is a complete lack of consensus over the weight our society should assign to each variable in the equation, we are doomed to disagree over the result of this equation.

The van den Haag rationale also necessitates the impossible task of estimating the odds of executing the innocent. A 1% error rate, for example, might be acceptable to those who tend to favor the death penalty, whereas an arbitrarily selected higher rate—say 5%—would not. Even if the odds could be calculated, it would be incorrect to use such a restricted notion of erroneous execution when debating whether or not to retain the death penalty. The criminal law defines innocence much more broadly than the narrow definition used in our research into Type II errors. Thus, a priori, the odds of executing the legally innocent (i.e., all those defendants who lack *mens rea*) are many times greater than are the odds of executing those who had literally nothing to do with causing the victim's death (Black, 1981). Nonetheless, for the reasons we have outlined above, any attempt to calculate the odds of executing the innocent, whatever the definition, is doomed to fail.

In any event, van den Haag's defense of the death penalty despite his concession that some innocent defendants will be executed can be criticized on grounds other than the impossibility of performing the calculations his argument requires. One could accept his cost-benefit logic for the sake of the argument, and still point to three objections. First, there is little or no empirical evidence on behalf of any of the alleged benefits of the death penalty that make it superior to long-term imprisonment. Second, van den Haag's comparison of the death penalty with other activities that cause the death of the innocent (building houses, driving a car, playing golf or football) is misleading for two reasons: Those who participate in the latter voluntarily consent to their exposure to risk, whereas there is no reason to believe that the *innocent* defendant has consented to the risk of being executed. Furthermore, the intention of the practice known as capital punishment is to kill the convicted, whereas this is not the intention of the practices to which van den Haag draws a parallel. Third, and most important, we need to consider basic issues of individual rights in a democratic society. We suspect that those who reason as van den Haag does might see the issue differently were they the innocent defendants facing the executioner. The right to life of all innocent citizens is beyond dispute. A worker cannot be required to risk certain death by being forced to repair a malfunctioning nuclear reactor, even if by doing so he or she would save hundreds of lives. Only volunteers—those who waive their right to life—can be asked to do such jobs. Given the irremediability of the death penalty and the availability of an adequate alternative punishment, the execution of *any* innocent defendant cannot be justified even if there were substantial benefits of capital punishment. The virtual certainty of executing the innocent in the future, as in the past, is sufficient ground for the abolition of the risk.

Defenders of the death penalty will dispute this conclusion. They could argue that abolitionists have forgotten the risk that elimination of the death penalty would force society to bear: the risk of recidivist crimes by persons previously convicted of murder but not incapacitated from future offenses by having been executed. Every time a guilty person is convicted of murder but not sentenced to death and executed, society runs the risk that such a person may kill again, or commit other crimes—against a fellow inmate, a prison visitor, prison employee, or even the general public. A comprehensive study of the incidence of recidivism by convicted murderers has yet to be done; still, evidence suggests that although the number of such crimes is not large (Bedau, 1982: 173-180), it exceeds the number of known innocents who have been executed. If this is indeed true, why should society run what appears to be the greater of the two risks?

An adequate reply to this important question is complex. First, it is not possible to know which risk is greater merely by knowing the difference between the two aggregate numbers (those wrongfully executed and those victims of recidivist murderers). The proper way to determine which risk is greater is to take a fixed population of persons condemned but not executed (e.g., all those spared execution by the 1972 *Furman* decision), and ask (1) how many were wrongfully convicted, and (2) how many committed another murder after their life was spared. Such a study has yet to be done. Second, by abolishing mandatory death penalties, society has implicitly agreed to run the risk of recidivism by convicted murderers in the vast majority of cases, since the effect of discretionary death sentencing is that only a small fraction of all those convicted of murder are sentenced to death and executed (Sellin, 1980: 69-74). Third, as things currently stand, society runs *both* the risk of executing the innocent and the risk of recidivist murder, whereas it is necessary that society runs only one or the other of these risks. To that extent, our current practice seems irrational unless it can be shown that a combination of these two risks is lower than either risk taken alone. Fourth, it is virtually impossible to imagine our society not running some risk of recidivist murder. Not only is the mandatory death penalty in general unconstitutional (*Woodson et al. v. North Carolina*, 428 U.S. 280, 1976), few American jurisdictions in this century enacted and enforced a truly mandatory death penalty even for murder during the years when it was a constitutionally permissible option. On the other hand, many nations and several American jurisdictions have decided not to run the risk of executing the innocent. So the real question to be asked is this: Which policy is more rational, running the risk of recidivist murder for 100% of convicted murderers (as abolitionists evidently believe), or (as defenders of the death penalty seem to prefer) running the risk for 95% or more of convicted murderers plus the risk of executing the innocent for the remaining 5% or less?

But even this does not state the true problem accurately. In addition to the two risks under discussion, there are other risks associated with the deterrent and incapacitative capacities of the death penalty that must be taken into account. For example, some have argued persuasively that the "brutalizing" effect of the death penalty is greater than its deterrent and incapacitating effects (Bowers and Pierce, 1980). Abolishing the death penalty involves running a slightly greater risk of recidivist murder than at present plus the alleged risk of lesser deterrence, whereas retaining or expanding the death penalty involves preserving or increasing the risks of brutalization and of executing the innocent. Although no adequate calculation of the relative risks involved is possible, the fact of erroneous death sentences and executions, the absence of any convincing evidence favoring the superior deterrent effect of the death penalty, and the low incidence of recidivism seems to us to show that abolition is the better policy.

In the Courts

Since the 1976 decisions in *Gregg v. Georgia* and related cases (428 U.S. 153), murder trials in American jurisdictions in which a defendant could be sentenced to death have been bifurcated. In the first phase the jury determines the defendant's guilt or innocence. If the verdict is guilty, the second phase of the trial begins, in which it is determined whether the death penalty should be imposed. Jurisdictions vary in the standards and procedures used to sentence a defendant to death (Gillers, 1980).

A recurring issue before the courts is what type of information a defendant should be able to present in mitigation during the sentencing phase of a capital trial. Since 1977, juries have been permitted to hear during the sentencing phase *any* evidence concerning the nature of the crime or defendant that would mitigate the offense and warrant a sentence of life imprisonment. As the Supreme Court declared:

The Eighth and Fourteenth Amendments require that the sentencer . . . not be precluded from considering, *as a mitigating factor*, any aspect of a defendant's character or record and any of the circumstances of the offense that the defendant proffers as a basis for a sentence less than death [*Lockett v. Ohio*, 438 U.S. 586, 604, 1977; emphasis in original].

One factor that jurors may consider in mitigation is the possibility that the defendant is really innocent. As the California Supreme Court declared:

[A] jury which determines both guilt and penalty may properly conclude that the prosecution has discharged its burden of proving defendant's guilt beyond a reasonable doubt but that it still may demand a greater degree of certainty of guilt for the imposition of the death penalty. . . . The lingering doubts of jurors in the guilt phase may well cast their shadows into the penalty phase and in some measure affect the nature of the punishment [*People v. Terry*, 390 P.2d 381, 387, 1964].

Or, in the more recent words of the U.S. Fifth Circuit Court of Appeals:

The fact that jurors have determined guilt beyond a reasonable doubt does not necessarily mean that no juror entertained *any* doubt whatsoever. There may be no *reasonable* doubt—doubt based upon reason—and yet some *genuine* doubt exists. It may reflect a mere possibility; it may be the whimsy of one juror or several. Yet this whimsical doubt—this absence of absolute certainty—can be real [*Smith v. Balkcom*, 660 F.2d 573, 580, 1981].

The admissibility of this "lingering doubt" argument was recently echoed by the U.S. Supreme Court in its decision in *Lockhart v. McCree* (106 S. Ct. 1758, 1986). There, the Court ruled that prospective jurors in a capital case who are opposed to the death penalty could be excluded from sitting not only when the jury is making its penalty decision, but also when it is deciding the prior issue of guilt. Writing for the majority, Justice Rehnquist argued that by having one jury make both guilt and penalty decisions, "the defendant might benefit at the sentencing phase of the trial from the jury's 'residual doubts' about the evidence presented at the guilt phase" (p. 1769).

As of the end of 1986, the Bedau-Radelet research has been presented during the penalty phase of three different California capital trials. In all three the jury voted to spare the defendant's life. These results are too few to test the power of the fruits of this research to buttress defense arguments for imprisonment rather than death. In each of these cases, the defendant was fortunate in having highly skilled counsel, and each case presented a solid basis of facts for the construction of the "lingering doubt" argument.

Admissibility of expert testimony regarding this research project during the penalty phase of a capital trial is a controversial matter. Some prosecutors have succeeded in preventing juries from hearing about the research, and appellate courts have yet to rule on their right to do so. Defense attorneys involved in these cases view the results of the research a powerful means to remind capital juries that virtually every year, somewhere or other in the nation, the wrong person is convicted of murder (Radelet, 1987). The earnest attempts by prosecutors to prevent jurors from learning about this study indicate that they apparently agree.

CONCLUSIONS

The power of the criminal justice system to make godlike judgments of who shall live and who shall die rests on an assumption that those who administer the system are possessed with a perfection of skills that make the execution of an innocent defendant impossible. Erroneous convictions and executions can be rationalized by death penalty proponents only by arguing that the alleged benefits of this punishment, over and above long imprisonment, outweigh this unavoidable cost. It is therefore ironic that among the justifications for capital punishment voiced by its supporters is a fear that a murderer imprisoned for life will be paroled only to commit another crime. This fear, for those who have it, is proof that they do not have complete confidence in the power of the criminal justice system to make infallibly correct decisions. The very explanation for this justified skepticism—the perceived imperfections of those who administer the system—also explains why no society can be trusted to use the death penalty itself with infallible reliability. Recognition of this contradiction should reduce our society's thirst for future executions.

REFERENCES

AVRICH, P. (1984) The Haymarket Tragedy. Princeton: Princeton University Press.
BEDAU, H. A. (1964) The Death Penalty in America. Chicago: Aldine.

BEDAU, H. A. (1982) The Death Penalty in America (3rd ed.). New York: Oxford University Press.

BEDAU, H. A. and M. L. RADELET (1987) "Miscarriages of Justice in Potentially Capital Cases." Stanford Law Review 40: 21-179.

BENNETT, E. W. (1978) "The Reasons for Michigan's Abolition of the Death Penalty." Michigan History 62: 42-55.

BLACK, C. (1981) Capital Punishment: The Inevitability of Caprice and Mistake. New York: W. W. Norton.

BORCHARD, E. M. (1932) Convicting the Innocent. New Haven: Yale University Press.

BOWERS, D. C. (1915) Life Imprisonment vs. the Death Penalty. To the Honorable Members of the Senate and Lower House of the 58th General Assembly and to the Chairman and Members of the Judiciary thereof. The Brief of Duke C. Bowers et al., Advocates, on Senate Bill, No. 242, and House Bill, No. 235, entitled "An Act to Abolish the Death Penalty in the State of Tennessee, and to Substitute Life Imprisonment Therefor." Privately published.

BOWERS, W. J. and G. L. PIERCE (1980) "Deterrence or Brutalization: What is the Effect of Executions?" Crime and Delinquency 26: 453-484.

BRANDON, R. and C. DAVIES (1973) Wrongful Imprisonment: Mistaken Convictions and their Consequences. London: Allen & Unwin.

BURBEY, L. H. (1938) "History of Execution in What is Now the State of Michigan." Michigan History Magazine 22 (Autumn): 493-457.

CHANDLER, D. (1976) Capital Punishment in Canada: A Sociological History of Repressive Law. Toronto: McClelland and Stewart.

DONNELLY, R. C. (1952) "Unconvicting the Innocent." Vanderbilt Law Review 6: 20-40.

EHRMANN, S. R. (1962) "For Whom the Chair Waits." Federal Probation 26: 14-25.

FRANK, J. and B. FRANK (1957) Not Guilty. London: Victor Gollancz.

GARDNER, E. S. (1952) The Court of Last Resort. New York: William Sloane.

GILLERS, S. (1980) "Deciding Who Dies." University of Pennsylvania Law Review 129: 1-124.

GROSS, S. (1987) "Loss of Innocence: Eyewitness Identification and Proof of Guilt." Journal of Legal Studies 16: 395-453.

HILL, P., M. YOUNG, and T. SARGENT (1985) More Rough Justice. Harmondsworth, England: Penguin.

HIRSCHBERG, M. (1940) "Wrongful Convictions." Rocky Mountain Law Review 13: 20-46.

HUIE, W. B. (1964) "The South Kills Another Negro," pp. 85-91 in E. G. McGehee and W. H. Hildebrand (eds.), The Death Penalty. Boston: D.C. Heath.

KENNEDY, L. (1961) 10 Rillington Place. New York: Simon and Schuster.

KENNEDY, L. (1985) The Airman and the Carpenter: The Lindbergh Kidnapping and the Framing of Bruno Richard Hauptmann. New York: Viking.

KLUGER, R. (1975) Simple Justice. New York: Vintage.

LEBOURDAIS, I. (1966) The Trial of Steven Truscott. Philadelphia: Lippincott.

MACKEY, P. E. (1974) " 'The Result May be Glorious'—Anti-Gallows Movement in Rhode Island, 1838-1852." Rhode Island History 33: 19-31.

MacKEY, P. E. (1976) Voices Against Death. New York: Burt Franklin.

MacNAMARA, D.E.J. (1969) "Convicting the Innocent." Crime and Delinquency 15: 57-61.

MILLER, G. (1975) Invitation to a Lynching. Garden City: Doubleday.

NORTH, J. W. (1870) The History of Augusta. Augusta, ME: Clapp and North.

POLLAK, O. (1952) "The Errors of Justice." The Annals of the American Academy of Political and Social Science 284: 115-123.

RADELET, M. L. (1987) "Sociologists as Expert Witnesses in Capital Cases: A Case Study" in Patrick R. Anderson and Thomas Winfree, Jr. (eds.), The Expert Witness: Theory, Practice, and Issues. New York: State University of New York Press.

RADIN, E. D. (1964) The Innocents. New York: William Morrow.

SCADUTO, A. (1976) Scapegoat: The Lonesome Death of Bruno Richard Hauptmann. New York: G. P. Putnam.

SELLIN, T. (1980) The Penalty of Death. Beverly Hills, Sage.

TEETERS, N. (1967) Hang by the Neck. Springfield, IL: Charles C Thomas.

VAN DEN HAAG, E. and J. P. CONRAD (1983) The Death Penalty: A Debate. New York: Plenum.

YOUNG, M. and P. HILL (1983) Rough Justice. London: Ariel.

CASES

Gregg v. Georgia, 428 U.S. 153 (1976).

Lockett v. Ohio, 438 U.S. 586 (1977).

Lockhart v. McCree, 106 S. Ct. 1758 (1986).

People v. Terry, 390 P.2d 381 (1964).

Smith v. Balkcom, 660 F.2d 573 (1981).

Woodson et al. v. North Carolina, 428 U.S. 280 (1976).

Chapter 5

RACIAL CONSIDERATIONS IN CAPITAL PUNISHMENT
The Failure of Evenhanded Justice

RAYMOND PATERNOSTER
ANNMARIE KAZYAKA

In 1971, in *McGautha v. California,* the United States Supreme Court rejected an explicit Fourteenth Amendment due process attack against the constitutionality of the death penalty as then practiced in the majority of U.S. states. What litigants in *McGautha* questioned was the constitutionality of allowing juries to have unguided discretion in making sentencing decisions, free to consider or not to consider countless factors, and free to decide how much or how little to weigh these factors in the selection of a life or death sentence. Such unfettered and untrammeled discretion, petitioners argued, produced nothing less than lawless decision making and a pattern of sentencing that failed to provide the rudiments of evenhanded justice. The solution, petitioners further argued, would be the extension of formal legal rules into the penalty phase of capital cases, an area previously untouched by legal formalism. Such rules would take the form of enumerated characteristics of the offense and offender, which the jury would explicitly consider before imposing sentence.

The majority of the Court in *McGautha,* however, rejected this Fourteenth Amendment claim. Justice Harlan, writing for the majority, noted that the promulgation of strict legal rules to guide the determination of who shall live and who shall die is beyond human intellectual power.[1] It is important to note what Justice Harlan both said and did not say. He did not conclude that the jury's sentencing decision in capital cases was capricious, irrational, or inevitably influenced by extra-legal criteria. In his opinion, Justice Harlan noted simply that juries do use morally and legally relevant criteria in imposing a sentence of death. He was pessimistic about the attempt to make rational such a process by the promulgation of formal legal rules.[2] Both sides in the *McGautha* debate took the position that the death penalty should be applied in a rational and evenhanded manner; they differed on the means through which this should be achieved. Justice Harlan was skeptical of the Court's ability to rewrite state statutes in order to reduce the jury's decision to precise legal rules. Justice Brennan, in dissent, claimed in essence that the jury's decision must be strictly and formally bounded by the rule of law.[3]

After *McGautha*, the next opportunity the Court had to consider the problem of the unfair imposition of capital punishment was the very next year, in *Furman v. Georgia*. *Furman* is a particularly interesting case for several reasons: (1) it is the longest written opinion to date in the Court's history, covering some 232 pages; (2) each of the nine justices felt compelled to write his own opinion, and the reasons for judgment "are stated in five separate opinions, expressing so many different rationales"(*Furman v. Georgia,* 408 U.S. 238, 414, 1972; J. Powell dissent), that many doubt whether *Furman* actually contains any "decision"; and (3) the Court essentially rereviewed the issue it had apparently decided the previous year in *McGautha*,[4] whether standardless, unstructured capital decision making was prohibited by the Constitution, this time, however under an Eighth Amendment attack.

Regarding the last point, Weisberg (1984: 315) noted that the majority opinions were essentially premised on the belief that the Eighth and Fourteenth Amendments had "very different things to say about standardless sentencing," and that the "wonderful fiction" the court had to entertain was the possibility that the *result* of standardless juries may violate the 8th Amendment prohibition against cruel and unusual punishment at the same time that the *process* did not violate the Due Process Clause of the Fourteenth Amendment. Whatever the strength or logic of the constitutional authority the Court acted under, it nevertheless declared existing schemes of capital punishment unconstitutional. Although it is not quite clear precisely what is "condemned in *Furman*," it can at least be concluded that three critical opinions of the majority, those of Justices Stewart, White, and Douglas, assailed the evils of capriciousness and discrimination found in patterns of standardless jury decision making.

Justice Stewart observed that because there was no rational basis to distinguish the few who are sentenced to death from the many who are spared it, current standardless jury sentencing is "cruel and unusual in the same way that being struck by lightening is cruel and unusual" (*Furman v. Georgia*, 408 U.S. 238,409 1972). Although not concluding that the product of unguided juries is a racially discriminatory one,[5] Justice Stewart did hold that those sentenced to death in such a standardless fashion "are among a capriciously selected random handful." Justice White's objection was premised on his belief that capital punishment had become so infrequently imposed that it failed to further legitimate state goals—retribution and deterrence. Even his concern for the functional rationality of the criminal justice system was touched with the idea of the evenhanded imposition of criminal penalties: "Nor could it be said with confidence that society's need for specific deterrence justifies death for so few when for so many in like circumstance life imprisonment or shorter prison terms are judged sufficient" (*Furman v. Georgia* 408 U.S. 238, 31 1-312, 1972; emphasis added). Justice Douglas expressed the infirmity of standardless sentencing, its lack of evenhandedness, in terms of its racially discriminatory product:

[W]e deal with a system of law and of justice that leaves to the uncontrolled discretion of judges or juries the determination whether defendants committing these crimes should die or be imprisoned. Under these laws no standards govern the selection of the penalty. People live or die, dependent on the whims of one man or of twelve.

Thus, these discretionary statutes are unconstitutional in their operation. They are pregnant with discrimination and discrimination is an ingredient not compatible with the idea of equal protection of the laws that is implicit in the ban on "cruel and unusual" punishments [*Furman v. Georgia* 408 U.S. 238, 253, 256-257, 1972].

Whatever else *Furman* condemned or ultimately required for capital sentencing the absence of evenhandedness was a central concern.[6] Furthermore, it is equally clear from *Furman* and subsequent cases that the notion of evenhanded sentencing has at least two dimensions: The infliction of the penalty of death can not be imposed (1) in an arbitrary or capricious manner, or (2) based upon the consideration of legally impermissible factors.[7] Capital-sentencing decisions can fail to be evenhanded, then, if they violate the first criterion, above, and are made randomly, or if they violate the second criterion and are systematically related to a legally impermissible characteristic of the defendant or victim, such as race.

In response to *Furman*, state legislatures revised their capital-sentencing schemes by either formally eliminating sentencing discretion or structuring and guiding it. The former solution took the form of various mandatory sentencing proposals, which made the death penalty automatic for specified types of murder. In 1976, the Court rejected these modifications of the substantive law of murder in *Woodson v. North Carolina* and *Roberts v. Louisiana*. The second solution entailed a procedural overhaul of capital sentencing by introducing formal legal rules into the penalty phase. In three cases, *Gregg v. Georgia, Proffitt v. Florida* and *Jurek v. Texas*, the Court approved so-called "guided discretion" statutes.[8] Generally, these took the form of lists of aggravating circumstances, of which the jury was required to find at least one before it could render a sentence of death. In essence, in these three cases the Court virtually required the states to do what Harlan said could not be done in *McGautha*—to create legal rules for the penalty phase of capital trials consistent with rational formality.

As Weisberg (1984) recently noted, with *Gregg* the Court embarked on an ill-fated journey of death penalty doctrine making. The intended outcome of this doctrine making would be the reduction of the lawlessness of standardless sentencing, at least two of its most pernicious features—capriciousness and discrimination—through the rule of law. More specifically, in approving Georgia's capital-sentencing scheme in *Gregg* the Court referred to three features: (1) a bifurcated trial in which the penalty issue is addressed in a separate hearing after conviction, (2) a statutory list of aggravating circumstances, and (3) rigorous and automatic appellate review. It was presumed by the majority in *Gregg* that the introduction of formal legal rules into the penalty phase of capital sentencing would sufficiently reduce the pattern of capricious and discriminatory sentencing of standardless juries "condemned" by the Court in *Furman*.[9]

The Court was quite optimistic in *Gregg* that the extension of formal legal rule making into the penalty phase would eliminate, or at least reduce to constitutionally tolerable levels, arbitrariness and racial discrimination in capital sentencing. Justice White, responding to petitioner's complaint that the changes in the Georgia statute were merely "cosmetic" and that the potential for arbitrary and racially discriminatory treatment at the hands of Georgia prosecutors and juries remained, claimed that such objections were "unsupported by any facts." At the time of the *Gregg* decision, of course, Justice White did not have any empirical evidence of his own to indicate that the suggested procedural reforms were likely to have their intended effects; in all three cases the new death penalty statutes were simply affirmed on their face.[10]

Since the time of *Gregg* and its companion cases, however, social scientific evidence has begun to accumulate regarding the effect of the Court's reshaping of the process of state administered capital punishment. In an early investigation of the capital-sentencing schemes of Florida, Texas, and Georgia, Bowers and Pierce (1980) reported evidence of racial discrimination. They found that in the most serious kinds of homicides, those that involved another statutory felony, Florida, Georgia, and Texas juries were more likely to impose a death sentence against killers of white victims. Black killers of whites were particularly likely to receive a death sentence in felony-type murders, whereas blacks who killed other blacks were far less likely to receive a death sentence than any other offender/victim racial combination. In Florida for felony-type murders, killers of whites were almost six times more likely to receive a sentence of death than were killers of blacks, and for similar homicides black killers of whites were over seven times more likely to receive a death sentence than black killers of other blacks. In Georgia, defendants who killed whites in felony-murders were over five times more likely to receive a death sentence than were killers of blacks. As in Florida, race of offender had an effect when the victim's race was considered. Blacks who killed whites were over nine times more likely to be sentenced to death than were blacks who killed other blacks. A pattern similar to this was found in Texas. It is clear from this study that the Court's introduction of rational formality into the penalty phase may have had only a limited impact.

Bowers and Pierce were not the only ones to have found racial discrimination in the administration of post-*Furman* capital-sentencing schemes. In his study of 600 homicide indictments in 20 Florida counties in 1976 and 1977, Radelet (1981) found that for murders involving strangers, those accused of killing whites were over two and a half times more likely to be sentenced to death than were killers of blacks. This difference in sentencing rates by race of victim was primarily caused by killers of whites being more likely to be indicted for first-degree murder, thus tracing the source of discrimination to decisions made by the prosecutor and grand jury—decisions untouched by *Gregg*. A similar pattern was also found by Zeisel (1981) with Florida data that overlap with those collected by Bowers and Pierce.

In a series of studies Paternoster reported that the prosecutor's decision to seek a death sentence in a given homicide was higher for white than black victim murders, particularly for black defendants who killed white victims. (Jacoby and Paternoster, 1982; Paternoster, 1983). Using data sources similar to Bowers and Pierce, Gross and Mauro (1984) found that in Georgia, Florida and Illinois, blacks who killed whites were most likely to be sentenced to death and blacks who killed blacks were least likely. They also found that the effect of the victim/offender's race varied by the region in each state, with the racial effect substantially more pronounced in rural than urban areas.

Although preliminary social science data had revealed post-*Furman* patterns of capricious and discriminatory capital sentencing, not all of the evidence was consistent, and much of the available evidence did not permit an unequivocal conclusion. In an analysis of homicides from Dade County Florida for the years 1973-1976 Arkin (1980) found that the probability of a death sentence was independent of the race of both the defendant and victim. In addition, the conclusions from many of the other studies on race and capital sentencing were suspect because researchers could not rule out the possibility that other legal and circumstantial factors accounted for observed racial differences in sentencing or charging decisions. For example, Bowers and Pierce's finding that killers of whites are more likely to be sentenced to death than killers of blacks may simply reflect the fact that white-victim homicides are more aggravated and brutal, or are committed by offenders with more violent criminal histories than are homicides involving black victims. Although Bowers and Pierce did control for the felony circumstances surrounding the murder, the limitations of their data precluded them from simultaneously controlling for several other important factors (relationship between victim and offender, number of victims and offenders, type of weapon, criminal history of defendant, brutality of the offense). A general criticism of much of this literature is that although a few legally relevant factors were considered, in no study was the full range of variation in type of offense or offender between death-imposed and life-imposed capital cases considered.

More recent research has tried to overcome these limitations by including simultaneous controls for several such factors. In a study of the charging of 1,400 Florida homicide cases from 32 counties between 1973 and 1977, Radelet and Pierce (1985) compared the initial police report of each homicide with its description in the court record. They found that white-victim homicides, particularly those involving black defendants, were more likely to be "upgraded" from a nonfelony or possible felony to a felony-type homicide, and less likely to be "downgraded" than those homicides with other racial characteristics. This pattern of upgrading white-victim and black-on-white homicides was found to exist even when statistical controls for eight variables that might affect prosecutorial behavior were made in a logistic regression. Also employing Florida data, Bowers (1983) found that the decision to indict a defendant for first-degree murder was significantly affected by the victim's race and the region of the state, even after controls for legally relevant factors were made.

Capital-sentencing practices also have been shown to be touched by racial influences. In a study of the capital-sentencing practices of Georgia, Florida, and Illinois, Gross and Mauro (1984) estimated a logistic regression equation for each state that included five legally relevant variables (felony circumstances, victim/offender relationship, number of victims, sex of victim, and type of weapon) and the race of the victim. They found that even when controlling for these five factors killers of whites in Georgia had a seven-times-greater likelihood of receiving a death sentence than killers of blacks. For Florida the effect was 4.8 times greater and defendants in Illinois with white victims were 4 times more likely to be sentenced to death than those with black victims.

The most comprehensive study to date of racial discrimination and arbitrariness in the imposition of capital punishment was conducted by Baldus and his colleagues using both pre- and post-*Furman* homicide data from Georgia (Baldus et al., 1983a, 1983b, 1985). Baldus collected data on over 400 variables thought to influence the legal processing of death cases, including richly detailed information on the manner in which the offense was committed, the kind and quality of evidence, and characteristics of the defendant including racial-demographic, educational, occupational, and criminal-history data. A discussion of the details and depth of Baldus' statistical analysis are beyond the scope of this chapter. Of direct relevance, however, are a series of multivariate analyses in which the effect of racial characteristics on the processing of death cases was estimated after controlling for scores of legally relevant factors. In spite of controlling for over 250 aggravating, mitigating, evidentiary, and suspect factors, Baldus and his colleagues found that the race of the victim had a significant effect on the imposition of a death sentence, with killers of whites more likely to be sentenced to death than killers of blacks. In several analyses of their data with different methodologies, Baldus and his colleagues (1983a, 1985) consistently found a significant race-of-victim effect on capital sentencing as did secondary analyses of the Baldus data by Barnett (1985).

Some 10 years of research since the beginning of the Supreme Court's introduction of legal formalism into the states' death penalty laws has shown that such rigorous doctrine making has been generally unsuccessful. This line of research, though striking in its consistency, cannot yet be used to provide unambiguous evidence of the Court's failure. Although much data has been collected and analyzed it has, for the most part, been restricted to one decision point in the legal processing of homicide cases—the decision to impose a death sentence—and in a limited number of states—Georgia and Florida. In addition, in only a few of these studies have researchers been able to eliminate confidently the influence of relevant legal factors as rival explanations.[11] Initially, a restrictive focus on these two states makes substantive sense. The capital punishment statutes of Georgia and Florida (along with Texas) were the first to be approved by the Court and a large number of Florida and Georgia capital defendants have since been sentenced to death, making detailed multivariate analysis more efficient and reliable. An analysis of the sentencing decision is also of critical importance since the penalty trial may be the most consequential point, and is the one most directly affected by the Court's doctrine making. It is now, however, important to analyze the legal administration of capital punishment in other states to establish the generality of the patterns found in Florida and Georgia. Further it is necessary to examine other points in the system since earlier decisions may significantly affect the magnitude and type of arbitrariness and discrimination observed at sentencing (Thompson and Zingraff, 1981; Berk, 1983; Klepper et al., 1983). In addition, it is necessary that the data should include a sufficient breadth of legal variables to eliminate confidently alternative explanations.

The research reported here concerns an investigation of the even-handedness of the administration of the death penalty in South Carolina. The South Carolina statute lists seven aggravating circumstances, one of which must be found beyond a reasonable doubt to make a defendant eligible for the death penalty. The state must forewarn the defendant 30 days in advance of the trial of its intention to seek the death penalty and the aggravating factor(s) for which it will argue. Because the statute essentially creates a new crime of capital murder, the filing of notice to seek the death penalty entails the prosecutor's charging decision. Unlike the Georgia statute, South Carolina's lists nine mitigating circumstances. Sentencers in South Carolina are implicitly instructed to weigh the factors in aggravation and mitigation before imposing sentence. The data discussed in this chapter will address two decision points within this statutory scheme—the decision of the prosecutor to charge a given homicide as a capital offense by seeking a death sentence and the decision of the sentencer to impose a death sentence. The analysis of evenhandedness will concern the effect of race variables on these decisions.

METHODS

The time interval covered by this study is from June 8, 1977, when South Carolina's new death penalty statute was enacted, until December 31, 1981. During this period approximately 1,800 nonnegligent homicide events occurred in the state. The unit of analysis in this research is the homicide event rather than a distinguishable crime of homicide. A homicide event is defined as a distinct act of homicide committed by a single defendant against one or more victims. If, for example, two offenders were to murder one victim in an armed robbery there would be two homicide events, each including the killing of a single victim during the course of an armed robbery by multiple offenders. On the other hand, if one offender were to kill two victims during the course of an armed robbery, then there would be only one homicide event, that involving a single defendant with multiple victims during an armed robbery. The event was selected as the unit of analysis, since in the first homicide described, two death sentences could be sought by the prosecutor and imposed by the jury, and the characteristics of each event would differ depending on the offenders' characteristics and culpability. In the second homicide type, generally only one death sentence is involved.

Of the original pool of 1,805 nonnegligent homicide events 119 were eliminated because there was no known offender. Not all of the offenders in the remaining 1,686 homicide events were eligible for the death penalty since they may not have committed one of seven aggravating factors enumerated in the state statute. In fact, only a small percentage (18%, N = 311) of these homicides included a statutory aggravating circumstance. A large proportion of these homicides (97%, N = 302) involved the commission of a felony as the requisite aggravating circumstance. The statistical analysis to follow is restricted to these cases. This restriction of the population of cases should present few problems of generalizability or comparability with other studies, since in other states that have been the subjects of published studies most death sentences are given in homicides involving an accompanying aggravating felony.

Data for this study came from several sources. Initial information on the 1,805 homicides were collected from the Supplemental Homicide Report (SHR). In South Carolina the SHR is completed for each homicide by a local police department and forwarded to a centralized public agency, the State Enforcement Division (SLED). Since all the enforcement departments in the state are included in SLED's SHR program there is virtually complete coverage for all homicides committed in the state. SLED supplied a computer generated copy of SHR information on each homicide committed during the study period. Since these data were generated by year, county, law enforcement agency, offense and offender characteristics, and date of offense, it was possible to construct each homicide as a homicide event and establish a preliminary data file. Unfortunately, the SHR contains only limited data on the victim, offender, and homicide event itself.

In order to obtain as much detail as possible about each homicide, the original police incident and investigation report was requested and received for approximately 95% of the entire pool of 1,800 homicide events and all 302 that involved a statutory felony. This investigation report contained detailed descriptive information pertaining to the offender, victim, crime scene, and the manner in which the crime was committed. This report often included data as to the nature and specific injury suffered by the victim. For example it often revealed whether the body had been moved or hidden, bound or gagged by the defendant; the number of knife wounds or bullet holes; if the victim struggled, resisted, or participated in any way; if there was pre- or postmortem abuse of the victim. It typically described the mental state of the offender, any previous arrests known to the investigator, and countless other features about the homicide that would allow a fairly complete reconstruction of the crime. In analyzing these reports, we found no obvious variation in their length or detail by year, agency, or type of homicide. This information was used to supplement the original data file constructed with the SHR.

In addition to this information compiled for all homicides, supplemental data were collected on all homicides that resulted in a conviction.

If a homicide results in an arrest and indictment, a record is kept by the State Office of the Attorney General. A computer listing of this record was obtained for each homicide committed from 1977 through the end of 1982, one year after the cut-off point for the collection of the homicide data. This computer record listed the date of the arrest and trial; county; name, race, sex, and birth date of the defendant; outcome of the trial; and the sentence imposed. It was then possible to code the disposition of each case. It was possible to match these two data sources with the SHR and incident report data. An additional source of data for these defendants was also obtained. Since all those defendants convicted of homicide received either a death sentence, life sentence, or a specified sentence of years in prison if convicted of a lesser offense, a check was made of their files at the State Department of Corrections. These inmate files also contained information about the offense from newspaper clippings, the defendant's own account and a detailed criminal history.

According to the state statute, prosecutors are required to notify the defense 30 days in advance of trial of the state's intention to seek the death penalty. The prosecutor is required to file a written copy of this notice with the State's Court Administrator, who then sends a copy to the staff of the state supreme court. The state supreme court research staff keeps an updated copy of all filed death requests and a copy of each of these notices was obtained. Since the defendant's name and trial county are included in this notice it was possible to code each homicide as to whether or not the death penalty was requested. Finally, as part of its direct review procedure, the state supreme court keeps a copy of the trial transcript in which a sentence of death is imposed. Together with the data on trial outcome supplied by the State Attorney General's office it was then possible to code the sentence received in each case.

FINDINGS

Table 5.1A reports the probability of the death penalty being sought by the prosecutor for the group of 302 felony-type capital murders by the racial characteristics of the victim and offender. Similar data pertaining to the decision of a sentencer to impose a death sentence are reported in Tables 5.1B and 5.1C. As a first point, it should be noted that by statute, local prosecutors in South Carolina have unrestricted discretion in seeking a death sentence for a given capital homicide, and the data indicate that they exercise that discretion with considerable frequency. Of the 302 homicides that were statutorily eligible to be "death penalty cases," prosecutors served notice that a death sentence would be sought in only 114 (38%). These simple analyses are consistent with other studies from different states under different statutory schemes in that they suggest that racial considerations may play a role in the legal process of deciding which homicide defendants shall live and which shall be put to death. Contrary to much of the pre-*Furman* literature, Table 5.1A indicates that the prosecutor's charging decision is independent of the race of the offender when considered apart from the race of the victim. In fact, the data show that white offenders are somewhat at a disadvantage. The probability that a death sentence will be sought is slightly higher for white offenders (.412) than for blacks (.355), although the difference is slight and nonsignificant.[12]

The data show, however, that the race of the victim, and the race of the offender and victim considered together do appear to be related to the prosecutor's charging decision. Killers of whites are over two times more likely to be charged with capital murder in a homicide involving a felony than are those who killed blacks. Black offenders who cross racial boundaries to kill whites are particularly likely to have the death penalty brought against them. Approximately half of the black-on-white felony killings resulted in a death request, but only 14% of the black-on-black killings, a ratio of three and a half to one. The overwhelming effect of the victim's race is seen when this is compared to white-on-white killings, which are about as likely as black-white murders to result in a death request. Intrarace homicides for whites are treated as harshly as cross race homicides for blacks and substantially more harshly than intrarace homicides for blacks. The last two panels of Table 5.1A show the direction of the racial influence on the prosecutor's charging decision; homicides not involving a black offender killing a black victim are over three times more likely to produce a death request, and blacks who kill whites are almost two times more likely to have the prosecutor request the death penalty compared with all other felony-type murders.

Tables 5.1B and 5.1C report the probability of a death sentence being imposed by the racial characteristics of the victim and offender. This and subsequent data pertaining to the decision to impose a death sentence should be viewed with some caution since only 26 death sentences were handed down from 1977 until the end of 1981. Additionally, there were only 19 convictions in 87 black-victim homicides (22%) compared with 116 convictions obtained in the 215 homicides involving white victims (54%). With such a small number of death sentences and convictions, in some subcells the estimated

TABLE 5.1A

Probability of Prosecutor Seeking the Death Penalty
for Capital Murder in South Carolina
by Race of Offender and Victim

	(Cases)	Probability	Ratio
Death sought			
White offender	(49/119)	.412	1.16
Black offender	(65/183)	.355	
White victim	(97/215)	.451	2.31[c]
Black victim	(17/87)	.195	
Black kills black	(10/72)	.139	3.56[a]
Black kills white	(55/111)	.495	
White kills black	(7/15)	.467	
White kills white	(42/104)	.404	1.23[b]
Black kills black	(10/72)	.139	3.25[c]
Black kills all others	(104/230)	.452	
Black kills white	(55/111)	.495	1.60[c]
Black kills all others	(59/191)	.309	

a. Ratio of black killing white to black killing black, race of offender is therefore held constant and the disparity is by race of victim.
b. Ratio of black killing white to white killing white, race of victim is therefore held constant and the disparity is by race of offender.
c. Significant association as measured by a standard chi-square test of statistical significance, $p < .01$.

probabilities are subject to substantial change with additional cases. Table 5.1B consists of all 302 capital homicides, whereas Table 5.1C reports the conditional probability of a death sentence being imposed given that a conviction was obtained. The results are, for the most part, consistent between the two tables.

Unlike the prosecutor's decision to seek a death sentence, the sentencer's decision to impose one is influenced by the race of the *offender* more than the race of the victim. The direction of this effect favors black offenders. When all felony-type murders are considered white offenders are over four times more likely to be sentenced to death than are black offenders (Table 5.1B: .160 versus .038), an effect that persists when the probability is conditioned on the offender's conviction (Table 5.1C: .317 versus .093). Although somewhat surprising from an historical viewpoint, given the magnitude of black offender-based racial discrimination in the pre-*Furman* literature (G. Johnson, 1941; Garfinkel, 1949; Wolfgang et al., 1962; E. Johnson, 1957; Wolfgang and

TABLE 5.1B

Probability of Death Sentence Being Imposed for Capital Murder
in South Carolina by Race of Offender and Victim

	(Cases)	Probability	Ratio
Death imposed			
White offender	(19/119)	.160	4.21[c]
Black offender	(7/183)	.038	
White victim	(20/215)	.093	1.35
Black victim	(6/87)	.069	
Black kills black	(1/72)	.014	3.86[a]
Black kills white	(6/111)	.054	
White kills black	(5/15)	.333	
White kills white	(14/104)	.135	2.50[b]
Black kills black	(1/72)	.014	7.78[c]
Black kills all others	(25/230)	.109	
Black kills white	(6/111)	.054	1.94
Black kills all others	(20/191)	.105	

a. Ratio of black killing white to black killing black, race of offender is therefore held constant and the disparity is by race of victim.
b. Ratio of white killing white to black killing white, race of victim is therefore held constant and the disparity is by race of offender.
c. Significant association as measured by a standard chi-square test of statistical significance, $p < .01$.

Reidel, 1975; Zimring et al., 1976), the finding that death sentences under South Carolina's post-*Furman* statute may work against white offenders is similar to other research during this period from different states (Bowers and Pierce, 1980; Gross and Mauro, 1984; Baldus et al., 1985).

In comparison with the pervasive race of victim effect observed in the prosecutor's decision to seek a death sentence, only a modest effect is observed when the decision to impose the death penalty is examined. In addition, the direction of this effect depends upon which pool of homicide cases is selected. When all 302 felony-type murders are examined a familiar, but weak, pattern of victim-based racial discrimination appears. Killers of whites are somewhat more likely to be sentenced to death than are killers of blacks (.093 versus .069). When the subset of those convicted are examined, however, the direction reverses, and killers of blacks are almost twice as likely to be sentenced to death than are killers of whites.

TABLE 5.1C

Probability of Death Sentence Being Imposed for Capital Murder
in South Carolina by Race of Offender and Victim —
Capital Murders Which Resulted in a Conviction

	(Cases)	Probability	Ratio
Death imposed			
White offender	(19/60)	.317	3.41^c
Black offender	(7/75)	.093	
White victim	(20/116)	.172	1.84
Black victim	(6/19)	.316	
Black kills black	(1/12)	.083	1.14^a
Black kills white	(6/63)	.095	
White kills black	(5/7)	.714	2.78^b
White kills white	(14/53)	.264	
Black kills black	(1/12)	.083	2.44^c
All others	(25/123)	.203	
Black kills white	(6/63)	.095	2.93^c
All others	(20/72)	.278	

a. Ratio of black killing white to black killing black, race of offender is therefore
held constant and the disparity is by race of victim.
b. Ratio of white killing white to black killing white, race of victim is therefore held
constant and the disparity is by race of offender.
c. Significant association as measured by a standard chi-square test of statistical
significance.

We can offer only a few speculations as to why this pattern exists. One
is that there are simply too few death sentences imposed (26 in all, and
only 6 that involved a black victim) in South Carolina during this period
to permit a clear analysis of patterns of racial disparity. Second, the low
conviction rate of black-victim homicides for capital murder (22%)
reduces substantially the denominator in the calculation of probabilities
in Table 5.1C. Had the conviction rate for black-victim homicides been
equal to that of white victims, the probability that a death sentence
would be imposed for convicted killers of blacks would have declined
from .316 to .127. The main contributor to the low capital murder
conviction rate in black-victim homicides comes from those involving
black defendants. Although only 17% (12/72) of all black-on-black
homicides result in a conviction, 47% (7/15) of the small number of
white-on-black homicides end in a conviction. The conviction rate for
blacks who kill whites is 57% and it is 51% for whites who kill other
whites. The black-on-black conviction rate for murder, then, is one-

third what it is for all other homicides.

What may account for the high death sentencing rates for black victims in Table 5.1C, then, may be the small number of death sentences imposed generally and in black-victim cases in particular, and the low rate with which killers of blacks are convicted, such that only cases involving certain convictions and excessive brutality are pursued. This differential handling of black-on-black homicides, which was clearly seen in the prosecutor's decision to seek a death sentence (Table 5.1A) and the decision to convict, persists in the sentencing decision. Not only are intrarace black homicides unlikely to result in a conviction, they are unlikely to end in the imposition of a death sentence. Here again, however, the few cases involved make any discussion speculative. In all felony-type murders, the probability of a death sentence for black defendants who kill other blacks is .014 (1/72; see Table 5.1B), whereas for blacks who kill whites it is almost four times higher (.054 versus .014). Comparing black-on-black with all other homicides, defendants in the latter categories are eight times more likely to receive a death sentence.

This pattern persists, though less strongly, among those who are eventually convicted (Table 5.1C). Of 12 black defendants convicted of killing another black, only one received a death sentence. This is roughly comparable to the probability for those blacks convicted of murdering a white (.083 versus .095). This finding is inconsistent with previous studies, which have found a more substantial race-of-victim effect at the sentencing stage, but, again, it probably reflects the infrequency of death cases and the low conviction rate of black-on-black homicides. Table 5.1C also reveals that the probability of a death sentence being imposed in a black-on-black homicide is less than half that for those involving all other racial combinations.

Differences in the likelihood that a death sentence would either be sought or imposed based upon the race of the offender or victim does not, of course, mean that such differences exist *because of race*. Differences in the treatment of these cases may reflect differences in the kinds of homicides involved or legally relevant characteristics of those who commit them. For instance, homicides committed against white victims may be more brutal than those against black victims. Killers of whites may have more extensive and violent criminal histories or may have behaved in ways that indicate to prosecutors and sentencers more culpability and less remorse (by trying to hide the body, for example). Although all of the homicides in this South Carolina data set are relatively homogeneous in that they all were eligible for the death penalty because an additional statutory felony was committed, felony-type murders can differ dramatically along any number of legally permissible factors. Before concluding that race influenced these outcomes such factors should be taken into account.

To estimate the effect of race and legally relevant variables, a series of logit regression equations were estimated. In the first set of equations the binary dependent variable was the prosecutor's decision to seek a death sentence in a felony-type homicide, with the affirmative decision coded as one. Two similar equations were estimated with the decision to impose a death sentence as the dependent variable. In one of these, the pool of all felony homicides was used in the equation, whereas in the other, only those homicides that resulted in a conviction were employed. In both of these equations, the decision to impose death was coded as a binary variable with the affirmative decision coded as one. In all three equations, nine legally relevant characteristics of the offense or offender were employed as prediction variables: (1) prior violent record of the defendant, (2) number of victims, (3) number of offenders, (4) victim/offender relationship, (5) number of mitigating circumstances, (6) type of weapon, (7) total number of statutory aggravating circumstances, (8) number of nonstatutory felony offenses committed, (9) number of nonstatutory aggravating factors.[13] In estimating these equations race variables were also included as independent variables in predicting the particular outcome variable.

Table 5.2 reports the results when the explanatory variables are regressed on the prosecutor's decision to seek a death sentence. The table supplies both the logistic maximum likelihood estimate,[14] the odds multiplier of a death sentence request for each explanatory variable, and a classification table to assess the overall fit of the model to the data.[15] Among the legally relevant variables, Table 5.2A indicates that offenders with prior violent records were 12 times more likely to have the death penalty requested than those with no violent history; offenders who committed a nonstatutory act of aggravation were over seven times more likely to have the death penalty requested; homicides involving two or more statutory aggravating circumstances were almost six times more likely to have the death penalty requested than those involving only one; and defendants killing with a gun were about twice as likely to have the death penalty requested as those who used some other weapon.

Regarding the effect of race on the prosecutor's decision to seek the death penalty, Table 5.2 indicates that this decision is made independent

TABLE 5.2A

Maximum Likelihood Logit Estimates for Prosecutor's Decision
to Seek a Death Sentence in South Carolina—Full Model

	ML Estimate	Odds Multiplier[b]
Prior violent record	2.4589[a]	11.69
Number of victims	−.2487	.78
Number of offenders	.0347	1.04
Victim/Offender relationship	.3117	1.37
Number of mitigating circumstances	−.2432	.78
Race of offender	−.1205	.89
Race of victim	.4856	1.62
Type of weapon	.6767[a]	1.97
Total number of statutory aggravating circumstances	1.7060[a]	5.82
Number of felony offenses in addition to murder	.9846[a]	2.68
Number of nonstatutory aggravating factors	1.9945[a]	7.35
Model classification:		
percent correctly classified by the model	85.10	
percent correctly classified by chance	53.31	
proportion reduction in error relative to chance	69.58	

a. $p < .10$.
b. The odds multiplier indicates how many times an offender's odds of receiving a particular outcome are increased (a multiplier greater than 1.00) or decreased (a multiplier less than 1.00) by the presence of a particular offender or offense characteristic. For example, an offender with a prior violent record has almost a 12 times greater likelihood of having the death penalty sought than one without a violent criminal history.

of the race of the offender. The maximum likelihood estimate is negligible and the odds multiplier for offender's race is not substantially different from one. As suggested by Table 5.1A, however, the race of the *victim* is influential in this decision. The regression coefficient is positive, and the magnitude of the odds multiplier indicates that those offenders who slay whites are over one and a half times more likely to have the death penalty requested than are killers of blacks. The effect for victim's race observed in Table 5.1A, then, persists even when important and legally relevant characteristics of the offense and offender are simultaneously controlled. The classification table provided at the bottom of Table 5.2A indicates that this 11-variable logistic regression model provides a fairly good fit to the data. The addition of other variables would only slightly improve the predictive ability of the model and would not substantially alter the estimated effects.

TABLE 5.2B

Maximum Likelihood Logit Estimates for Prosecutor's Decision
to Seek a Death Sentence in South Carolina—Reduced Model

	ML Estimate	Odds Multiplier[b]
Prior violent record	2.3382[a]	10.36
Type of weapon	.6186[a]	1.86
Race of victim	.5233[a]	1.69
Total number of statutory aggravating circumstances	1.7673[a]	5.86
Number of felony offenses in addition to murder	.9429[a]	2.57
Number of nonstatutory aggravating factors	1.9623[a]	7.12
Model classification:		
percent correctly classified by the model	85.10	
percent correctly classified by chance	52.65	
proportion reduction in error relative to chance	69.03	

a. $p < .10$.
b. See note b at Table 5.2A.

Table 5.2B reports the estimates of a more parsimonious version of
the preceding model. In this equation only those variables in the 11-
variable model that were statistically significant ($p < .10$) were included,
along with the race of the victim. The results of this model are
substantively similar to that found for the more complete one. The
prosecutor's decision to seek a death sentence is affected by the
offender's violent history, the appearance of a nonstatutory factor in
aggravation, the number of statutory aggravating factors, the commission of additional felonies, and the type of weapon. As before, even
when these factors are taken into account, the race of the victim has an
important effect, with killers of whites over one and a half times more
likely to face the possibility of a death sentence than slayers of blacks.
The model classification table suggests that the result of greater
parsimony in eliminating some nonsignificant explanatory variables
was not to reduce the model's overall predictive ability.

Two other models of prosecutorial decision making were estimated.
In both models the race of victim and race of offender variables were
replaced with a dichotomous dummy variable, which considers the
victim and offender's race in combination. In the first of these, the race
variable consisted of a comparison between blacks who killed blacks
with all other homicide cases, whereas the other compares black
defendants who slay whites with all others. In both instances the same

nine legally relevant explanatory variables shown in Table 5.2 were entered into the equation. First, these models revealed that significant predictors of the prosecutor's charging decision are: offender's prior violent record, type of weapon, number of statutory aggravating circumstances, the commission of a nonstatutory felony, and the existence of a nonstatutory aggravating factor. In addition, these models showed that even after controlling for nine important and legal considerations, the influence of race is substantial. In comparison with those homicides in which a black has killed another black, those slayings involving all other racial combinations are over twice as likely to result in a death sentence (odds multiplier of 2.12). The second model indicated that black killers of whites are over one and a half times more likely to have the death penalty requested than homicides involving all other racial combinations.[16]

These data from the first few years of the administration of South Carolina's capital punishment statute thus far suggest that the Supreme Court's doctrinal reform of the death penalty has not been completely successful in purging some forms of racial discrimination. It remains to be seen whether or not the decision to sentence a defendant to death is similarly touched by racial disparities. Table 5.3 reports the results of both a full variable (Table 5.3A) and reduced variable (Table 5.3B) logistic regression model when the outcome variable is the sentencer's decision to impose a death sentence.[17] The same nine legally permissible explanatory variables are included in this equation as in the one modeling prosecutorial behavior. Having a prior violent record is significantly related to the decision to impose the death penalty, with those who have a violent criminal history twice as likely to be sentenced to death than those with no violent past. This factor was also a significant element in the prosecutor's decision to seek a death sentence but its effect is diminished in the sentencing decision.[18] Other significant predictors of the sentencing decision are the total number of statutory aggravating circumstances, the commission of a nonstatutory felony, and the existence in the case of a nonstatutory aggravating factor (Table 5.3A). There are two explanatory variables that are significant predictors of the sentencing decision that were unimportant at the charging stage. Defendants who killed more than one victim are almost three times more likely to be sentenced to death than are those who killed a single victim. In addition, although the prosecutor's decision to charge an offense as a capital murder is independent of any mitigating factors in the case (See Table 5.2), capital sentencers are significantly influenced

TABLE 5.3A

Maximum Likelihood Probit Estimates for Sentencer's
Decision to Impose a Death Sentence—Full Model

	ML Estimate	Odds Multiplier[b]
Prior violent record	.7660[a]	2.15
Number of victims	1.0500[a]	2.86
Number of offenders	.5994	1.82
Victim/Offender relationship	.2451	1.28
Number of mitigating circumstances	−1.1255[a]	.32
Race of offender	1.3594[a]	3.89
Race of victim	−.5355	.58
Type of weapon	.0668	1.07
Total number of statutory aggravating circumstances	1.5804[a]	4.86
Number of felony offenses in addition to murder	1.0904[a]	2.98
Number of nonstatutory aggravating factors	1.1615[a]	3.19
Model classification:		
percent correctly classified by the model	92.38	
percent correctly classified by chance	85.10	
proportion reduction in error relative to chance	52.34	

a. $p < .10$.
b. See note b at Table 5.2A.

by such elements in mitigation. Those defendants who proffered factors in mitigation are one-third as likely to be sentenced to death as those presenting no obvious factors in mitigation.[19]

The effect of race is also somewhat different at the sentencing stage than at charging. The race of the offender has a significant and *positive* effect on the decision to impose death, with white defendants almost four times more likely to be sentenced to death than black defendants, even after controls for legally relevant factors and the race of the victim are taken into account. This finding is contrary to much of the pre-*Furman* empirical evidence on race, which found substantial bias against black defendants but is consistent with other post-*Furman* studies of racial factors in capital sentencing (Baldus et al., 1985). The difference in the two sets of studies may reflect differences in methodology, the effect of post-*Furman* procedural reforms in capital sentencing, or obvious attempts to make the current administration of capital punishment more fair, which, in the short run, produces a type of "white liability." These sentencing data from South Carolina should be viewed with some caution, however, since only 26 death sentences are

TABLE 5.3B

Maximum Likelihood Probit Estimates for Sentencer's
Decision to Impose a Death Sentence—Reduced Model

	ML Estimate	Odds Multiplier[b]
Prior violent record	.6933	2.00
Number of victims	1.2955[a]	3.65
Number of mitigating circumstances	−1.0074[a]	.36
Race of offender	1.3783[a]	3.97
Total number of statutory aggravating circumstances	1.6040[a]	4.97
Number of felony offenses in addition to murder	1.1356[a]	3.11
Number of nonstatutory aggravating factors	1.2893[a]	3.63
Race of victim	−.4396	.64
Model classification:		
percent correctly classified by the model	92.39	
percent correctly classified by chance	83.77	
proportion reduction in error relative to chance	54.21	

a. $p < .10$.
b. See note b at Table 5.2A.

involved, and only 7 are against black defendants.

Regarding victim's race, contrary to other published reports, these data indicate that the race of the victim is not significantly related to the decision to impose a death sentence. Moreover, the effect that is found is *negative*; killers of whites are about half as likely to be sentenced to death as killers of blacks. The model classification table for each equation suggests that the sentencing model provides a reasonable fit to the data, although it shows less predictability than the charging decision.

As for the prosecutor's decision to seek a death sentence, the effect of victim and offender's race taken in combination on the sentencing decision were estimated. One logistic regression model compared black-on-black killings with all other racial combinations, after controlling for the full complement of legally relevant factors. In this case, when a capital homicide does not involve a black defendant killing a black victim the probability of a death sentence increases by a factor of 3 (data available from first author). A second model compared black-on-black killings with all others. This equation revealed that homicides involving black defendants who kill white victims are somewhat (about one-third) less likely to be sentenced to death when compared with homicides involving all other racial combinations. This is inconsistent with studies conducted in Georgia, which found that black-on-white homicides are more likely to result in the imposition of a death sentence even after controlling for factual differences between them (Baldus et al., 1983b) Again, it is not clear to what extent this difference in observed results is due to the idiosyncrasies of the small sample of death cases analyzed here.

Racial Discrimination and Prosecutorial Discretion: Contingent Effects

Although the data with regard to capital sentencing in South Carolina are too meager to permit a definitive conclusion and await further research, the information on prosecutorial discretion allows a more refined analysis. Recent research by Baldus and his colleagues (1983a, 1983b, 1985) has suggested that defendants convicted of killing white victims were particularly more likely to be sentenced to death than those who killed blacks at the midrange of homicide aggravation. Once a severity threshold was crossed, white- and black-victim homicides were treated similarly.

Table 5.4 reports the probability of the prosecutor seeking the death penalty by the racial characteristics of the homicide at each of five levels of homicide aggravation.[20] An examination of the death request rates for various racial combinations reveals an interesting and consistent pattern. With the exception of the race of the offender, which is unrelated to the decision to seek a death sentence, the observed magnitude of racial disparity is substantially greater at lower levels of homicide aggravation. For example, at the lowest two levels of homicide aggravation, defendants who slay white victims are twice as likely to have the death penalty requested against them as those who kill blacks. This racial difference disappears at the upper three levels of homicide severity in which white-victim and black-victim homicides are treated similarly.

Although the number of death requests is small, the pattern found for black-on-black killings is similar. At the lowest two levels of homicide aggravation the probability that the prosecutor will seek a sentence of death in a murder involving a black offender and a black victim is .06. For all other homicides at the same level of aggravation it is over three times higher (.184). For the three highest levels of aggravation the probabilities are both substantially higher and roughly comparable, 1.00 (6/6) for black/black killings and .840 (79/94) for all others. The pattern is essentially the same when black-on-white homicides are compared with all others. At the very lowest level of aggravation, in which the probability of a death request is less than .10, blacks who kill whites are somewhat less likely to face a death sentence request compared with all other homicides (.049 versus .061). At the middle range of homicide aggravation, where most of the homicides and death penalty requests are found, blacks who slay whites are more likely to have the death penalty requested compared with all other cases. At the most aggravated level homicides involving the two groups are treated equally.

Similar to research involving the sentencing decision, these data suggest that racial disparity in the handling of death cases is greatest when the aggravation level of the homicide is in the low to middle range. It is within these groups of cases that the prosecutor has the most discretion, since the brutality of the homicide is not particularly glaring and the decision to seek a death sentence is not clear cut. Once the aggravation of the homicide crosses a certain threshold (which itself is different for white and black victim cases), however, the racial differences observed at lower levels disappear and equally severe cases are handled similarly.

The effect of race may not be contingent only upon the magnitude of the homicide's aggravation, but also upon the location of the crime. In one of the earliest post-*Furman* studies, Bowers and Pierce (1980: 606) reported that in Florida the probability of a defendant receiving a death sentence varied from .750 for the murder of a white victim in the panhandle of the state to .026 for the murder of a black in the north.

Tables 5.5 and 5.6 report the results of a second series of logistic regressions involving the prosecutor's decision to seek a death sentence in different parts of South Carolina. As before, in each table the results of two equations are reported. The first estimation (Tables 5.5A and 5.6A) includes all nine legally relevant explanatory factors included in previous equations (plus race). The second equation (Tables 5.5B and 5.6B) is a more parsimonious one including only those effects that were significant in the more complete equation (as well as the race variable). Each equation is now estimated twice, for both urban and rural counties.[21] In this way the effect of race in different geographic contexts can be determined after controlling for legally relevant differences in the kinds of homicides committed in those locales.

Table 5.5 examines the separate effects of race of offender and race of

TABLE 5.4

Probability of Prosecutor Seeking the Death Penalty
for Capital Murder in South Carolina
by Racial Characteristics of the Homicide and
Level of Aggravation

Death Requested	Level of Aggravation				
	1	2	3	4	5
White victim	.071	.405	.758	.895	.882
	(6/85)	(17/42)	(25/33)	(34/38)	(15/17)
Black victim	.036	.200	.833	1.00	1.00
	(2/55)	(4/20)	(5/6)	(4/4)	(2/2)
Ratio	1.97	2.02	.91	.90	.88
Black offender	.034	.317	.889	.957	.917
	(3/89)	(13/41)	(16/18)	(22/23)	(11/12)
White offender	.098	.381	.667	.842	.857
	(5/51)	(8/21)	(14/21)	(16/19)	(6/7)
Ratio	.347	.83	1.33	1.14	1.07
All others	.076	.409	.750	.800	.889
	(7/92)	(18/44)	(27/36)	(36/40)	(16/18)
Black kills black	.021	.167	1.00	1.00	1.00
	(1/48)	(3/18)	(3/3)	(2/2)	(1/1)
Ratio	3.61	2.45	.75	.90	.89
Black kills white	.049	.435	.867	.952	.909
	(2/41)	(10/23)	(13/15)	(20/21)	(10/11)
All others	.061	.282	.708	.857	.875
	(6/99)	(11/39)	(17/24)	(18/21)	(7/8)
Ratio	.80	1.54	1.22	1.11	1.04

NOTE: The ratios represent the comparison between the following sets of racial characteristics: white to black victims, black to white offenders, all homicides to those where a black offender killed a black, homicides involving black offenders with white victim to all other capital murders.

victim on the prosecutor's charging decisions in urban counties. Table 5.6 examines the same set of effects in rural counties. In comparing the two tables, an important contextual effect emerges. First of all, some explanatory factors have similar effects regardless of region, although the magnitude of the effect may vary. Prosecutors in both urban and rural jurisdictions are more likely to seek a death sentence when the offender has a prior violent record and when the homicide involves more than one statutory aggravating circumstance, an additional non-

TABLE 5.5A

Maximum Likelihood Logit Estimates for the Prosecutor's Decision
to Seek a Death Sentence for Urban Counties—Full Model

	ML Estimate	Odds Multiplier[b]
Prior violent record	2.8943[a]	18.07
Number of victims	−2.2985[a]	.10
Number of offenders	−.5016	.61
Type of weapon	3.3845[a]	29.50
Victim/Offender relationship	1.0174[a]	2.76
Race of victim	1.2992[a]	3.67
Race of offender	2.0642[a]	7.88
Total number of statutory aggravating circumstances	2.0066[a]	7.44
Number of felony offenses in addition to murder	1.3045[a]	3.68
Number of nonstatutory aggravating factors	2.0558[a]	7.81
Number of mitigating circumstances	−.3304	.72
Model classification:		
percent correctly classified by the model	89.19	
percent correctly classified by chance	56.76	
proportion reduction in error relative to chance	75.00	

a. $p < .10$.
b. See note b at Table 5.2A.

statutory felony, or at least one nonstatutory aggravating factor. Other factors are significant predictors in urban counties but not in rural ones; such as the number of victims, victim/offender relationship, and type of weapon. More important, however, are the effect of the race variables that have different consequences in different jurisdictions.

In urban counties prosecutors are almost four times more likely to seek a death sentence when the victim is white than black, and almost eight times more likely to seek death against whites as compared to black offenders. In rural counties, however, killers of white victims are less likely to face a possible death sentence, and black defendants are nearly twice as likely as white offenders to be charged with a capital murder. The finding reported in Table 5.2 that the decision to seek a death sentence was independent of the offender's race reflects the fact that it has opposite effects in different parts of the state.

An additional series of logistic regression equations was estimated comparing different pairs of race of offender/victim combinations in rural and urban counties. As before, all equations also contain legally relevant factors. In the first of these equations, the race variable is now a

TABLE 5.5B

Maximum Likelihood Logit Estimates for the Prosecutor's Decision
to Seek a Death Sentence for Urban Counties—Reduced Model

	ML Estimate	Odds Multiplier[b]
Prior violent record	2.666[a]	14.38
Number of victims	−2.4015[a]	.09
Type of weapon	3.1938[a]	24.38
Victim/Offender relationship	.9670	2.63
Race of victim	1.3490[a]	3.85
Race of offender	1.8928[a]	6.64
Total number of statutory aggravating circumstances	2.0334[a]	7.64
Number of felony offenses in addition to murder	1.0672[a]	2.91
Number of nonstatutory aggravating factors	2.1732[a]	8.79
Model classification:		
percent correctly classified by the model	90.99	
percent correctly classified by chance	56.76	
proportion reduction in error relative to chance	79.16	

a. $p < .10$.
b. See note b at Table 5.2A.

dummy variable comparing the effect of black-on-black homicides with all other racial combinations. The results again show the importance of geography as a contextual effect. In urban counties interracial homicides and intraracial white homicides are 10 times more likely to produce a request for the death penalty than those involving a black offender and black victim ($b = 2.30$). In rural counties this effect is nonexistent ($b = .099$; odds multiplier $= .91$); the prosecutor shows no greater disinclination to seek death in a black-on-black killing.

Race does, however, influence the prosecutor's decision to seek a death sentence in rural South Carolina counties. In the second series of equations, black-on-white killings were imposed with all other homicides in both rural and urban counties. These models indicate that urban prosecutors are no more likely to seek death in a black-on-white killing compared with all others. The logit regression coefficient for this factor ($b = -.067$) was negligible and the odds multiplier in the complete equation is not substantially different from 1.0. However, rural prosecutors are influenced by this particular interracial characteristic of a homicide. In rural counties prosecutors are approximately twice as likely to seek the death penalty in homicides that involved a black

TABLE 5.6A

Maximum Likelihood Logit Estimates for the Prosecutor's Decision
to Seek a Death Sentence for Rural Counties—Full Model

	ML Estimate	Odds Multiplier[b]
Prior violent record	2.1333[a]	8.44
Number of victims	.4755	1.61
Number of offenders	.1844	1.20
Type of weapon	.3298	1.39
Victim/Offender relationship	−.0982	.91
Race of victim	−.5172	.60
Race of offender	−.5265	.59
Total number of statutory aggravating circumstances	1.1637[a]	3.20
Number of felony offenses in addition to murder	.5166[a]	1.68
Number of nonstatutory aggravating factors	2.3152[a]	10.13
Number of mitigating circumstances	−.0197	.98
Model classification:		
percent correctly classified by the model	84.83	
percent correctly classified by chance	50.34	
proportion reduction in error relative to chance	71.44	

a. $p < .10$.
b. See note b at Table 5.2A.

slaying a white than for all other types combined (b = −.681; odds multiplier = 1.98).[22]

SUMMARY AND CONCLUSION

From 1976-1983 the U.S. Supreme Court attempted a doctrinal revision of the states' administration of capital punishment (Weisberg, 1984). In this endeavor the Court sought to promote greater even-handedness in the administration of capital punishment by introducing legal formalism. The purpose of this chapter has been to examine the effect of the Court's doctrinal revision of the death penalty on the administration of capital punishment in South Carolina. More specifically, the data reported on herein examined the influence of race variables on: (1) the prosecutor's decision to seek a death sentence, and (2) the sentencer's decision to impose one.

The data revealed a substantial amount of racial disparity at both decision points. Even after controlling for nine legally relevant and

TABLE 5.6B

Maximum Likelihood Logit Estimates for the Prosecutor's Decision
to Seek a Death Sentence for Rural Counties—Reduced Model

	ML Estimate	Odds Multiplier[b]
Prior violent record	2.2073[a]	9.09
Race of victim	−.2658	.77
Race of offender	−.6115	.54
Total number of statutory aggravating circumstances	1.1230[a]	3.07
Number of felony offenses in addition to murder	.6614[a]	1.94
Number of nonstatutory aggravating factors	2.2944[a]	9.92
Model classification:		
percent correctly classified by the model	82.07	
percent correctly classified by chance	50.34	
proportion reduction in error relative to chance	63.89	

a. $p < .10$.
b. See note b at Table 5.2A.

permissible variables, we found that local South Carolina prosecutors
were more likely to seek a death sentence in a white-victim homicide,
particularly if it crossed racial lines and involved a black offender. They
were much less likely to request the death penalty if a black killed
another black. Racial effects on the prosecutor's decision were concentrated within the lower and middle levels of homicide aggravation.
When the seriousness of the offense was not so glaring as to constitute an
"obvious capital punishment case," giving prosecutors greater opportunity to exercise their discretion, racial effects were strong. Once a
homicide passed a certain level of aggravation, however, prosecutors
requested a death sentence with greater frequency regardless of race.

The decision to sentence a defendant to death was not entirely free of
racial influences, but the low conviction rate for black-victim homicides
and small number of death sentences during the study period precludes
any definitive conclusions. The data did suggest, however, that the
probability that a death sentence would be imposed was greater for
white offenders and for black offenders who killed white victims. A
death sentence was unlikely to be given if both the offender and victim
were black.

Finally, an important geographical effect was observed regarding the
prosecutor's decision to seek a death sentence. In comparison with their
counterparts in rural areas of the state, urban South Carolina prose-

cutors were much more inclined to seek the death penalty in white-victim than black-victim homicides. In urban jurisdictions, white offenders were more likely to face the prospect of a death sentence, and homicides involving black offenders who killed black victims were substantially less likely to result in a death penalty request. In contrast, prosecutors in rural areas were more likely to request a death sentence in cross-racial homicides involving black offenders and white victims than they were in other types of cases.

Despite procedural revisions, the administration of capital punishment in South Carolina continues to be influenced by racial variables. The strongest evidence of racial discrimination was observed at an early decision point—the decision of the local prosecutor to seek the death penalty. At a later stage—the decision to impose a death sentence—racial effects were somewhat diminished. Whether this reflects an idiosyncratic feature of the data (the infrequency of death sentences in the first few years of the statute) or is due to the "filtering" effects of earlier but more discriminatory decisions is as yet unknown and requires additional research. The evidence regarding the effect of race variables on prosecutorial decision making is worrisome, since such decisions are not part of the explicit review process of capital sentencing. Although some may argue that only evenhanded *sentencing* is required, such an argument ignores the masking effect that early decisions may have on later ones. This point may not have gone unnoticed by Chief Justice Burger when he spoke in *Furman* of "evenhanded justice" rather than evenhanded sentencing (*Furman v. Georgia,* 408 U.S. 238, 399, 1972).

NOTES

1. "To identify before the fact those characteristics of criminal homicides and their perpetrators which call for the death penalty, and to express these characteristics in language which can be fairly understood and applied by the sentencing authority, appear to be tasks which are beyond present human ability" (*McGautha v. California*).

2. "The states are entitled to assume that jurors confronted with the truly awesome responsibility of decreeing death for a fellow human will act with due regard for the consequences of their decision and will consider a variety of factors, many of which will have been suggested by the evidence or by the arguments of defense counsel. For a court to attempt to catalog the appropriate factors in this elusive area could inhibit rather than expand the scope of consideration, for no list of circumstances would ever be really complete. The infinite variety of cases and facets to each case would make general standards either meaningless 'boiler plate' or a statement of the obvious that no jury would need" (*McGautha v. California,* 402 U.S. 183, 208, 1971).

3. Justice Brennan cites *Marbury v. Madison's* thesis that our system of government has been "termed a government of laws, and not of men." He concludes that:

the Due Process Clause of the Fourteenth Amendment . . . require[s] that, if state power is to be exerted, these choices must be made by a responsible organ of state government. . . . If there is no effective supervision of this process to insure consistency of decision, it can amount to nothing more than government by whim. . . . Government by whim is the very antithesis of due process" [*McGautha v. California*, 402 U.S. 153, 188, 1975].

4. In this regard, Justice Powell in his dissent noted "the shattering effect this collection of views has on the root principles of *stare decisis,* federalism, judicial restraint and most importantly—separation of powers" (*Furman v. Georgia*, 408 U.S. 238, 417, 1972). In a later opinion, Justice Stewart, who voted with the majority in *Furman* to essentially overturn *McGautha*, also observed that *Furman* "is in substantial tension with a broad reading of *McGautha's* holding" (*Gregg v. Georgia*, 428 U.S. 153, 195-196, 1976).

5. "My concurring Brothers have demonstrated that, if any basis can be discerned for the selection of these few to be sentenced to die, it is the constitutionally impermissible basis of race. . . . But racial discrimination has not been proved, and I put it to one side"(*Furman v. Georgia*, 408 U.S. 238, 310, 1972).

6. This position was also held by the dissenters in *Furman,* with Chief Justice Burger noting that "The decisive grievance of the opinions . . . is that the present system of discretionary sentencing in capital cases has failed to produce evenhanded justice" (*Furman v. Georgia*, 408 U.S. 238, 398, 1972). In their opinion in *Gregg*, Justice Stewart joined by Justice Powell and Justice Stevens observed that "Because of the uniqueness of the death penalty, *Furman* held that it could not be imposed under sentencing procedures that created a substantial risk that it would be inflicted in an arbitrary and capricious manner" (*Gregg v. Georgia*, 428 U.S. 153, 188, 1976).

7. *Furman v. Georgia*, 408 U.S. 238, 1972; *Gregg v. Georgia*, 428 U.S. 153, 1976; *Zant v. Stephens*, 456 U.S. 410, 1983; *Spenkelink v. Wainwright*, 578 F. 2d 582, 1978.

8. Although the specific form of these statutes varied, a common element is the enumeration of factors a jury had to consider before imposing a death sentence. Guided discretion statutes have included a great variety of sentencing schemes. The Georgia statute, for example, lists 10 aggravating but no mitigating circumstances. Under Georgia law the jury may recommend a death sentence if it finds one aggravating circumstance, but does not have to, and a jury's recommendation is binding on the judge. Florida's statute, approved in *Proffitt*, lists both aggravating and mitigating circumstances and requires the jury to weigh both sets before recommending a sentence. Unlike Georgia law, the jury's sentencing recommendation may be overridden by the presiding judge. The Texas scheme in *Jurek* is probably the most formal of the three. Texas juries are required to answer three questions and an affirmative answer to all three mandates a death sentence. To save the Texas statute from a *Woodson* infirmity, the Court has read the second question (regarding the offender's future potential for violence) quite broadly, to include a consideration of both aggravating and mitigating circumstances. For a more complete description of various capital-sentencing schemes, see Steven Gillers's, "Deciding Who Dies," *University of Pennsylvania Law Review,* Vol. 129, No. 1, 1-124.

9. "In summary, the concerns expressed in *Furman* that the penalty of death not be

imposed in an arbitrary or capricious manner can be met by a carefully drafted statute that ensures that the sentencing authority is given adequate information and guidance" (*Gregg v. Georgia,* 428 U.S. 153, 195, 1976).

10. The issue regarding the Court's evaluation of discrimination claims is, however, far from settled. More recently, the Court in 1983 (*Zant v. Stephens*) claimed that the death penalty statutes approved in its 1976 cases "promised to alleviate" the lack of evenhanded sentencing condemned in *Furman.* It is clear from *Zant* that the Court has not determined that its doctrine making in *Gregg* would be self-fulfilling and that it apparently would evaluate death penalty statutes on how the states met that promise—an empirical demonstration. On April 22, 1987, the Court, in *McCleskey v. Kemp,* decided that the Georgia death penalty statute is not unconstitutionally discriminatory even though studies have shown that the death penalty in Georgia is disproportionately imposed on black defendants and defendants killing white victims. The Court held that to prevail in such a case, the petitioner must prove that the decision makers in *his* case acted with discriminatory intent.

11. There are some important exceptions to these observations. Prosecutorial behavior has been the subject of research undertaken by Radelet and Pierce (1985), Paternoster (1983, 1984) and Baldus et al. (1983a); the appellate review of death cases has been examined by Radelet and Van Diver (1983), Baldus et al. (1983a, 1985) and Dix (1979). In addition to Georgia and Florida, the capital-sentencing schemes of Illinois (Gross and Mauro, 1984), South Carolina (Paternoster, 1983, 1984) and Texas and Ohio (Bowers and Pierce, 1980) have been examined in some detail.

12. In a strict sense statistical significance tests are inappropriate here since the pool of cases examined constitutes a population of all capital cases from June 8, 1977 until December 31, 1981, rather than a sample. Since the reported values here have no sampling distribution all reported differences are substantively important ones.

13. The coding for these variables was as follows: a code of 1 was recorded (1) if the defendant had a previous arrest for a violent crime, (2) if there was more than one victim, (3) if there was more than one offender, (4) if the victim was a stranger, (5) if one or more mitigating circumstances existed, (6) if a gun was used, (7) if more than one statutory aggravating factor, (8) if there were one or more nonstatutory felonies committed, (9) if one or more nonstatutory aggravating factors existed. If the specified condition did not apply, a code of 0 was assigned. The coding for the race variable was 1 for white victims and white offenders.

14. Since all variables were coded as 0,1 dichotomies, the procedure was a binary logistic regression. In logistic regression analysis the underlying probability function is logistic and the logistic estimator is a maximum likelihood one. In this model the estimated coefficient represents the change in the log of the odds on the dependent variable associated with a unit change in the independent variable. Since the effect parameters are in the form of an odds ratio the magnitudes may be compared to determine relative effects of each exogenous variable.

15. In ordinary least squares analysis the overall fit of the model is usually determined by the amount of variance explained, R^2. Although there is an R^2 analogy in logit and probit models (McKelvey and Zavoina, 1975), its sampling distribution is unknown and may substantially underestimate the model's true fit. In its place, the Model Classification Table reported at the end of the logistic regression tables is employed. This table estimates the overall goodness-of-fit of the model in terms of its ability to predict the outcome on the dependent variable. The percent correctly classified by the model estimates the accuracy of the prediction based upon the marginals predicted by the model. The percent correctly

classified is the sum of the cells in which the predicted outcome equals the actual outcome divided by the total. The percent correctly classified by chance is based upon marginal distributions assuming the actual outcome and predicted outcomes are independent (this procedure is similar to that done for expected cell frequencies used in chi-square tables). The proportion reduction in error relative to chance measures the percent of classification error by chance that is reduced by using the model. It reflects, then, the percentage of errors one would have made but no longer makes based on predictions from the model.

16. Complete results of these models are not shown here. The interested researcher can obtain these from the senior author upon request. In addition to these models, moreover, a series of logistic regressions were run in which the four-category race of offender/race of victim variable was treated as a dummy variable and included in a full variable equation similar to that reported in Table 5.2A. Two equations were estimated. In both, race of offender/victim was expressed as three dummy variables; in one black-on-black killings was the suppressed category and in the other white-on-white killings was the suppressed category. In this way, the obtained coefficients for each race dummy variable could be expressed as the difference in intercepts between the two racial groups. The magnitude and sign of the coefficient would reflect, then, a reduction or enhancement in the probability of the prosecutor requesting the death penalty in comparison with the suppressed category. The first dummy-variable analysis revealed the following coefficients; black kills white (2.74), white kills black (3.66), and white kills white (1.76). In comparison with the suppressed category of black-on-black killings, homicides involving all other racial combinations are more likely to result in a death penalty request. When the suppressed category is white-on-white slayings the coefficients are; black kills black (-.5658), black kills white (.44362), and white kills black (.7319). Compared with white-on-white killings, then, homicides involving a black defendant and victim are less likely to result in a death penalty request and both black-on-white and white-on-black homicides are more likely to result in a death penalty request. The dummy-variable analysis confirms the previously reported findings that prosecutors are much less inclined to seek the death penalty in an intraracial black homicide and generally more inclined to do so when a black offender crosses racial lines and slays a white.

17. In these logistic regressions the complete population of 302 capital felony-type murders was employed. A separate series of regressions was estimated using the pool of 135 cases in which the defendant was convicted. These results do not differ substantively from the complete-group regressions and are not reported here. These may be obtained from the first author upon request.

18. The effect of these and other factors, such as race variables, may be diminished at the sentencing phase of processing capital cases if they play important roles in earlier decisions. This is the effect of sample selection bias (Berk, 1983; Klepper et al., 1983), and is produced when earlier decisions homogenize a sample at later decision points.

19. The phrase "no obvious factors in mitigation" does not mean that there were no factors in mitigation offered at any point. It simply means that there were no immediate factors about the crime or offender recorded in the SHR or police incident report to warrant mitigation, such as the victim's own involvement in the offense, mental/emotional impairment of the offender, youthful age of offender, or if the offender was retarded or of diminished intelligence. If the case proceeded to a penalty trial, in all likelihood character witnesses were introduced to attest to the defendant's essential goodness—a factor in mitigation that is probably a constant in these cases.

20. These aggravation levels are based upon a scale created by the logistic regression of significant explanatory and legally permissible variables on the prosecutor's decision to

seek a death sentence. Five aggravation levels were created by employing cut off points at approximately equally spaced intervals. This regression equation included all nine legally relevant variables reported in Table 5.2, plus race of victim and offender. The weights for the aggravation scale are the estimated logistic regression coefficients from this equation. The scale was created by summing the weights of those *legally relevant* factors that were statistically significant ($p < .10$). Although race variables were included in the equation that estimated the scale's weights, they were excluded from the final scale (see Blumstein et al., 1983).

21. Urban counties included those that contained the four SMSA's in South Carolina: Columbia, Charleston, Spartanburg, and Greenville. All other counties were designated as rural.

22. The results of the full regression equation are not reported here but are available from the first author upon request. These results are confirmed and expanded by a specific comparison of racial groups. A dummy-variable logistic regression analysis identical to that reported in Note 16 was done separately for urban and rural jurisdictions. In rural areas the coefficient representing the difference in probabilities of death request between black-on-black and black-on-white homicides was modest (.40618), whereas in urban jurisdictions it was quite large (1.2951). Translated into more meaningful terms, compared with black-on-black homicides, murders involving a black offender and white victim are 1.5 times more likely to result in a death penalty request in rural counties and 3.65 times more likely in an urban county. In a rural jurisdiction whites who kill whites are about half as likely to have the death penalty requested as blacks who kill blacks but in urban jurisdictions they are over 28 times more likely to have the prosecutor seek the death penalty. A different contextual effect occurs for white-victim homicides. In urban jurisdictions a black-on-white homicide is approximately one-tenth as likely to produce a death request but is three times more likely to do so in a rural area.

REFERENCES

ARKIN, S.D. (1980) "Discrimination and arbitrariness in capital punishment: An analysis of post-Furman murder cases in Dade County, Florida, 1973-1976." Stanford Law Review 33 (November): 75-101.

BALDUS, D. C., C. PULASKI, and G. WOODWORTH (1983a) "Comparative review of death sentences: An empirical study of the Georgia experience." Journal of Criminal Law and Criminology 74 (Fall): 661-753.

BALDUS, D. C., C. PULASKI, and G. WOODWORTH (1983b) "Discrimination and Arbitrariness in Georgia's Capital Charging and Sentencing System: A Preliminary Report." Unpublished manuscript, University of Iowa.

BALDUS, D. C., C. PULASKI, and G. WOODWORTH (1985) "Monitoring and evaluating contemporary death sentencing systems: Lessons from Georgia." U.C. Davis Law Review 18 (Summer): 1375-1407.

BARNETT, A. (1985) "Some distribution patterns for the Georgia death sentence." U.C. Davis Law Review 18 (Summer): 1327-1374.

BERK R. A. (1983) "An introduction to sample selection bias in sociological data." American Sociological Review 48 (June): 386-397.

BLUMSTEIN, A., J. COHEN, S. E. MARTIN, and M. H. TONRY (1983) Research on Sentencing: The Search for Reform. Washington, DC: National Academy Press.

BOWERS, W. J. (1983) "The pervasiveness of arbitrariness and discrimination under post- Furman capital statutes." Journal of Criminal Law and Criminology 74 (Fall): 1067-1100.

BOWERS, W. J. and G. L. PIERCE (1980) "Arbitrariness and discrimination under post-Furman capital statutes." Crime and Delinquency 26 (October): 563-575.

DIX, G. E. (1979) "Appellate review of the decision to impose death." Georgetown Law Review 68 (October): 97-161.

GARFINKEL, H. (1949) "Research note on inter- and intra-racial homicides." Social Forces 27 (May): 369-380.

GILLERS, S. (1980) "Deciding who dies." University of Pennsylvania Law Review 129 (November): 1-124.

GROSS, S. R. and R. MAURO (1984) "Patterns of death: An analysis of racial disparities in capital sentencing and homicide victimization." Stanford Law Review 37 (November): 27-153.

JACOBY, J. E. and R. PATERNOSTER (1982) "Sentencing disparity and jury packing: Further challenges to the death penalty." Journal of Criminal Law and Criminology 73 (Spring): 379-387.

JOHNSON, E. H. (1957) "Selective factors in capital punishment." Social Forces 36 (December): 165-169.

JOHNSON, G. (1941) "The Negro and crime." Annals of the American Academy of Political and Social Science 217 (September): 93-104.

KLEPPER S., D. NAGIN, and L. TIERNEY (1983) "Discrimination in the criminal justice system: A critical appraisal of the literature." pp. 55- 128 in A. Blumstein, J. Cohen, S. E. Martin, and M. H. Tonry (eds.) Research on Sentencing: The Search for Reform, Vol. 2. Washington, DC : National Academy Press.

MCKELVEY, R. D. and W. ZAVOINA (1975) "A statistical model for the analysis of ordinal level dependent variables." Journal of Mathematical Sociology 4, 1: 103-120.

PATERNOSTER, R. (1983) "Race of victim and location of crime: The decision to seek the death penalty in South Carolina." Journal of Criminology and Criminal Law 74 (Fall): 754-785.

PATERNOSTER, R. (1984) "Prosecutorial discretion in requesting the death penalty: A case of victim-based racial discrimination." Law and Society Review 18, 3: 437-478.

RADELET, M. L. (1981) "Racial characteristics and the imposition of the death penalty." American Sociological Review 46 (December): 918-927.

RADELET, M. R. and G. L. PIERCE (1985) "Race and prosecutorial discretion in homicide cases." Law and Society Review 19, 4: 587-621.

RADELET, M. R. and M. VANDIVER (1983) "The Florida Supreme Court and death penalty appeals." Journal of Criminal Law and Criminology 74 (Fall): 913-926.

THOMPSON, R. J. and M. T. ZINGRAFF (1981) "Detecting sentencing disparity: Some problems and evidence" American Journal of Sociology 86 (January): 869-880.

WEISBERG, R. (1984) "Deregulating death," pp. 305-395 in P. Kurkland (ed.) Supreme Court Review. Chicago: University of Chicago Press.

WOLFGANG, M. E., A. KELLY, and H. C. NOLDE (1962) "Comparison of the executed and the commuted among the admissions to death row." Journal of Criminal Law, Criminology and Police Science 53 (September): 301-311.

WOLFGANG, M. E. and M. REIDEL (1975) "Rape, race and death penalty in Georgia." American Journal of Orthopsychiatry 45 (July): 658-668.

ZEISEL, H. (1981) "Race bias in the administration of the death penalty: The Florida experience." Harvard Law Review 95 (December): 456-468.

ZIMRING, F. E., J. EIGEN, and S. O'MALLEY (1976) "Punishing homicide in Philadelphia: Perspectives on the death penalty." University of Chicago Law Review 43 (Winter): 227-252.

CASES

Furman v. Georgia, 408 U. S. 238 (1972)

Gregg v. Georgia, 428 U. S. 153 (1976)

Jurek v. Texas, 428 U. S. 153 (1976)

McCleskey v. Kemp, 107 S. Ct. 1756 (1987)

McGautha v. California, 402 U. S. 183 (1971)

Proffit v. Florida, 428 U. S. 242 (1976)

Roberts v. Louisiana, 428 U. S. 325 (1976)

Spenkelink v. Wainwright, 578 F. 2d 582 (1978)

Woodson v. North Carolina, 428 U. S. 280 (1976)

Zant v. Stephens, 456 U. S. 410 (1983)

Chapter 6

DEATH BY JURY

VALERIE P. HANS

The American jury plays a central role in sending men and women to the executioner. In all but a handful of states that retain capital punishment, the jury has sole responsibility for pronouncing the death sentence.[1] Although it is the majority practice, the jury's involvement in the death sentencing process is not constitutionally mandated. In *Spaziano v. Florida* (1984), the U.S. Supreme Court held that Florida's practice of restricting the jury to an advisory role was permissible, and commented that even a complete exclusion of juries from the penalty phase would not violate the Constitution.

Although the contemporary jury's prominent role in deciding death is not surprising when considered in historical perspective, it is notable when viewed against the declining role of the jury in the remainder of the criminal justice system. Estimates are that between 85% to 90% of contemporary criminal cases are decided without a jury. Massive numbers of cases are settled through plea agreements between the parties, and even in contested cases, defendants frequently choose bench trials. The jury's fact-finding abilities have been called into question, and important limits have been placed on it. Jury sentencing in noncapital crimes is almost extinct, and there have been many

AUTHOR'S NOTE: *This chapter was written while the author was a Visiting Fellow in the Department of Psychology, Stanford University, and a Visiting Scholar at Stanford Law School. Writing was facilitated by a fellowship in law and psychology from NIMH, and by the helpful comments of Phoebe Ellsworth, Samuel Gross, Reid Hastie, Carol Krafka, Deana Logan, Vicky Smith, and Robert Weisberg. The chapter on juries and the death penalty in* Judging the Jury *(1986), which I coauthored with Neil Vidmar, provided the foundation for a number of ideas developed here.*

recommendations to abolish it entirely (ABA Standards for Criminal Justice, 1980; Hans and Vidmar, 1986).

Why, then, should juries remain so central in death penalty decisions? Legislatures have taken the view that the imposition of the death penalty is fundamentally a normative decision. The notion that a person "deserves" to die has little meaning when construed as a traditional fact-finding task; the fact-finding dimensions of a typical penalty decision are minor. Since deciding to impose the death penalty is essentially a moral judgment, the jury's ability to represent the public's sentiment, to speak as the authentic voice of the community, makes it the most appropriate decision maker (Gillers, 1980; *Spaziano v. Florida*, 1984, Stevens, J., concurring in part and dissenting in part). The political and symbolic functions of the jury are also critical. Vesting the state's power to execute in the hands of a representative group of its citizens rather than state officials serves as an important limit on state power. And there is a strong practical reason for the prevalence of the capital jury. Defendants typically forego jury trials in exchange for some benefit from the prosecutor. Once the prosecutor has insisted on charging them with a capital offense, defendants have little incentive to waive a trial by jury.

Evidence suggests that defendants facing death benefit from reliance on juries. In their classic study of jury decision making, Kalven and Zeisel (1966) asked judges to render hypothetical judgments when they presided over jury trials. Comparing the judges' decisions to the actual jury verdicts and sentences in capital trials, Kalven and Zeisel discovered that in most cases, both judge and jury agreed on the appropriate penalty. But in the 19% of cases in which judge and jury disagreed, juries were twice as likely as judges to recommend a prison sentence over a death sentence (Kalven and Zeisel, 1966, Table 117, p. 436). Radelet's work on the frequency of judicial overrides of jury recommendations for mercy in Florida capital cases also indicates that judges are more willing than juries to pronounce the death sentence (Radelet, 1985, pp. 1413-1414).

Despite the impressive amount and quality of legal scholarship on capital sentencing, there is woefully little empirical evidence about how the jury actually goes about its task. Partly this is because the penalty phase jury is a modern judicial creation; researchers have had only limited time to examine its operations. Another reason is that the penalty phase is difficult to study. Because real jury deliberations are hidden from public view, researchers interested in jury decision making often employ the method of jury simulation, in which participants are asked to role-play jurors. Yet the penalty phase does not lend itself easily to simulation; mock jurors are unlikely to feel the profound sense of responsibility for a fellow citizen's life or death that characterizes actual penalty phase jurors.[2]

Understanding the penalty phase, however, is essential. Given the Supreme Court's recent decisions and the public's support for the death penalty, juries are going to be deciding between life and death in the foreseeable future. Using research findings and legal cases on jury decision making and the penalty phase in capital trials, this chapter attempts to develop a portrait of the penalty phase jury, including who the jurors are, what views they hold, and what reactions they are likely to have to courtroom proceedings, evidence, and instructions. Taking something of a juror's-eye view of the penalty phase, we will assess whether the penalty jury is equipped to handle its awesome responsibility.

THE JURORS

Our starting point is the jurors themselves. Capital jurors differ from the community at large and from jurors in other cases in several notable ways. This is because death penalty jurors must undergo death qualification, whereby prospective jurors whose attitudes regarding capital punishment would preclude them from being fair and impartial in deciding on the guilt or sentence are excluded for cause from the capital jury. Because opposition to the death penalty is more characteristic of certain subgroups of society than of others, death qualification detrimentally affects the ability of the jury to represent the entire community. Significant numbers of women and blacks are excluded by virtue of their capital punishment opposition; Jews, agnostics, atheists, the poor, and Democrats are also disproportionately eliminated. Jurors who survive death qualification are demographically distinctive: They are more likely to be male, to be white, to be well-off financially, to be Republican, and to be Protestant or Catholic (Fitzgerald and Ellsworth, 1984).

Because views of the death penalty are part of a cluster of crime and justice attitudes, death-qualified jurors also possess other distinctive perspectives that predispose them to view evidence in a manner more negative to the defense. For instance, compared to those who would be excluded from a capital jury because of their opposition to the death penalty, death-qualified jurors are more likely to trust prosecutors and distrust defense attorneys, consider inadmissible evidence even if a judge instructed them to ignore it, and infer guilt from a defendant's silence (Fitzgerald and Ellsworth, 1984). Death-qualified jurors are more hostile to psychological defenses such as schizophrenia (Ellsworth et al., 1984). They tend to view prosecution witnesses as more believable, more credible, and more helpful (Cowan et al., 1984). They are less likely to believe in the fallibility of the criminal justice process, and less likely to agree that even the worst criminal should be considered for mercy (Fitzgerald and Ellsworth, 1984).

Survey evidence indicates that supporters of capital punishment assume that the death penalty is a more effective deterrent than is life imprisonment, although two-thirds of them say they would still support the death penalty even if it proved not to be a deterrent (Ellsworth and Ross, 1983). Half agree that they would favor capital punishment even if it *caused* (via a "brutalization" effect) as many murders as it prevented. Proponents think that capital punishment is necessary to provide support and protection for the police, and that society benefits more if murderers are executed than if they are imprisoned for life. Proponents are more likely to disagree that there is too much danger of executing an innocent man, and to disagree that some people sentenced to death could be rehabilitated and could contribute to society (Ellsworth and Ross, 1983).

All of these attitudinal predispositions, taken together, have some implications for how penalty phase jurors will interpret testimony and arguments by counsel. Compared to the community at large, penalty phase jurors should be more likely to believe the prosecution testimony than the testimony presented by the defense; they should be less sympathetic to psychological excuses for the defendant's behavior; they should be less willing to believe in the possibility of rehabilitation for the defendant. In short, the penalty phase jury constitutes a relatively unreceptive audience for arguments for life.

The representativeness of the capital jury, on both demographic and attitudinal dimensions, is further modified by the exercise of peremptory challenges. Bruce Winick (1982) studied peremptory challenge practices in 30 Florida capital cases and discovered that both prosecution and defense peremptories were strongly related to prospective jurors' expressions of scruples against the death penalty during voir dire. If jurors voiced some opposition to the death penalty but survived a challenge for cause, prosecutors typically eliminated them with a peremptory challenge. Defense attorneys tended to exercise their peremptories only rarely against those prospective jurors who expressed hesitancy over the death penalty. Nevertheless, because the number of jurors expressing some opposition was small, the prosecutorial peremptories eliminated all but a fraction of them from juries. Peremptory challenge practices thus exacerbate the nonrepresentativeness of capital juries in a manner unfavorable to the defense.

THE VOIR DIRE PROCESS

In addition to the distinctive demographic and attitudinal characteristics of death-qualified jurors, their experiences during voir dire may affect their views of the penalty phase. During capital voir dire, of course, prospective jurors are questioned extensively about their opinions of capital punishment and their ability to decide on a death sentence in the case before them. For many years, courts followed the *Witherspoon* standard of eliminating prospective jurors for cause if they made it "unmistakably clear" that they could never give a death sentence (*Witherspoon v. Illinois*, 1968). *Wainwright v. Witt*, decided in 1985, relaxed that rule, holding it was necessary for the judge to believe only that jurors' views about capital punishment would "substantially impair" their ability to be fair and impartial. Whatever standard is employed, questioning must continue until the judge is satisfied that the juror meets or fails it.

Eric Schnapper (1984) analyzed voir dire exchanges in 76 capital cases and concluded that courtroom assessment of juror attitudes was problematic. In response to questions about their views on the death penalty, jurors sometimes displayed confusion, indecision, and vacillation. It is not surprising that jurors have some difficulty predicting how they might respond in a penalty hearing. Despite evidence that many people hold robust views regarding capital punishment, their attitudes contain a strong symbolic component (Tyler and Weber, 1982). It is one matter to tell friends or an interviewer that one is for or against capital punishment, and another affair entirely to speculate in the formal setting of the courtroom about whether or not one could render a death sentence (Vidmar and Ellsworth, 1974). In addition, the juror's verbal description of the likelihood of this future behavior must match some (to him or her, probably unknown) predetermined legal criterion. The pressure to respond honestly and to be a good juror can produce apparently conflicting answers that do not fit neatly into the requisite formulaic response.

Schnapper provided some interesting examples of the way jurors articulated views that did not comport with the legal standard. One juror commented: "I don't believe in [capital punishment] in a way and in a way I do believe in it" (Schnapper, 1984, p. 997, fn. 67). Several jurors pointed out that having never been faced with the decision presented them with problems of predicting their own behavior: "Well, since I have never been faced with that before, I could not say definitely 'yes' or 'no,' so I could not really answer." "I don't know. I have never been put in that position, and I am not sure that I could make a truthful answer to that." "I have never been posed with that question. I don't know yet." (all quotes from Schnapper, 1984, p. 999, fn. 78). Another said he didn't think he could vote for death, "but a fellow never knows till the times [sic] comes." (Schnapper, 1984, p. 1048, fn. 262).

Sometimes, jurors alter their views after contemplating them. For instance, one juror who had testified the first day that he could vote for the death penalty changed his mind the next day: "I have given the matter more thought. I had never thought about it as being a personal responsibility in this case. I seem to be going the other way today. Up to this point I had never thought I was against capital punishment, but for some reason I tend to be drifting that way." (Schnapper, 1984, p. 1000, fn. 82).

Different questioning strategies of judges, prosecutors, and defense attorneys may succeed in shifting juror responses regarding the death penalty. Prosecutors often take the approach of restating the tentatively expressed opposition of the juror in firmer language, whereas defense attorneys frequently pose a hypothetical extreme and heinous case and inquire whether a prospective juror could impose the death penalty in that instance. Leading questions may produce unreliable answers, as illustrated by the example of one juror who, in response to the prosecutor's question, "You couldn't give anybody the death penalty, could you?" answered an apparently unequivocal "No." However, when the defense attorney queried, "Could you possibly vote for the death penalty in a certain case depending on what the facts were, depending on what the evidence is in that particular case?" the juror replied, "I guess possibly I could then, I guess. I don't know." (Schnapper, 1984, p. 1026, fn. 190).

Trial judges may respond to vacillation by demanding a clear response: for example, "Would your feeling against or your opposition to the death penalty irrevocably compel you to vote against capital punishment. Would it or wouldn't it? One time you said 'No,' and then you said 'Yes.' I have got to rule on it, and I don't know how to rule" (Schnapper, 1984, p. 1022, fn. 173). They can also become exasperated: "He's asked you two or three times, lady. I know it's new to you, but can you do it or can't you do it?" (Schnapper, 1984, p. 1000, fn. 83). Each of these approaches to soliciting jurors' views can produce different answers, and that is an important matter. Since opinions about capital punishment are related to other criminal justice attitudes, verbal responses that lead to exclusion can produce a biased jury.[3]

The mandatory voir dire questioning about prospective jurors' death penalty attitudes has another effect: It operates to predispose jurors to render a death sentence. Craig Haney (1984a) has pointed out a unique structural problem with capital trials. Even before prospective jurors decide on a defendant's guilt or innocence, they must try to anticipate their own behavior at the penalty phase of the trial. This forecasting task may set in motion a number of psychological processes, any one of which may bias jurors against the defendant. The time and energy spent on questions related to capital punishment may suggest to the prospective jurors that the defendant's guilt is a foregone conclusion and that the penalty phase will be necessary. Imagining that the penalty phase will occur, even as a hypothetical exercise during voir dire, should make jurors more likely to believe that it will occur, since imagining events generally makes them subjectively more likely (Tversky and Kahneman, 1973). Being questioned about one's willingness to impose the death penalty is likely to desensitize a juror to this task. The public affirmation and behavioral commitment required of capital jurors during voir dire also may increase their likelihood of rendering a death sentence. Finally, there is the danger that jurors will perceive legal disapproval of those opposed to the death sentence, since those who express extreme opposition are eliminated from the jury. In group voir dire, in which jurors have ample opportunity to observe the elimination of death penalty opponents and the retention of death penalty supporters, the impact of these psychological processes should be most pronounced.

Haney (1984b) tested some of these hypotheses about the process effects of capital voir dire in an inventive laboratory experiment.

Recruiting adults from Santa Cruz County, California, he randomly assigned them to watch one of two videotapes of a simulated voir dire. Half of the subjects watched an experimental tape that included a 30-minute segment depicting death penalty questioning, while the remainder watched a control tape of voir dire without any questions about the death penalty. The results of his study were dramatic: Inclusion of the death penalty questions introduced systematic biases. Subjects who observed them were more conviction-prone[4] and they thought the judge and the prosecutor were more supportive of capital punishment, compared to subjects who saw only the control voir dire questions. The experimental subjects were also more likely to think that the law disapproved of people who opposed the death penalty. The subjects were asked to imagine that they were jurors in a hypothetical case in which the defendant had been convicted of first-degree murder and to indicate an appropriate penalty. Just 22% of the control-condition jurors said that the death penalty was appropriate, whereas 57% of the experimental-condition jurors selected the death penalty. On the basis of these and other research findings, the California Supreme Court ordered that death penalty questioning be done individually and in a sequestered fashion to minimize potentially negative effects from observing the questioning of other panel members (*Hovey v. Superior Court*, 1980).

In addition to procedural reforms, judges and attorneys could try to minimize negative process effects. Consider the following material from a post-*Hovey* voir dire in the capital trial of Kenneth Gay and Raynard Cummings (*People v. Gay*, 1984). After the judge described the complicated California death penalty scheme involving the guilt phase, the finding of special circumstances, and the penalty phase, she embarked on questioning prospective jurors about their attitudes toward the death penalty but noted: "You understand I am asking these questions because I am mandated to do so in this case and we have no way of knowing at this time whether in fact we will ever reach the penalty phase. Do you understand that?" (*People v. Gay*, transcript, p. 4076) The defense attorney expanded on the theme:

DEFENSE ATTORNEY: One last question. This procedure is required by the law to bring jurors in one at a time and ask them about their views on the death penalty, which could only be imposed if there is a previous conviction. I am worried that by asking you your views on the possible penalty or punishment that could be imposed before you have heard a stitch of evidence that we might give you the impression the only issue before this jury is the penalty and not the trial on the guilt or innocence. In other words, I am worried that we might by putting the cart before the horse precondition you to believe that my client is guilty and the only question that remains to be decided is his penalty. Do you think that would have an effect on you?

JUROR: No.

DEFENSE ATTORNEY: At the appropriate time I intend to argue to the jury that the defendant is not guilty of the murder. Is there anything about this process that would make you less than neutral or fair and objective in listening to that argument?

JUROR: No [*People v. Gay*, transcript, p. 4140].

In this case, even the prosecutor got into the act, albeit with a somewhat different theme:

PROSECUTOR: We are talking about these lawyers asking questions about whether or not you are going to be influenced by the process itself. You said you wouldn't be, so let me ask you a couple of questions about that. [The defense attorney] asked jurors questions about rejecting the prosecutor's evidence and just because the prosecutor said something you don't have to believe him, et cetera. That process isn't going to condition you, is it?

JUROR: I think what he said was that opinions or matter-of-fact statements that you might make won't influence me as opposed to factual information. Factual information that is proven, I can say yes or not [sic] to.

PROSECUTOR: My opinions, Mr._____, are irrelevant to what we are doing here. I am not supposed to even voice them. If I do do that, you ignore them. Actually, all of these people, their opinions are not relevant. Just the evidence [*People v. Gay*, transcript, pp. 4128-4129].

At present we do not know how frequently judges and attorneys try to circumvent the biases inherent in the death qualification process, nor whether these strategies are successful. (The jury actually sentenced both Gay and Cummings to death.) But they might well prove useful. Just as one's public expression of willingness to deliver a death sentence may increase the likelihood of voting for that penalty, so too might a public affirmation of impartiality encourage jurors to set their biases aside.

Faced with evidence of negative process effects, defense attorneys are forced to consider whether it is better to minimize questioning of prospective jurors in efforts to limit the biases created by death qualification. Psychological research indicates, however, that for the purpose of detecting prejudice in jurors, individual, sequestered, open-ended questioning is the superior method (Hans, 1986). Furthermore, at least one study suggests that, under such expansive conditions, defense attorneys are better able to "rehabilitate" prospective jurors who might otherwise be eliminated because of their opposition to the death penalty. In a Kentucky study of voir dire methods in 13 capital cases, Nietzel and Dillehay (1982) discovered that individual, sequestered voir dire benefited the defense in two ways. First, when jurors were questioned individually and outside the presence of other jurors, judges were more likely to eliminate prospective jurors for cause for defense reasons (e.g., pretrial publicity, prior knowledge, preformed opinions). Second, fewer jurors were eliminated because of their opposition to the death penalty when questioning was sequestered. Interestingly, just one of the four juries that had experienced the most extensive form of sequestered voir dire returned the death sentence, compared to seven of the nine juries that had experienced other forms of voir dire. Because the Nietzel and Dillehay project was a field study of actual trials, differences among the cases themselves could have contributed to these results. However, they are quite consistent with an extensive literature on the psychology of prejudice that shows individualized, open-ended questioning is the most suitable approach for detecting bias.

THE TRIAL

We know very little about how events during a defendant's trial affect the jury's decision at the penalty phase. However, it is reasonable to assume that the experience of hearing trial evidence and deciding on the guilt of the defendant will influence penalty phase decision making. Certainly the possibility of such influence controls trial strategy. Goodpaster (1983) has noted that if defendants deny having committed the offense completely at their trial, and they are convicted, they are in a double bind in the penalty phase. If they then admit the offense at the penalty phase but ask for mercy, their credibility is likely to be low indeed. Goodpaster gave the example of the 1981 California case of Robert Harris, who at his trial denied he had murdered two young boys. During the penalty phase, Harris admitted the murders but expressed his sorrow for them. The jury's death sentence was one of the handful upheld by the California Supreme Court during that time period (Goodpaster, 1983, p. 330, fn. 134).

Even if trial tactics during the guilt phase are unsuccessful in securing an acquittal, they might be used to set the stage for a penalty phase argument for mercy. Hence lawyers might advance a reasonable-doubt defense or cross-examine witnesses during the trial to illustrate positive features of the defendant (Goodpaster, 1983). The trial presents a protracted time period in which to present the defendant as a human being and to begin to defuse any stereotype of him or her as an "icy killer." Just as death qualification desensitizes jurors to imposing the death sentence, listening to extensive testimony relating to a killing may also desensitize jurors to some of its more shocking features. Jurors might also feel more of a commitment to the defendant; there is less diffusion of responsibility when the same jury decides guilt and penalty. Another factor jurors consider in deciding to impose the death penalty is their certainty that the defendant is a deliberate killer (Barnett, 1985). Even if a jury is convinced beyond a reasonable doubt of a defendant's guilt, any residual doubts could create reluctance to impose the death penalty (*Lockhart v. McCree*, 1986).[5]

Do jurors actually reach an initial decision about whether the defendant deserves to die in the guilt phase? Does the possibility of the death penalty strongly influence their guilt phase deliberations? Do they insist on a higher standard of proof in a capital case compared to other trials? These and other questions about the interaction between the guilt and penalty phase remain unanswered to date, although they have important implications for trial strategy.

STRUCTURING JURY DECISION MAKING IN THE PENALTY PHASE

In *McGautha v. California* (1971), Justice Harlan, writing for the Court, asserted that any regulation of the penalty phase was likely to be futile, since the decision to render a death sentence was essentially a complex moral decision by jurors. Nevertheless, following closely on the heels of *McGautha, Furman v. Georgia* (1972) established the constitutional requirement of "guided discretion" in the imposition of the death penalty. Over a decade and a half after *McGautha*, in the wake of countless efforts by the courts and legislatures to regulate capital decision making by structuring the decision around the weighing of aggravating and mitigating factors, Justice Harlan's pronouncement seems to have anticipated current dilemmas over guided discretion of the jury's penalty decision (Weisberg, 1984).

The aim of guided discretion is to heighten the "rationality" of the decision making process and to lessen the arbitrary imposition of the death penalty. Under a guided discretion scheme, state death penalty statutes list specific aggravating and mitigating factors that are to be considered in the decision to impose death. Thus, in the penalty phase of a capital trial, jurors are presented with evidence bearing on statutorily defined factors. They are instructed to weigh these factors in their decision making, although they may also consider other relevant information about the defendant and the crime. Jurors may not impose death unless they find that at least one statutorily defined aggravated circumstance exists beyond a reasonable doubt. It is an open question whether juries have actually become less arbitrary in delivering death sentences as a result of the "guidance" they are now receiving from the courts. Some commentators have applauded guided discretion, pointing to the fact that capital juries now decide a smaller subset of cases than ever before. By narrowing the pool of cases that may be considered for capital punishment, legislatures, courts, and prosecutors have removed from jury consideration some outlying cases—crimes that do not involve a death (*Coker v. Georgia*, 1977), or that do not involve at least one aggravating circumstance. Arguably, guided discretion has at the very least minimized the potential amount of arbitrariness by the jury.

Other scholars dispute this conclusion by noting that the scope of statutory aggravating circumstances is so sweeping that most killings can be readily described as possessing at least one of them. And even operating under guided discretion statutes, penalty juries appear to be affected by extra-legal factors such as the race of the victim (Baldus et al., 1983; Gross and Mauro, 1984; Gross, 1985; *McCleskey v. Kemp*, 1987). The key question is whether those effects would be even greater if the jury were left to its own devices.

Whether or not court guidance attenuates the impact of extra-legal variables, there is an inherent tension in the concept of guided discretion. A certain amount of freedom is implied in the granting of discretion to a decision maker, yet deference to discretionary judgment increases the chance that racial or other undesirable factors will affect the verdict. *McCleskey v. Kemp* (1987), recently decided by the U.S. Supreme Court, exemplifies the acute strain in the notion of guided discretion. McCleskey, a black man, was sentenced to death in Georgia for killing a white victim. In the teeth of a record showing striking statistical evidence that blacks who kill whites are more likely to be sentenced to die than other defendant-victim racial combinations, the Supreme Court bowed to the McCleskey jury's discretion and upheld its death penalty. Although acknowledging the strength of the statistical data, the Court said that there was no *direct* evidence that McCleskey's jury itself had been affected by racial factors, and noted that "exceptionally clear proof" that the jury had abused its discretion would be necessary before its decision would be overturned.

MODELS OF JURY DECISION MAKING

The ultimate success of guided discretion statutes depends partly on how jurors undertake the decision making task. Although there are no published studies of jurors' decisional processes in the penalty phase, let me propose two different methods, derived from psychological research, that jurors might employ in deciding whether a defendant deserves to die. First, jurors might take an algebraic approach, in which they assess the value and weight of each piece of evidence and average them together to form an overall judgment (Anderson, 1981; Arkes and Hammond, 1986).[6] If the defendant's total exceeds some cut-off point along the juror's subjective continuum of deservingness to die, then the juror chooses death; if it falls below the cut-off, then the juror decides life. An algebraic model of jury decision processes seems to reflect rather closely the legal assumptions underlying guided discretion statutes and penalty phase jury instructions. If jurors decide death in this manner, then judicial instructions to evaluate and weigh aggravating and mitigating evidence and to reach a summary judgment would reflect their natural decision processes. The instructions would be comprehensible and perhaps even effective in guiding juror discretion.

Other work on jury decision making, however, indicates that jurors do not follow a weighing and summing procedure in judging a defendant's criminal responsibility. Psychologists Nancy Pennington and Reid Hastie (1986, in press; see also Bennett and Feldman, 1981) have argued persuasively that jurors instead employ a story model to evaluate the guilt of an accused. This work shows that jurors arrange trial evidence in the form of a plausible sequence of motivated human actions, or story, much as any narrative about human events would be organized. Next, jurors assess the extent to which their story of the event matches the available verdict categories.

The Pennington and Hastie work implies that capital jurors begin the penalty phase with a story developed during the guilt phase. This story contains important events, circumstances of the crime, states of mind, and inferences about the character of the defendant. The story may indicate prognoses that the defendant has rehabilitative potential, is a hopeless case, or is dangerous, conclusions that have obvious implications for sentencing. Most importantly, once the story has been developed, jurors are likely to resist reconstruction of it. Hence, the guilt and penalty phases are necessarily interdependent, pointing to the need for integrated trial phase and penalty phase strategies.

The success of the story model in describing jurors' guilt decisions suggests that an algebraic model may not adequately explain jurors' penalty decisions. One alternative approach, which is more in the spirit of the story model, is a category-based strategy (Smith and Medin, 1981). In this model, jurors are presumed to possess general stereotypes (called "prototypes") of criminals who deserve the death penalty. The prototypes might represent an amalgamation of specific individuals, let us say Charles Manson or Richard Speck, who jurors feel deserve to be executed. To decide whether a defendant deserves to die, jurors would match the central figure in their story, the defendant, to the abstract prototype. If the defendant is quite similar to the prototype, the match is close, and the juror decides on death; if there are significant discrepancies, then the juror decides on life. Interestingly, lawyers' arguments to the capital jury often incorporate stereotypes or specific instances of defendants who deserve the death penalty or mercy. If penalty phase arguments reflect lawyers' intuitions about how jurors decide death, then attorneys appear to believe that jurors employ a category-based approach rather than a weighing approach. If jurors do operate with such categories, then instructions to weigh aggravating and mitigating evidence would be at odds with their "natural" decision making strategy, and might be less successful in governing their decisional processes.

Whichever model best captures the approach jurors actually employ in deciding death, the structure of the penalty phase is critical. By specifying what evidence is introduced, and by allowing certain forms of argument by counsel, guided discretion statutes circumscribe the amount and value of the information or the content of jurors' stories.

The statutory listing of aggravating and mitigating factors carries a message of social and legal approval. This may cause jurors to redefine the weights or the penalty categories in deciding who constitutes an appropriate candidate for life or for death.

JURY INSTRUCTIONS

Debates about the impact of guided discretion statutes raise the related issue of whether jury decision making can be satisfactorily guided by judicial instructions. Although jury researchers have a generally positive view of jurors' ability to decide factual issues, they routinely point out jurors' difficulty with understanding and applying judges' instructions (Elwork and Sales, 1985; Hans and Vidmar, 1986; Hastie et al., 1983). Studies of juror comprehension of traditional instructions have revealed disappointingly low levels of understanding, although when such instructions are rewritten using psycholinguistic principles, understanding improves (Charrow and Charrow, 1979; Elwork et al., 1982; Severance and Loftus, 1982). Problems of jury comprehension are compounded by inappropriate application of the instructions. Jurors do not always set aside legally irrelevant evidence in accordance with a judge's limiting instruction (e.g., Doob and Kirshenbaum, 1972; Hans and Doob, 1976; Wissler and Saks, 1985). Confusion stemming from poorly worded instructions may be partly to blame; or the instructions may be disregarded because they do not comport with jurors' cognitive abilities or views of justice.

Penalty phase instructions are likely to be particularly problematic for jurors. As outlined above, weighing instructions may run counter to jurors' natural decision-making strategy. In addition, judicial instructions admonish jurors to focus only on aggravating and mitigating evidence and to ignore illegitimate factors in determining the appropriateness of a death sentence. The aim is admirable: to channel the jury's discretion so that it is based on clear and objective standards rather than improper sentiments. Yet, like other limiting instructions, the admonition to disregard illegitimate factors is based on two questionable premises: that jurors know when an illegitimate factor is influencing them, and that they are able to subtract the influence of this factor in the decisional calculus. Psychological research has demonstrated that people's estimates of factors influencing their judgments are often quite inaccurate (Nisbett and Wilson, 1977).

The difficulty of instructing jurors to disregard illegitimate factors is magnified in the penalty phase because the decision maker must be allowed to consider any relevant mitigating evidence of the defendant's background and character and the circumstances of the offense (*Lockett v. Ohio*, 1978; Hertz and Weisberg, 1981). The juror must perform the mental gymnastic of distinguishing "legitimate" from "illegitimate" feelings of sympathy flowing from such evidence.

This quandary was highlighted in *California v. Brown* (1987), in which the U.S. Supreme Court held that warnings to the jury to avoid relying on sympathy did not violate the defendant's right to have any evidence considered in mitigation. At issue was California's instruction to the penalty phase jury that it "must not be swayed by mere sentiment, conjecture, sympathy, passion, prejudice, public opinion, or public feeling." Chief Justice Rehnquist, joined by three other justices, wrote that a reasonable juror would most likely interpret the instruction to mean that he or she should ignore only the sort of sympathy that derived from illegitimate factors. The reasonable juror would see that sympathy based on the aggravating and mitigating evidence presented in court was an appropriate consideration. But in her concurrence, Justice O'Connor pointed out that jurors might well be misled into believing that legitimate mitigating evidence about the defendant's background and character must also be ignored. And in *Brown*, the prosecutor's closing arguments directly fostered this reading. After noting that numerous relatives had testified about Brown's character and background during the penalty phase, the prosecutor asserted:

> They did not testify, ladies and gentlemen, regarding any of the factors which relate to your decision in this case. Their testimony here, ladies and gentlemen, I would suggest, was a blatant attempt by the defense to inject personal feelings in the case, to make the defendant appear human, to make you feel for the defendant, and although that is admirable in the context of an advocate trying to do his job, you ladies and gentlemen must steel yourselves against those kinds of feelings in reaching a decision in this case. As the Judge will instruct you, you must not be swayed by sympathy [*California v. Brown*, 1987, p. 845].

Jurors hearing the prosecutor's comments would in all likelihood interpret the judge's antisympathy instruction as forbidding any reliance on the legitimate sympathy arising from Brown's background and character evidence, as O'Connor observed. Thus Rehnquist's contention that jurors were able to differentiate legitimate and illegitimate sources of sympathy seems far-fetched. The *Brown* case illustrates why knowing more about how jurors react to penalty phase instructions would be valuable.

AGGRAVATING CIRCUMSTANCES

In the penalty phase, jurors are first presented with evidence relating to aggravating features of the murder that might justify the imposition of the death penalty. Enumerated in state statutes, these aggravating circumstances typically include the defendant's past history of violent criminal conduct, the existence of more than one killing, and the commission of a murder while engaged in another felony such as robbery or rape. The purpose of the killing may also constitute an aggravating circumstance, as in the case of a murder committed for pecuniary gain or for the purpose of avoiding arrest. Probably the most controversial, potentially aggravating element is that the murder was "especially heinous, atrocious, or cruel." Before imposing the death penalty, juries are usually required to find that at least one aggravating circumstance exists beyond a reasonable doubt. But as already noted, the typical list of aggravating factors is so all-inclusive that almost all killings can easily be classified as aggravated, and the "beyond a reasonable doubt" criterion is often irrelevant. Proof of most aggravating circumstances, such as the felony-murder rule or past criminal conduct, is a straightforward matter.

Another problem is that different aggravating factors can apply to the same evidence. Kaplan and Weisberg (1986, pp. 452-453) have pointed out that killings committed during a robbery or burglary could be readily described as having the purpose of "pecuniary gain." And if liberally construed, the purpose of "avoiding arrest" could apply to the killings of many victims. "Double-counting" the same factual circumstances as multiple aggravating factors may have pernicious effects on the jury. Instructed to weigh aggravating and mitigating features of the crime, jurors may twice penalize the defendant on the identical evidence. Juries' decisions to impose the death penalty are directly related to the quantity of aggravating circumstances (e.g., Gross and Mauro, 1984, Table 21, p. 71). They may take the legislative specification of such multiple aggravation as notice of public support and redefine who deserves to die. Jurors may perceive the prosecution as having the edge if the absolute number of aggravating circumstances is larger than the number of mitigating circumstances.

Some aggravating circumstances, such as the continuing dangerousness of the defendant, or certain questions about the intent of the
defendant in committing the crime, may be more debatable issues. Here
the state benefits from the prosecution-proneness of death-qualified
jurors. They are more likely than the community at large to give
prosecution witnesses greater credence (Cowan et al., 1984), and are less
sanguine about rehabilitation prospects of the defendant (Ellsworth et
al., 1984). Doubts may be resolved in favor of the prosecution.

In some states, Texas being a notable example, the future dangerousness of the defendant constitutes an aggravating circumstance. Many
psychologists and psychiatrists have concluded that the prediction of
dangerousness is prone to substantial error (Monahan, 1981). Two out
of every three predictions are likely to be incorrect, and there is a bias
toward overpredicting dangerousness.

The constitutional status of future dangerousness as an aggravating
factor was assessed in *Barefoot v. Estelle* (1983). Thomas Barefoot was
convicted by a Texas jury of the capital murder of a police officer. At
Barefoot's penalty hearing, jurors heard the prosecution psychiatrist,
Dr. Grigson, testify that Barefoot was an incurable sociopath who had a
"one hundred percent and absolute" likelihood of committing future
violent acts, whether he was imprisoned or not. Barefoot was sentenced
to die. Despite an *amicus curiae* brief from the American Psychiatric
Association indicating that predictions of future dangerousness are
highly unreliable, the Supreme Court ruled that such testimony at the
penalty phase did not violate the Constitution. After all, Justice White
wrote for the Court, "[n]either petitioner nor the Association suggests
that psychiatrists are always wrong with respect to future dangerousness,
only most of the time." The psychiatric testimony would be subject to
cross-examination, and jurors could assess the reliability of the
predictions.

In a stinging dissent, Justice Blackmun, joined by Justices Brennan
and Marshall, criticized the Court's willingness to permit unreliable
psychiatric testimony in the penalty phase, noting "[o]ne can only
wonder how juries are to separate valid from invalid expert opinions
when the 'experts' themselves are so obviously unable to do so." When
death hangs in the balance, they said, a defendant should not have to
face the burden of convincing lay jurors of the unreliability of
psychiatric predictions of dangerousness.

It is interesting tu speculate about how death-qualified jurors
consider psychiatric predictions of dangerousness. Support for the
death penalty is linked to the personality variable of authoritarianism,

which is characterized by respect for authority figures. Other research indicates that death-qualified jurors are skeptical of psychological excuses for criminal behavior (Ellsworth et al., 1984; White, 1987). Taken together, these research findings suggest that death-qualified jurors may perceive prosecution psychiatrists favorably and might be reluctant to criticize their testimony, although they may take a dim view of defense psychiatrists who use psychological data to mitigate the defendant's responsibility.

Although guided discretion statutes require the jury to focus on aggravating and mitigating evidence, a study of attorneys' final arguments in the penalty phase revealed that prosecutors tended to concentrate on moral as opposed to evidentiary arguments when asking the jury for the death sentence (Logan, 1982). They often recreated the scene of the crime, emphasized its horror, and asserted that the defendant showed a lack of humanity. Interestingly, prosecutors mentioned deterrence and the protection of society in less than half of the final arguments, although both of these factors are prominent in scholarly discussion of the death penalty. The very last statement made by prosecutors was most likely to be a statement relating to justice. Although it was also typical for prosecutors to state that the aggravating circumstances outweighed the mitigating circumstances, the overall pattern of their arguments in the penalty phase suggested that they perceived the emotional dimensions of the decision to be paramount.

Psychological research challenges the basis for some appellate decisions regarding unconstitutional aggravating factors (*Zant v. Stevens*, 1983). After declaring as unconstitutional certain aggravating factors that the jury was allowed to consider in the penalty phase, some appellate courts nevertheless have upheld the defendant's death sentence, reasoning that the remaining evidence would have been sufficient for the jury to impose capital punishment. These decisions ignore the fact that once a decision is made, it is usually impossible to "substract" an element. Neither the decision maker nor an observer can accurately estimate the weight of that factor; furthermore, hindsight bias could convince the observer that the same result would have been obtained (Nisbett and Wilson, 1977).

MITIGATING CIRCUMSTANCES

In 1980, drug dealer Robert Nelson stood trial on charges that he had murdered a business partner and his girlfriend over a payment dispute.

The case looked grim: Nelson's alleged associate in the crime had immunity and was prepared to testify that Nelson had killed the two victims. Furthermore, relatives and others were willing to swear that Nelson had boasted of the murders and professed complete responsibility for them. That's when defense attorney Thomas Nolan took the novel step of hiring journalist Lacey Fosburgh. As a member of the defense team, Fosburgh employed her investigative talents to assemble a massive quantity of information about the defendant's background, family life, character, habits, strengths, and flaws. Friends, relatives, and the defendant testified about some of these matters during the guilt phase. After Nelson was convicted of the two murders, close family members provided even more background information during the penalty phase. No psychiatrist ever testified. The aim was to use journalistic skills to create an engaging, understandable, and sympathetic picture of a defendant whom the jury would not want to kill. The jury ultimately concluded that Nelson should not receive a death sentence; as one juror stated, the homicides were "out of character" for him (Fosburgh, 1986).

Although the guidance of a journalist in a capital trial is unusual, the Nelson case illustrates what is becoming an increasingly common feature of the penalty phase. Responding to the Supreme Court's holding in *Lockett v. Ohio* (1978) that capital defendants must be allowed to introduce any factors they wish in mitigation of their crimes, many defense attorneys are using the penalty phase to present the personal background, psychological dynamics, and social history of their clients. As one defense advocate explained, presenting the defendant as a multidimensional human being makes it more difficult to "dispose" of him or her (De Falla et al., 1984). And if jurors take a category-based approach to sentencing, differentiating the defendant from the prototype of the criminal who deserves death should be advantageous.

The "humanization" of the defendant can be accomplished through different types of witnesses, including family, friends, coworkers, teachers, and psychologists. For instance, psychologist Craig Haney testified in the penalty phase hearing of one Mr. Dolan. He had reviewed court documents and psychological test results, interviewed family, friends, and employers of Dolan, and talked to Dolan himself. After constructing a social history of Dolan and sharing that material with the jury, Haney concluded that despite psychological problems, Dolan was a good prospect for adjustment to prison life. Haney avoided burdening the jury with technical jargon; rather, he employed lay language to describe the defendant's traumatic childhood and his psychological makeup. Taking into account the fact that the death-qualified jury tends to be hostile to psychological excuses for the defendant's behavior, social history information was presented not as an "excuse" but as an explanation (De Falla et al., 1984).

We really know little about how jurors evaluate mitigating evidence. Causal attributions concerning a defendant's behavior are linked to sentencing recommendations and thus it is useful to offer them. However, a punishment-oriented juror is not likely to turn into a rehabilitation-oriented juror overnight (Carroll et al., 1987). It is possible that jurors discount much mitigating evidence. Consider the following notes from a penalty phase juror in the case of a Vietnam veteran:

> We decided to start by listing all the aggravating and mitigating factors we could think of—not to see which number was larger, but just to keep track so we'd know what we had to talk about. Karen, sitting by the blackboard, volunteered to write it down. We ended up with aggravations outnumbering mitigations about ten to eight, and a general feeling that aggravation outweighed mitigation as well. After all, we'd been allowed to throw in any consideration, however trivial or unprovable, on the mitigation side, but the aggravating factors were necessarily those with some clout behind them [Lakoff, 1987, Chap. 8, p. 16].

Even though the jurors agreed that aggravating factors "outweighed" mitigating ones, they decided that the Vietnam vet deserved a life sentence. That hints that this jury did more than simply weigh factors, or, alternatively, that they were not able to articulate mitigating factors that influenced their decision.

Deana Logan (1982, 1986) analyzed the themes of 21 final penalty phase arguments by defense counsel in capital cases and concluded that many arguments were unlikely to be effective with the jury. The most common themes in defense arguments were that the death penalty itself is equivalent to murder and that vengeance is a base motive. Perhaps these arguments seem persuasive to many defense attorneys who are deeply committed to fighting capital punishment. But it is doubtful that they are convincing to the death-qualified jurors, all of whom have expressed some support for the death penalty during voir dire. Because death penalty attitudes are so tightly interwoven with other views, only those jurors with relatively mild support for the death penalty are likely to be swayed by these arguments.[7]

Logan suggests avoiding direct attacks on jurors' values. She recommends that defense counsel concentrate instead on underscoring the subjective nature of the weighing process, on making the defendant's behavior understandable, and on stressing the severity of the life imprisonment sentencing option. Taking into account the values and likely perspectives of the jurors, these tactics illustrate how the desires to punish the defendant and protect society can be satisfied without the imposition of a death sentence in this particular case. These approaches can transform the penalty phase into, in Goodpaster's (1983) words, a "trial for life."

IMPACT ON THE JURORS

Serving on the penalty jury can be emotionally difficult. Take the case of David Steffen, a door-to-door salesman, who had sexually assaulted and murdered a young woman about to be married. Although none of the jurors was conscientiously opposed to the death penalty, they found listening to the evidence and deciding on a death sentence upsetting. In the words of one juror, it was "traumatic. It was terrible, and I'm still shaken. I just hope I never have to go through something like that again." The juror responded to a question over the death sentence by crying and saying, "I didn't want to do it, but I had to" (Kaplan, 1985, pp. 49-50).

Psychiatrist Stanley Kaplan interviewed jurors who served in the Steffen case and observed severe stress reactions in several jurors as long as two months after the trial. Exposed to bloody photographs of the victim and graphic evidence concerning her death, the jurors were forbidden to talk to friends and family about their experiences during the trial. They had to deal with their anxieties in the absence of their usual support systems. Furthermore, the decision to sentence the defendant to death was made despite their profound ambivalence. One juror expressed the dilemma: "I was doing the right thing, but it was a horrible thing to do. It would be on my conscience if he hurt someone else. . . . Well, when you heard the horrible things about his childhood; his stepfather, his mother is an alcoholic. He turned on the children and mistreated them.-. . . That's when you feel sorry for him . . . feel that if someone gave him some love at an early age. Now, it's hopeless" (Kaplan, 1985, p. 52). Despite the fact that the jurors felt that they had reached the correct decision to sentence the defendant to death, most experienced remorse and guilt. Several even expressed the desire to communicate their regrets to the defendant, to say, "I'm sorry, but this is the best we could do" (Kaplan, 1985, p. 52).

CONCLUSION

It is not surprising that capital jurors experience distress, for the penalty phase presents significant incongruities. The jurors are charged with representing the community's judgment, yet the voir dire and challenge processes have eliminated significant segments of the public from the jury. Jurors have been influenced by preceding events during voir dire questioning and the trial in pivotal ways, yet they are instructed to focus only on aggravating and mitigating evidence. They are told to ignore their emotions in perhaps one of the most emotionally charged decisions they will ever make, when a human life quite literally hangs in the balance. The court's assistance is limited to technical legal advice, likely to be mysterious and difficult to follow. And nearly all capital jurors have no prior experience to guide them.

Whether the penalty phase jury is fully equipped to handle its burden remains an unanswered question. Despite considerable legal scholarship, there are gaps in our knowledge of how the jury confronts the problem of deciding death. Our juror's-eye review of aspects of the penalty phase indicates a number of issues requiring further analysis and study. These include the interaction between the guilt and penalty phases of capital trials, the decision process jurors employ in arriving at a penalty, the understandability and impact of judicial weighing instructions, and the effect of specific aggravating and mitigating circumstances. Aggregate analyses of capital jury decisions reveal substantial variability in death penalty verdicts that cannot now be explained. How jurors deliberate to reach a sentence is also unknown.

Although rare to date, jury simulation studies of the penalty phase could serve a useful function. For some issues such as jurors' interpretation of legal instructions, they might inform judicial speculation by providing concrete evidence about jurors' understanding. Other questions might best be addressed by interviewing capital jurors after their service. Results from such studies could be combined with archival and other analyses of actual jury sentences to develop a fuller understanding of the factors affecting jury decisions on death.

NOTES

1. In 30 of the 37 states with capital punishment, the jury alone decides on the death penalty. In three other states, the jury makes a recommendation for life or death, but the judge may override the jury's decision. Just four states exclude the jury's voice completely (*Spaziano v. Florida*, 1984, pp. 463-464, fn. 9). Of course, in all states, death penalty decisions are subject to judicial review.

2. Here I would distinguish jury simulation of guilt decisions and jury simulation of penalty decisions. There has been much debate over the use of experimental methods to study jury decision making (see, e.g., *Lockhart v. McCree*, 1986). I conclude, along with the majority of psychologists, that jury decision processes in the guilt phase can often be adequately captured by simulation methods. Whether the same is true of penalty phase decision making is an open question. Surely certain penalty phase topics are amenable to experimental investigation: e.g., the ability of jurors to understand judges' instructions, or the impact of knowledge about specific aggravating or mitigating circumstances. Whether the life or death nature of the decision so substantially affects jurors' decision making that it is impossible to simulate other dimensions of the task is unclear.

3. It should be noted that Schnapper's picture of the voir dire process may not reflect current voir dire practices. Schnapper's analysis drew primarily on actual voir dires reported in published opinions prior to *Witt*. Reliance on appellate opinions may overestimate the problem of juror vacillation. Furthermore, because the post-*Witt* standard does not demand that jurors be unalterably opposed to the death sentence before a challenge for cause, questioning strategies may have changed as well.

4. Although it might seem that conviction-proneness is relevant only to the guilt phase of a capital trial, conviction-proneness effects are also critical to the penalty phase. For instance, Barnett (1985) has documented that the certainty that a defendant is an intentional killer is related to jurors' willingness to impose the death penalty.

5. In *Lockhart*, faced with impressive evidence of the biasing effects of death qualification, the state raised the residual doubt issue to justify the practice of employing a single capital jury to decide guilt and penalty. Although the residual doubt argument does not seem unreasonable, to date it has no empirical support.

6. In another context, some business organizations have adopted structured approaches to decision making in attempts to enhance the reliability of their decisions (Arkes and Hammond, 1986). Using this strategy, a decision maker specifies factors that would be affected by the decision, assigns weights to each factor, and calculates the desirability of different decisions in light of their impact on those factors. Typically, however, decision makers employ this strategy over multiple, successive decisions. An inexperienced group like a jury, charged with making a single decision, faces additional obstacles in structuring its decision making.

7. A recent jury simulation of the penalty phase by White (1987), however, demonstrated that college student subjects were swayed by defense attorney arguments that the death penalty was outdated, morally reprehensible, and an ineffective deterrent. White's college student subjects, some of whom were moderately opposed to capital punishment, may have been more responsive than other audiences to principled arguments against the death penalty. Whether such arguments are persuasive to people likely to survive capital voir dire and peremptory challenges awaits empirical investigation.

REFERENCES

ABA (1980) ABA Standards for Criminal Justice, 2nd. ed.

ANDERSON, N. H. (1981) Foundations of Information Integration Theory. New York: Academic Press.

ARKES, H. R., and K. R. HAMMOND [eds.] (1986) Judgment and Decision Making: An Interdisciplinary Reader. Cambridge: Cambridge University Press.

BALDUS, D. C., C. PULASKI, and G. WOODWORTH (1983) "Comparative review of death sentences: An empirical study of the Georgia experience." Journal of Criminal Law and Criminology 74: 661-753.

BARNETT, A. (1985) "Some distribution patterns for the Georgia death sentence." U.C. Davis Law Review 18: 1327-1374.

BENNETT, W. L. and M. FELDMAN (1981) Reconstructing Reality in the Courtroom. New Brunswick, NJ: Rutgers University Press.

CARROLL, J. S., W. T. PERKOWITZ, A. J. LURIGIO, and F. M. WEAVER (1987) "Sentencing goals, causal attributions, ideology, and personality." Journal of Personality and Social Psychology 52: 107-118.

CHARROW, R. P. and V. R. CHARROW (1979) "Making legal language understandable: A psycholinguistic study of jury instructions." Columbia Law Review 79: 1306-1374.

COWAN, C. L., W. C. THOMPSON, and P. C. ELLSWORTH (1984) "The effects of death qualification on jurors' predisposition to convict and on the quality of deliberation." Law and Human Behavior 8: 53-79.

DE FALLA, E., L. HEANEY, and T. WALLER [eds.] (1984) Capital Trials: Juror Attitudes and Selection Strategies. Oakland: National Jury Project.

DOOB, A. N. and H. KIRSHENBAUM (1972) "Some empirical evidence on the effect of s.12 of the Canada Evidence Act upon the accused." Criminal Law Quarterly 15: 88-96.

ELLSWORTH, P. C., R. M. BUKATY, C. L. COWAN, and W. C. THOMPSON (1984) "The death-qualified jury and the defense of insanity." Law and Human Behavior 8: 81-93.

ELLSWORTH, P. C. and L. ROSS (1983) "Public opinion and capital punishment: A close examination of the views of abolitionists and retentionists." Crime and Delinquency 29: 116-169.

ELWORK, A. and B. D. SALES (1985) "Jury instructions," pp. 280-297 in S. M. Kassin and L. S. Wrightsman (eds.) The Psychology of Evidence and Trial Procedure. Beverly Hills, CA: Sage.

ELWORK, A., B. D. SALES, and J. J. ALFINI (1982) Making Jury Instructions Understandable. Charlottesville, VA: Michie.

FITZGERALD, R. and P. C. ELLSWORTH (1984) "Due process vs. crime control: Death qualification and jury attitudes." Law and Human Behavior 8: 31-51.

FOSBURGH, L. (1986) "The Nelson case: A model for a new approach to capital trials." Reprinted in M. G. Millman (ed.) California Death Penalty Defense Manual. Los Angeles, CA: California Attorneys for Criminal Justice and California Public Defenders Association.

GILLERS, S. (1980) "Deciding who dies." University of Pennsylvania Law Review 129: 1-124.

GOODPASTER, G. (1983) "The trial for life: Effective assistance of counsel in death penalty cases." New York University Law Review 58: 299-362.

GROSS, S. R. (1985) "Race and death: The judicial evaluation of evidence of discrimination in capital sentencing." U.C. Davis Law Review 18: 1275-1325.

GROSS, S. R. and R. MAURO (1984) "Patterns of death." Stanford Law Review 37: 27-153.

HANEY, C. (1984a) "Examining death qualification: Further analysis of the process effect." Law and Human Behavior 8: 133-151.

HANEY, C. (1984b) "On the selection of capital juries: The biasing effects of the death qualification process." Law and Human Behavior 8: 121-132.

HANS, V. P. (1986) "The conduct of voir dire: A psychological analysis." Justice System Journal 11: 40-58.

HANS, V. P. and A. N. DOOB (1976) "Section 12 of the Canada Evidence Act and the deliberations of simulated juries." Criminal Law Quarterly 18: 235-253.

HANS, V. P. and N. VIDMAR (1986) Judging the Jury. New York: Plenum.

HASTIE, R., S. D. PENROD, and N. PENNINGTON (1983) Inside the Jury. Cambridge, MA: Harvard University Press.

HERTZ, R. and R. WEISBERG (1981) "In mitigation of the penalty of death: *Lockett v. Ohio* and the capital defendant's right to consideration of mitigating circumstances." California Law Review 69: 317-376.

KALVEN, H. and H. ZEISEL (1966) The American Jury. Boston: Little, Brown.

KAPLAN, J. and R. WEISBERG (1986) Criminal Law: Cases and Materials. Boston: Little, Brown.

KAPLAN, S. M. (1985, July) "Death, so say you all." Psychology Today, pp. 48-53.

LAKOFF, R. (1987) Unpublished manuscript, University of California, Berkeley.

LOGAN, D. D. (1982) "Why you should not kill this man." Presented at the British Psychological Society's International Conference on Psychology and Law, Swansea, Wales.

LOGAN, D. D. (1986) "Pleading for life: An analysis of penalty phase final arguments." In M. G. Millman (ed.) California Death Penalty Defense Manual. Los Angeles, CA: California Attorneys for Criminal Justice and California Public Defenders Association.

MONAHAN, J. (1981) The Clinical Prediction of Violent Behavior. Rockville, MD: U.S. Department of Health and Human Services.

NIETZEL, M. T. and R. C. DILLEHAY (1982) "The effects of voir dire procedures in capital murder trials." Law and Human Behavior 6: 1-13.

NISBETT, R. E. and T. D. WILSON (1977) "Telling more than we can know: Verbal reports on mental processes." *Psychological Review* 84: 231-259.

PENNINGTON, N. and R. HASTIE (1986) "Evidence evaluation in complex decision making." Journal of Personality and Social Psychology 51: 242-258.

PENNINGTON, N. and R. HASTIE (in press) "Explanation-based decision making: The effects of memory structure on judgment." Journal of Experimental Psychology: Learning, Memory, and Cognition.

RADELET, M. L. (1985) "Rejecting the jury: The imposition of the death penalty in Florida." U.C. Davis Law Review 18: 1409-1431.

SCHNAPPER, E. (1984) "Taking *Witherspoon* seriously: The search for death-qualified jurors." Texas Law Review 62: 977-1084.

SEVERANCE, L. and E. F. LOFTUS (1982) "Improving the ability of jurors to comprehend and apply criminal jury instructions." Law and Society Review 17: 153-198.

SMITH, E. E., and MEDIN, D. L. (1981) Categories and Concepts. Cambridge, MA: Harvard University Press.

TVERSKY, A. and D. KAHNEMAN (1973) "Availability: A heuristic for judging frequency and probability." Cognitive Psychology 5: 207-232.

TYLER, T. R. and R. WEBER (1982) "Support for the death penalty: Instrumental response to crime, or symbolic attitude?" Law and Society Review 17: 21-45.

VIDMAR, N. and P. C. ELLSWORTH (1974) "Public opinion and the death penalty." Stanford Law Review 26: 1245-1270.

WEISBERG, R. (1984) "Deregulating death," pp. 305-395 in P. B. Kurland, G. Casper, and D. J. Hutchinson (eds.) The Supreme Court Review, 1983. Chicago: University of Illinois Press.

WHITE, L. T. (1987) "Juror decision making in the capital penalty trial: An analysis of crimes and defense strategies." Law and Human Behavior 11: 113-130.

WINICK, B. J. (1982) "Prosecutorial peremptory challenge practices in capital cases: An empirical study and a constitutional analysis." Michigan Law Review 81: 1-98.

WISSLER, R. and M. J. SAKS (1985) "On the inefficacy of limiting instruction: When jurors use prior conviction evidence to decide guilt." Law and Human Behavior 9: 37-48.

CASES

Barefoot v. Estelle, 463 U.S. 880 (1983).

California v. Brown, 107 S. Ct. 837 (1987).

Coker v. Georgia, 433 U.S. 584 (1977).

Furman v. Georgia, 408 U.S. 238 (1972).

Hovey v. Superior Ct., 28 Cal. 3d 1, 616 P. 2d 1301, 168 Cal. Rptr. 128 (1980).

Lockett v. Ohio, 438 U.S. 586 (1978).

Lockhart v. McCree, 106 S. Ct. 1758 (1986).

McCleskey v. Kemp, 107 S. Ct. 1756 (1987).

McGautha v. California, 402 U.S. 183 (1971).

People v. Gay, Cal. Super. Ct., Los Angeles Cty. (1984).

Spaziano v. Florida, 468 U.S. 447 (1984).

Wainwright v. Witt, 105 S. Ct. 844 (1985).

Witherspoon v. Illinois, 391 U.S. 510 (1968).

Zant v. Stevens, 462 U.S. 862 (1983).

Chapter 7

UNPLEASANT FACTS
The Supreme Court's Response to Empirical Research on Capital Punishment

P H O E B E C. E L L S W O R T H

Slowly at first, and then with accelerating frequency, the courts have begun to examine, consider, and sometimes even require empirical data. From 1960 to 1981, for example, use of the terms "statistics" and "statistical" in Federal District and Circuit Court opinions increased by almost 15 times.[1] Of course, citation rates indicate only that a topic is considered worthy of mention, not that it is taken seriously, or even understood. Nonetheless, in a number of areas, such as jury composition and employment discrimination, the courts have come to rely on empirical data as a matter of course.

In the last 25 years, empirical research has been central to most major challenges to the constitutionality of capital punishment. The research involved has covered an enormous range of methods, from surveys to simulations, from econometric analyses to laboratory experiments, and the presentation of the research to the courts has generally been both comprehensive and sophisticated. There is probably no other area of

AUTHOR'S NOTE: *This chapter was written while the author was a Fellow at the Center for Advanced Study in the Behavioral Sciences. I am grateful to the John D. and Catherine T. MacArthur Foundation and to the James McKeen Cattell Fund for financial support, and to the Center Staff and Fellows for time, space, unsurpassable services, and intellectual stimulation. Joseph B. Kadane and Samuel R. Gross read the first draft of this chapter and made it better.*

177

criminal law in which the Supreme Court has been faced with such well-organized and wide-ranging empirical demonstrations. It is quite likely that comparable empirical data about some other issue would be persuasive to the Court; when the issue is the death penalty, however, the Court is not persuaded. In case after case, the majority of the Justices have been faced with empirical research that supports an outcome they do not want.

Three major empirical questions have been brought before the Court in relation to capital punishment. The first is the issue of deterrence: Is the death penalty more effective than life imprisonment as a deterrent to murder? The second is the issue of discrimination: Are decisions about which criminals should be executed and which should be allowed to live based in part on the race of the person accused or on the race of the victim? The third is the issue of the fairness of capital juries: Does the common practice of removing strong opponents of capital punishment from the jury create juries that are biased toward a guilty verdict? The Court has dealt with the data on each of these issues somewhat differently—sometimes by calling them inconclusive, sometimes by calling them irrelevant, and sometimes by evading them. I shall examine the Court's use of the data presented on each of these three questions, the first two briefly, and the third at greater length.

DETERRENCE

Most people who favor the death penalty believe that it deters murderers (Ellsworth and Ross, 1983). It seems commonsensical that a person contemplating murder would be deterred by the threat of death. If so, then the existence of a death penalty is morally justified because it saves innocent lives. Opponents of the death penalty reason differently. They argue that few homicides are the product of such rational calculation. Most murderers do not stop to weigh the costs and benefits of their act. Those who do may figure (correctly) that the odds of execution are vanishingly small, so it is worth the risk. At any rate the likelihood of getting killed at the time of committing the murder is considerably greater than the likelihood of getting killed after conviction. Also, an argument for a powerful deterrent effect of capital punishment requires that it be a significantly more effective deterrent than life imprisonment. That is, the hypothetical person contemplating murder would go ahead with it if he considered the prospect of spending the rest of his life in prison, but not if he considered the prospect of execution.[2]

Until 1974, the empirical research on the deterrent effects of the death penalty was completely consistent: No researcher claimed to have found a significant deterrent effect. The research was dominated by the work of Thorsten Sellin (1959, 1980), who had carried out a comprehensive series of studies covering many different times and places, and using a variety of complementary research designs. He examined neighboring states with and without the death penalty, and found that homicide rates were no lower in the death penalty states (in fact they were usually slightly higher). Over time the levels of homicide in contiguous states tended to rise and fall in synchrony, providing some indication that the states were in fact comparable, that similar forces affected the homicide rate. He also examined states and countries that had a death penalty and then abolished it to see if the homicide levels would rise; and he examined states that instituted a death penalty after a period without it to see if the number of homicides would fall. The death penalty had no noticeable effect in either case. He looked at crimes that are especially likely to be punished by death, such as killing police officers, killing for hire, and killing by prisoners serving life sentences, and again found no differences between the rates of these crimes in jurisdictions with and without a death penalty. One of the great beauties of Sellin's work is that each study answers a question left unanswered or compensates for a methodological shortcoming in the previous works, in a classic demonstration of the incremental elegance of converging research methods. Numerous other researchers, working independently, reached the same conclusion: The death penalty has no detectable long-term effect on homicide. It is not a more effective deterrent than life imprisonment (see, Lempert, 1981; Dike, 1982, for comprehensive reviews).

Another possible type of deterrence might be called "immediate deterrence." Maybe deterrent effects exist, but are very short-lived, so that right after an execution when the death penalty is particularly salient in the mind of the potential murderer, homicide rates will drop. Although there is considerably less research on this topic, there is no evidence whatsoever of such deterrence. In fact there is some evidence that executions stimulate potential killers to kill sooner (Dann, 1935; Bowers and Pierce, 1980).

In 1972, in *Furman v. Georgia*, the constitutionality of the nation's death penalty laws became an open question. The Court held that all the capital punishment statutes then in effect violated the Eighth Amendment prohibition against cruel and unusual punishment, but stopped short of saying that capital punishment itself was unconstitutional. Most of the basic empirical questions that have figured in subsequent cases were raised in the opinions in *Furman,* but none were decided. Each of the Justices wrote an opinion detailing the considerations that he felt were important in deciding whether the death penalty was cruel and unusual. Instead of a coherent majority position, there were five separate one-vote opinions. Although deterrence was mentioned in several of the *Furman* opinions, only Justice Marshall explicitly cited the research, concluding that it proved that the death penalty was excessive, because its deterrent function could be served just as well by other penalties. Chief Justice Burger stated that no one had definitely proven that the death penalty was not a superior deterrent. However, in his view, empirical research on the issue was of no consequence, because deciding that sort of factual issue was not necessary or appropriate in interpreting the Eighth Amendment. Justice White accepted the argument that current death penalty laws had little deterrent effect (without citing studies), but reasoned that they were ineffective because hardly anyone was actually executed.

Although the social science research on deterrence was not discussed in any of the *Furman* opinions besides Justice Marshall's, it was probably influential in preventing any of the Justices from maintaining the simplistic common sense argument that the threat of death must be an effective deterrent, and therefore capital punishment is acceptable because it saves lives. The influence of empirical data cannot be completely evaluated by focusing only on what is said; it is also important to consider what might have been said had there been no data, or different data.

Since *Furman* had not said that capital punishment itself was unconstitutional, state legislatures hurried to enact death penalty laws that would pass constitutional muster. By 1976, when the next major capital punishment case was decided, 35 states had enacted new legislation. It was generally assumed that the main reason the pre-*Furman* laws were declared unconstitutional was that they permitted such unbridled discretion that there was no principled or systematic way of distinguishing among those who were sentenced to death and those who were not. Thus the *arbitrariness* of the death penalty was the central issue, but the issue of deterrence was also raised.

By 1976, however, the empirical record had also changed. Against the unanimity of the pre-*Furman* research on deterrence, a single new study was presented as part of the solicitor general's brief, purporting to show that executions deterred homicide. The study, by Isaac Ehrlich (1975) used complex statistical analysis and economic theory, and found a small but significant deterrent effect. Unlike Sellin's research, which could be readily understood by any graduate student or Supreme Court Justice who chose to read and consider it thoughtfully, Ehrlich's work could not easily be evaluated without specialized expertise. The brief against capital punishment included several equally complex analyses by other experts discrediting Ehrlich's work. By now it has been established that Ehrlich's claims were unfounded. The research record still shows no evidence that the death penalty is a more effective deterrent than life imprisonment (see, Dike, 1982; Lempert, 1981; Blumstein et al., 1986, for reviews of the empirical evidence).

In fact, most of the important criticisms of Ehrlich's work were before the Supreme Court in 1976, along with Ehrlich's study. The briefs on both sides devoted considerable space to equations, technical discussions, and theoretical and methodological disputes. Yet the deterrence question is mentioned in only one of the five cases that the Court considered in deciding whether capital punishment was constitutional, and even in that one it receives only the most superficial attention. Justice Stewart, in his lead opinion in *Gregg v. Georgia*, concluded that the evidence on deterrence is ambiguous, presumably because there was disagreement among the researchers: On the one hand, Ehrlich claimed to have found a deterrent effect; on the other hand, everyone else claimed not to, whether they were analyzing their own data or Ehrlich's. Stewart goes on, illogically, to argue that since the research record is inconclusive, the death penalty must be a significant deterrent to some people, and therefore that capital punishment is not without justification. Since 1976, research on deterrence has not played a major role in any of the numerous Supreme Court decisions on the death penalty.

Had Ehrlich's study not existed, or had its inadequacies been recognized, at least some of the Justices might have felt compelled to deal with the massive body of scientific research indicating that the death penalty could not be justified on the grounds that it prevents murders from occurring, because it does not.

Recognizing the inadequacies of Ehrlich's study would not have been an easy task for a Supreme Court Justice. Statistical analysis was not a form of reasoning that was familiar to the Justices, and the presentations in the briefs were quite abstruse; nonetheless, given a real willingness to try to understand the data, the task would not have been impossible.

Indeed, Justice Marshall's dissenting opinion contains an excellent critical analysis of the research, concluding that no deterrent effect had been found by Ehrlich or anyone else. It still stands as one of the most lucid analyses of complex empirical data to be found in a Supreme Court opinion.

The Justices joining the lead opinion chose a much easier method of dealing with the social science data, simply noting that there was disagreement in the scientific community, and apparently deciding, therefore, that such an "inconclusive" record need not be considered at all. Behind this is a tacit requirement of complete consensus within the social science community before its research on an issue even need be *considered,* a standard far beyond what is required for any other sort of evidence. The issue of deterrence was erased from serious consideration by a *single* dissenting voice from the research community. It is distressing to think that the most influential thing a social scientist can do is to give the Court an excuse to ignore some body of research.

If a similar body of research had been presented on a different issue, such as the relative deterrent efficacy of different sanctions in some area of administrative law, the Court's reaction probably would have been different. But when the death penalty is involved, lay people reason less rationally (Ellsworth and Ross, 1983), and so do Supreme Court Justices. When the data compel a conclusion that might threaten the institution of capital punishment, something must be done about the data. In the case of deterrence, the existence of one flimsy study contradicting a mass of consistent research allowed the Court to avoid considering the evidence on the grounds that "experts disagree."

RACIAL DISCRIMINATION

Although advocates of the death penalty readily incorporated Ehrlich's study into their arguments for capital punishment (e.g., van den Haag, 1975, and the brief for petitioner in *Gregg*), evidence of deterrence is not essential to a principled position in favor of the death penalty. An advocate might argue that even if the utilitarian functions of capital punishment could be served equally well by sentencing murderers to life in prison, the death penalty is justified because it is *just.* Those who commit the very worst crimes deserve the very worst penalty.

Evidence of racial discrimination in the imposition of the death penalty is disastrous to the argument that capital punishment is serving the ends of justice, because it means that many of those who actually receive the worst penalty are not those who have committed the worst crimes, but those who have the darkest complexions. The deterrence argument is that the death penalty is cruel and unusual because it is excessive—other penalties would work as well; the discrimination argument is that the death penalty is cruel and unusual because it is unfair. And the basis for this unfairness is one that the Court has found completely unacceptable in numerous other contexts. Being born black is no fault of the person, and it generally means a lifetime of slights, risks, and disadvantages, most of which are beyond the reach of the law to correct. The Supreme Court has been stern in combating racial discrimination in other contexts, such as racially imbalanced juries (*Strauder v. West Virginia*, 1880; *Batson v. Kentucky*, 1986), school segregation (*Brown v. Board of Education*, 1954), and employment discrimination (*Griggs v. Duke Power and Light Co.*, 1971). If the death penalty discriminates on the basis of race, not only the Eighth Amendment prohibition against cruel and unusual punishment is involved, but also the Equal Protection clause of the Fourteenth Amendment.

Like research on deterrence, research on discrimination in the application of the death penalty has a long history. In the nineteenth century, several state laws made certain crimes punishable by death if the offender was black, but not if he was white (Bowers, 1974). By the twentieth century the laws were gone, but most studies still showed that when arrested, blacks were more likely than whites to be indicted for capital crimes; when charged with capital crimes, blacks were more likely to be convicted; when convicted, blacks were more likely to be sentenced to death; and when sentenced to death, blacks were more likely to be executed (see Bowers, 1974; Dike, 1982). Racial effects were substantial across a variety of potentially criminal acts, and enormous for the crime of rape. Over the last hundred years hardly anyone has been executed for rape except in the southern and border states, and hardly any white man has been executed for rape anywhere in the country (Bowers, 1984). The most striking data were presented by Wolfgang and Reidel (1973) in a study of rape convictions and executions in 11 southern states from 1945 to 1965. They found that death sentences for rape had virtually disappeared except in cases in which the rapist was a black man and the victim was white: Black men accused of raping white women were 18 times more likely to sentenced to death than white rapists or black men accused of raping black women. Similar trends have been found in studies of death sentences for homicide (e.g., Zimring et al., 1976), although the disparities are less extreme.

Wolfgang and Reidel's data were considered and rejected by the Eighth Circuit in the case of *Maxwell v. Bishop* (1968) on the grounds that very few of the cases came from the jurisdiction in which Maxwell was tried; some factor other than race or the other variables that Wolfgang and Reidel had considered might have accounted for the disparity; and the study did not show that Maxwell's particular jury had been motivated by racial prejudice when they sentenced him to death. The Supreme Court vacated the judgment in *Maxwell* on other grounds, without touching the discrimination issue.

In 1972 the data on racial discrimination came before the Court again in *Furman*, as part of the more general argument that the death penalty was unconstitutional because the people who were executed were not the people who most deserved to die. If there was any systematic difference between those who were killed and those who were allowed to live, it was an unacceptable one, such as income, class, or, most obviously, race.

What little consensus there was in the *Furman* case seemed to converge on the conclusion that the imposition of the death penalty laws then in effect produced no *legitimate* distinction between the few who were selected to die and the many who were not. At best, death sentences were arbitrary and capricious. Most of the Justices shied away from addressing Wolfgang and Reidel's study directly, although it is difficult to imagine that it had no effect on their decision that the imposition of the death penalty under current laws was unfair. Only Justice Douglas and Justice Marshall explicitly asserted that the death penalty discriminated against the poor and the black. Justice Stewart based his opinion on arbitrariness. Death sentences were "cruel and unusual in the same way that being struck by lightning is cruel and unusual," although he also acknowledged that if there were any factor that particularly characterized those sentenced to death, it was the "constitutionally impermissible basis of race" (*Furman*, 1972, p. 310).

Like the research on deterrence, the research on discrimination was barely mentioned in the *Furman* opinions, but it was probably influential. The Court could have concluded that those who were sentenced to death were those who had committed the most heinous crimes. The Justices could have concluded that those who were sentenced to death were in the same groups that were the victims of discrimination in other social contexts. Or they could, as they did, conclude that there was no valid basis for distinguishing between those who were sentenced to death and those who were not: The system was arbitrary. The social science data may have persuaded a majority away from the first position, but some Justices may have chosen to emphasize the more neutral problem of arbitrariness rather than endorsing the much more inflammatory idea that black lives had been treated as more dispensable than white lives. After all, the immediate practical outcome was the same. Current death penalty laws were struck down, and current death sentences were canceled.

In *Gregg v. Georgia* (1976) and its companion cases, arbitrariness was the central issue. State laws that provided for mandatory death sentences for certain crimes were struck down, whereas state laws that provided standards by which the unbridled discretion rejected in *Furman* could be "suitably directed and limited" were upheld. Racial discrimination was not mentioned. Presumably a law that prevented arbitrariness by limiting the aggravating factors that could be considered in imposing the death penalty would also prevent racial discrimination. Once again, it is quite likely that the research on racial discrimination was disturbing to the majority Justices, but that they felt that in endorsing the guided discretion statutes they could solve the problem without acknowledging it.

In 1977, a case came before the Supreme Court that many observers felt would force the Court to deal with the issue of racial discrimination directly. It was the case of *Coker v. Georgia,* raising the issue of the constitutionality of capital punishment for the crime of rape. The evidence, as we have seen, indicated that the death penalty for rape had long since been practically abandoned, except for black men who raped white women. Racial prejudice seemed the unavoidable conclusion.

The Court in *Coker* did avoid reaching that conclusion, however. In fact it avoided any mention of the research on racial patterns in capital sentencing for rape. Instead, the Court held that capital punishment for rape was unconstitutional because it was grossly disproportionate to the severity of the crime and therefore excessive. Again, the Court reached the conclusion that would be compelled by the data on racial discrimination, but reached it on other grounds. Curiously enough, the Court actually based its finding that the death penalty was disproportionate on empirical data, of a sort. Justice White, in the lead opinion, argued that public attitudes toward a penalty should be considered in deciding whether that penalty was excessive for a particular crime. As a means of ascertaining public attitudes, he examined the history of the death penalty for rape, pointing out that few national or international jurisdictions still punished rape by death, and that although after the *Furman* decision many states reenacted death penalty statutes for murder, they did not do so for rape. He also pointed out that even when the death penalty was allowed for rape, juries hardly ever imposed it, opting for a lesser penalty in 9 out of 10 cases, thus indicating that the public felt it was excessive. (Of course he avoided all mention of the racial factors distinguishing those rare cases in which the juries did sentence rapists to death. He also neglected to mention that the jury chooses a penalty less than death in 8 out of 10 murder cases.)[3] He even cited public opinion poll data. In sum, it is hard to resist the conclusion that the Court went out of its way to avoid basing its decision on the powerful empirical evidence of racial discrimination, even to the extent of citing much more fragmentary empirical data on another issue.

After 1972 state legislatures that favored the death penalty drafted new statutes designed to protect against the arbitrary and discriminatory imposition of capital punishment that had been held unconstitutional in *Furman*. In *Gregg v. Georgia* (1976) the Court found acceptable Georgia's new statute, which provided for a bifurcated trial with guilt decided at the first phase, followed by a separate sentencing phase in which new evidence might be introduced to help the jury decide whether the defendant should live or die. Factors that the jurors were permitted to consider as aggravating or mitigating the crime were enumerated, and provision was made for the Georgia Supreme Court to review all cases to make sure that the system was working properly—that the death penalty was reserved for the most aggravated cases. Similar statutes in Texas and Florida were upheld in the companion cases to *Gregg* (*Jurek v. Texas,* 1976; *Proffitt v. Florida,* 1976), and, by implication, all statutes employing comparable methods of limiting the jury's discretion were held to be constitutional.

Because the laws had changed, pre-*Furman* data were no longer sufficient to demonstrate racial discrimination. The question now was whether the new guided discretion statutes did what they were intended: to prevent arbitrariness and discrimination. A crude examination of America's death row population suggested no improvement: In 1971, just before the *Furman* decision, 53% of the people on death row were nonwhite; in 1978, 62% were nonwhite (Reidel, 1976). Raw figures, however, were no longer enough. Research on discrimination had become substantially more sophisticated, and the courts were becoming much more accustomed to complex statistical analyses in other kinds of discrimination cases. However overwhelming the raw figures, litigators assumed that they would be insufficient to prove discrimination. They had to prove not only that blacks were disproportionately sentenced to death, but that they were sentenced to death *because they were black,* not because they had committed more aggravated murders. If they could not prove that race was the reason, they had at least to prove that no other *legitimate* reason distinguished the blacks on death row from murderers who were sentenced to life imprisonment.

By 1980, eight years after the *Furman* decision, studies of the racial consequences of the post-*Furman* guided discretion statutes began to appear. Bowers and Pierce (1980) found that in Georgia, Florida, Texas, and Ohio (these states accounted for about 70% of the death sentences in the time period studied), a familiar pattern emerged: "Black killers and the killers of whites were more likely to receive the death penalty in all four states, with black killers of white victims overwhelmingly more likely to receive the death sentence" (Dike, 1982, p. 49; see also Zeisel, 1981). With increasingly sophisticated statistical controls, later studies found that the effect of the defendant's race could not conclusively be shown to have an effect independent of the effects of legitimate aggravating factors such as committing murder in the course of another felony or killing a stranger. This means that it is impossible to tell whether the reason blacks are more likely than whites to be sentenced to death is that they are black. The race-of-victim effect, however, continues to show up strongly in the best-controlled studies; killing a white person is much more likely to result in a death sentence than is killing a black person (Radelet, 1981 [Florida]; Radelet and Pierce, 1985 [Florida capital charges]; Jacoby and Paternoster, 1982 [South Carolina capital charges]; Gross and Mauro, 1984 [eight states]). In one study the researchers collected data on over 400 variables in over a thousand Georgia homicide prosecutions and found that nothing could explain away the discrimination against defendants who killed white people (Baldus et al., 1983). Some 10 years later, it is clear that the guided discretion statutes endorsed in *Gregg v. Georgia* have not succeeded in preventing capital sentencing from being contaminated by the "constitutionally impermissible basis of race."

The issue and the new data came before the Court in the recent case of *McCleskey v. Kemp* (1987). The social science research on race-of-victim effects were the core of the case, and this time there was no way the Court could avoid facing the problem of racial discrimination in capital sentencing.

Writing for the majority, Justice Powell made a faint-hearted attempt to question the conclusiveness of the research by arguing that the correlational data presented could not actually *prove* that race was the cause of the sentencing disparities. However, the Baldus study had controlled for over 200 other variables and found that none of them, alone or in combination, could explain the pattern of racial discrimination, and neither Justice Powell nor anyone else was able to come up with any other explanation for the racial effects. History, common sense, and the data all overwhelmingly supported the simple, obvious explanation. The racial effects were due to race. The majority, however, repeatedly referred to the correlation of death sentences with race as "unexplained," for example, "where the discretion that is fundamental to our criminal process is involved, we decline to assume that what is unexplained is invidious" (*McCleskey v. Kemp*, 107 S. Ct. 1756, 1778 [1987]).

The opinion is also written to make the death penalty invulnerable to any future statistical challenges based on race, by holding that proof of racial discrimination requires a demonstration of conscious, intentional racial discrimination in the drafting of the law or the decision in the particular case. That is, in order to succeed with a claim of racial discrimination, a defendant must prove either (1) "that the decision makers in *his* case acted with discriminatory purpose" [emphasis in original] (107 S. Ct. at 1766), or (2) "that the Georgia legislature enacted or maintained the death penalty statute *because of* an anticipated racially discriminatory effect" [emphasis in original] (107 S. Ct. at 1769).

A juror or a prosecutor must come forth and admit that McCleskey was sentenced to death because he was black and he killed a white man, a highly unlikely event because neither jurors nor prosecutors are asked to account for their decisions, and even if they were, they would almost always be unable or unwilling to say that race was a factor. Or, a legislature must come forth and admit that the capital punishment statute was designed to produce racial bias. Otherwise, the Equal Protection clause does not apply.

Once again it is clear that the majority Justices (five of them, in *McCleskey*) value the death penalty so highly that they are willing to ignore the inescapable implications of the social science research and to undermine fundamental constitutional guarantees. The majority admitted that the system for deciding who lives and who dies is imperfect, and conceded that the evidence of discrimination found in the Baldus study would have been persuasive if the case had involved discrimination in jury selection or employment. Traditionally, the Court has assumed that the decision to impose the death penalty should be safeguarded with higher standards of fairness than other sorts of legal decisions. In *McCleskey*, the Court has reversed this traditional attitude. Empirical evidence that would be sufficient to protect McCleskey's job was not considered sufficient to save his life.

Finally, the majority spent some time describing the sanctity of trial by jury, and their reluctance to tamper with the collective discretion of a representative jury of one's peers. The jury, "representative of a criminal defendant's community, assures a 'diffused impartiality,' in the jury's task of 'expressing the conscience of the community on the ultimate question of life or death'" (107 S. Ct. at 1776, citations omitted). However, as we shall see in the next section, the Court had already held that juries in capital cases are not required to be as fair or as representative of community opinion as juries in other cases.

DEATH-QUALIFIED JURIES

The issue of death qualification also raises questions about the fairness of the administration of capital punishment laws, but it is limited to a procedure—the refusal to allow citizens who adamantly oppose the death penalty to serve as jurors in capital cases. Jurors who state that they cannot consider imposing the death penalty are not allowed to participate in the decision between death and life imprisonment, and hardly anyone has seriously questioned this practice.[4] However, these opponents of the death penalty are also excluded from the jury that decides whether a person charged with a capital crime is guilty or innocent of the crime, even when they state that they would be entirely fair and impartial in weighing the evidence on guilt or innocence. Thus in capital cases, unlike all other cases, the jury that decides guilt or innocence is made up exclusively of people who would be willing to sentence a person to death. The empirical question is: Is such a "death-qualified" jury more likely than an ordinary jury to decide that the defendant is guilty?

Most trial attorneys assume the biasing effects of death qualification as a matter of common sense. Jurors who favor executions tend to favor the arguments of the prosecution, whereas jurors who reject the death penalty are more sympathetic to the defense. Even prosecutors occasionally admit to using death qualification in order to get a jury that is more likely to convict (Oberer, 1961). But lawyers' intuitions are not evidence. The issue first came before the U.S. Supreme Court in 1968 in the case of *Witherspoon v. Illinois* (1968). Nearly half of the jurors called to hear Witherspoon's case had been excused because of their "conscientious scruples" against the death penalty, and Witherspoon argued that his jury was therefore biased toward conviction. He supported his case with preliminary reports of three unpublished studies showing a relationship between attitudes toward capital punishment and propensity to convict. The Court rejected the empirical data as "too tentative and fragmentary" to demonstrate a bias toward conviction, and it held that a modified form of death qualification, excluding only the most adamant opponents of the death penalty, was constitutionally permissible. However, the Court acknowledged that the question was an empirical one, that its decision was a provisional one, made "in the light of the presently available information" (*Witherspoon v. Illinois,* 1968, p. 518), and that future research might demonstrate that Witherspoon's claims were correct.

By the time the issue came back to the Supreme Court in 1968, there were 15 empirical studies in the record. They had been conducted over a span of three decades, using a variety of samples from different areas of the country, a variety of questions designed to identify the excluded group, and a variety of different research methods. Attitude surveys of random samples of the public were used to discover the size and racial composition of the excluded group and to examine the correlation between attitudes toward the death penalty and predispositions to favor the prosecution or defense. Simulations were used for a direct examination of the relation between death penalty attitudes and verdicts across a range of cases. Interviews with actual jurors were used to establish that attitudes toward the death penalty predicted verdicts in real cases. Another study examined the biasing effects of the death-qualifying voir dire itself, and still others looked at the effects of death qualification on the quality of jury deliberation. Without exception, the studies found that death-qualified jurors were more favorable to the prosecution and more likely to vote guilty than the citizens who are excluded from the jury.

For many reasons, death qualification is a particularly interesting context in which to examine the Court's response to empirical data related to capital punishment. First, the empirical question was posed by the Court itself, in *Witherspoon.* Thus the Court ought to be unusually receptive to empirical research specifically designed to answer that question. And the Court not only posed the question, but stated that the holding in *Witherspoon* might be reversed if new evidence established that death-qualified juries were "less than neutral with respect to *guilt*" (*Witherspoon v. Illinois,* 1968, p. 520, n. 18, emphasis in original).

Second, the constitutional issue was a Sixth Amendment issue, one involving the fairness of the jury, rather than an Eighth Amendment issue challenging the constitutionality of capital punishment per se. In the past, the Court had shown considerable willingness to consider social science data in cases involving jury composition (cf. *Williams v. Florida,* (1968); *Colgrove v. Battin,* (1973); *Ballew v. Georgia,* (1978).[5]

Third, the studies themselves were easy to understand. In most of the studies two groups of people were compared, and the main data took the form of percentages of each group favoring proprosecution attitudes or voting guilty. The basic argument did not hinge on complex regression equations or mathematical models. And of course the data agreed with the "common sense" of most people familiar with the criminal justice system.

Fourth, the social science data were immune from the criticism that the data were introduced into the decision making process too late to have received careful critical evaluation from the lower courts. This criticism was clearly stated by Justice Powell in his concurring opinion in *Ballew v. Georgia* (1978):

> I have reservations as to the wisdom—as well as the necessity—of Mr. Justice Blackmun's heavy reliance on numerology derived from statistical studies. Moreover, neither the validity nor the methodology employed by the studies cited was subjected to the traditional testing mechanisms of the adversary process. The studies relied on merely represent unexamined findings of persons interested in the jury system [p. 246].

The new data on death qualification had been introduced in an evidentiary hearing that lasted several weeks, with testimony by five expert witnesses for the defense and two for the prosecution (*People v. Moore,* August-September, 1979). The California Supreme Court, in *Hovey v. Superior Court* (1980), carried out an extraordinarily thorough evaluation of the empirical record, perhaps the most knowledgeable analysis of social science data yet to appear in an appellate court opinion. The California Supreme Court concluded that excluding jurors according to the *Witherspoon* standard did create juries that were unconstitutionally biased toward guilty verdicts, but questioned the applicability of the research to California juries, because in California, jurors at the opposite end of the attitudinal spectrum could also be excluded for cause. These are the jurors who state that they would be unable to consider a penalty less than death for anyone convicted of a potential capital crime, regardless of the circumstances.

Subsequent research indicated that the number of people so bloodthirsty that they would automatically vote for death without regard for the evidence is minuscule—only 1% of the population (Louis Harris, 1981), far too few to correct the bias toward guilty verdicts created by death qualification (Kadane, 1984). In 1981 an evidentiary hearing was conducted before the U.S. District Court for the Eastern District of Arkansas, when all the *Hovey* research was presented in addition to the new evidence on "automatic death penalty" jurors. Again, experts testified on both sides, and the *Hovey* record was introduced in evidence. Again, the court evaluated the research very carefully and concluded that the practice of death qualification created juries that were unconstitutionally biased against the defendant (*Grigsby v. Mabry,* 1983). The state appealed but the Eighth Circuit affirmed (*Grigsby v. Mabry,* 1985). The *Grigsby* record, which included the *Hovey* record, reached the U.S. Supreme Court in the case of *Lockhart v. McCree* (1986).[6] Thus the data on death qualification had abundantly fulfilled Justice Powell's requirement that they be subjected to the "traditional testing mechanisms of the adversary system," having been scrutinized in 26 days of evidentiary hearings and evaluated in 145 pages of appellate court opinions.

Fifth, the Justices could not avoid evaluating the data, as they had avoided the data on deterrence, by concluding that there was a lack of consensus among the experts. Although the state tried to argue that the social scientists' use of different research *methods* revealed a lack of consensus, all 15 of the studies reached the same *result*. As the American Psychological Association (APA) argued in its amicus brief, "the use of diverse subjects, stimulus materials, and empirical methods does not reveal a 'lack of consensus' but comports fully with the goal of 'generalization,' the accepted rubric for evaluating how far beyond the specific facts of any one particular study one can apply its findings." Few bodies of social science research have shown such consistency across times, places, groups, and methods. The only "study" that failed to find a difference in conviction rates is one that simply compared conviction rates in murder trials with those in robbery and burglary trials. No prosecution expert was willing to present this study as evidence, and no lower court found it worthy of consideration. In general, the prosecution experts made minor methodological criticisms and conceded many of the defense's empirical claims. No studies were introduced that contradicted those claims; the research record was uncontroverted. The state's brief attacked the research primarily with vague global statements about the "pseudoscientific" nature of social science research in general.

Finally, it would be very difficult for the Court to do what it did with the issue of racial discrimination in the pre-*McCleskey* cases—make a decision consistent with the research without mentioning the research itself. The whole case was built on the empirical proposition, raised in *Witherspoon*, that death qualification creates juries that are unlike all other juries in that they are "less than neutral with respect to guilt."[7]

However, by 1986 there were over 1,500 people on death rows across the country, most of whom had been convicted by death-qualified juries. There were many more people serving life sentences who had also been convicted by death-qualified juries. If the Court admitted that death qualification unfairly prejudices the jury against capital defendants, what would happen to these people? A decision in line with the evidence would raise enormous legal and moral questions about retroactivity. It seems quite possible, even probable, that if the practice of death qualification had not existed before, and some state had attempted to introduce it as a new restriction on the normal process of jury selection, the Court would have found the data persuasive, and declared the procedure unconstitutional. But the political and practical consequences of such a decision in 1986 were extremely unpalatable. Thus, as in *McCleskey*, the Court was faced with a substantial, consistent, and highly persuasive body of data that pointed to a conclusion opposite to the one the majority wanted to reach.

Given that the Court was determined to come out in favor of death qualification, its decision was bound to be disappointing to the social science research community. The actual decision was worse than disappointing; it was lamentable. Justice Rehnquist, writing for the majority, first attacked the research in ways that suggested that the majority Justices had either not understood it or not read it, or that they just didn't care. He then declared that it didn't matter how compelling the data might be, because it is constitutionally permissible to try capital cases before juries that are biased toward guilty verdicts. In short, "we don't believe the data, but if we did it wouldn't matter."

In the discussion that follows, I shall review the *Lockhart* opinion's criticisms of the empirical data. In most instances, the same issues had been reviewed in the *Grigsby* and *Hovey* opinions, and, when appropriate, I shall compare the three courts' methods of dealing with them.

1. *The data are insufficient.* In 1968, the Court in *Witherspoon* rejected the existing studies as "too tentative and fragmentary to establish that jurors not opposed to the death penalty tend to favor the prosecution in the determination of guilt" (p. 527). Most social scientists would have agreed with this assessment. The Court had before it incomplete, preliminary versions of three studies. Most social scientists would recognize, however, that as new investigations accumulated, all confirming the original conclusions, the research became less tentative and fragmentary, and correspondingly more definite and complete. Courts, however, have sometimes seemed to regard the phrase "tentative and fragmentary" as having a binding precedential force on all research that might be done on death qualification (Gross, 1984).

In *Lockhart*, Justice Rehnquist also concluded that the data were insufficient to form the basis of a constitutional rule, but he did so in a slightly more sophisticated manner. The 15 studies were lined up, and each of them was found to have a flaw; each time a flaw was discovered, the study was eliminated from the set until only one study was left. "Surely," concluded Justice Rehnquist, "a 'per se constitutional rule' as far-reaching as the one McCree proposes should not be based on the results of the lone study that avoids this fundamental flaw" (*Lockhart*, 1986, p. 1764).

The first "flaw," accounting for the elimination of 8 of the 15 studies, was that the studies "dealt solely with generalized attitudes and beliefs about the death penalty and other aspects of the criminal justice system" (*Lockhart* 1986, p. 1762). In fact, several of these studies measured attitudes about the death penalty precisely in the terms defined by *Witherspoon*, and in all of them the attitudes about "other aspects of the criminal justice system" directly reflected a proprosecution (and therefore proconviction) bias. Among these attitudes, for example, are the belief that defense attorneys are less trustworthy than prosecutors are, that defendants who do not testify are guilty, that the insanity defense is a loophole for guilty defendants, and that a confession should be considered even if the judge rules it inadmissible. The emergence of the same relation between death penalty and proprosecution attitudes in every study indicates that the exact wording of the question is not important. Wherever the line between death-qualified and excludable citizens is drawn, the former group will hold attitudes more favorable to the prosecution. The relevance of studies involving attitudes toward the criminal justice system is strongly suggested by (1) the direct connection between the attitudes measured and the jurors' task, (2) the argument that the excluded jurors share a perspective that is different from that of the qualified jurors, and (3) the fact that the attitudinal studies and the more direct studies of conviction rates reach identical conclusions. Both the *Hovey* opinion and the *Grigsby* opinion explicitly considered the relevance of the attitudinal studies, and found that, *taken in conjunction with the other studies*, they were important. Here, as elsewhere, the *Lockhart* opinion chose to ignore the conclusions reached by the "traditional testing mechanisms of the adversary system."

One study (Haney, 1984) showed that the very process of questioning jurors intensively about their attitudes toward capital punishment before the trial suggested to the jurors that the defendant was probably guilty. Thus added to the bias caused by the composition of the jury was a bias caused by the experience of the death-qualifying *voir dire*. This study was dismissed from consideration because it "would not, standing alone, give rise to a constitutional violation," (*Lockhart*, 1986, p. 1763). Again the Court's logic seems to be that if each study is insufficient evidence on its own, then all 15 put together must also be insufficient. If one payment, standing alone, is insufficient to buy a house, then it should not be considered in conjunction with others in assessing the means of the purchaser.

Three studies were rejected because they were the studies that had been before the Court in *Witherspoon*, albeit in preliminary form: "It goes almost without saying that if these studies were 'too tentative and fragmentary' to make out a claim of constitutional error in 1968, the same studies, unchanged but for having aged some 18 years, are still insufficient to make out such a claim in this case" (*Lockhart*, 1986, p. 1763). In fact, the studies were not "unchanged"; preliminary drafts had become completed, fully-documented reports. The briefs and the lower court opinions were clear on this point. More important, the conclusions of the first study on a new research topic are nearly always "tentative." It takes replication to establish the truth and generality of a scientific finding and in turn to establish the validity of the early work. Having been replicated, the early conclusions were no longer tentative. The Supreme Court's assessment of the early research is analogous to claiming that Alexander Fleming's discovery of penicillin is of trivial medical importance because in 1930 the scientific community felt that the prospects for using it to cure infections in humans were discouraging.

Two of the studies demonstrating conviction-proneness were rejected because they did not include jury deliberation and because they did not identify and exclude jurors who might admit to being unable to make a fair decision on the guilt of a capital defendant. No explanation was given for why deliberation is essential, and indeed, research on juries has consistently shown that the distribution of individual first-ballot verdicts is a very good predictor of the final jury verdict (Kalven and Zeisel, 1966; Hastie et al., 1983). Several of the studies rejected on other grounds did identify and exclude people who could not judge guilt fairly, and the overall bias was demonstrated in these studies as strongly or more strongly than in the studies that did not take this precaution.

The "flaws" identified in individual studies were in no instance fatal flaws. But more important, the one-by-one elimination of studies from a consistent body of research shows an ignorance of the principle of convergent validity. The idea that new scientific truths are proven by means of a single, perfect, definitive experiment is generally mistaken. Typically there are numerous sources of error and numerous confounding variables that must be controlled, and typically it is impossible to control them all in a single study. Thus the scientist must triangulate in on the truth by ruling out some alternative explanations in some experiments and other alternative explanations in other experiments until only one explanation is left that can account for the results of all the experiments. This is the method of convergent validation. If all the studies share the same shortcoming, then that shortcoming may be a possible alternative explanation that has not yet been ruled out. But if the experiments have different limitations, then none of the limitations can serve as an explanation for a result that is consistent across all the experiments.

For example, in order to show that death-qualified jurors vote guilty more often than the jurors who are normally excluded, it is important to demonstrate that in response to the *very same trial* more of the death-qualified jurors vote guilty. Since in the "real world" each case is tried only once, before a single jury, the only way to expose many juries to the very same trial is to conduct a simulation, as Cowan et al. (1984) did. Simulations can always be criticized, however, on the grounds that people may behave differently on real juries.

In this case, the argument might be that on real juries people's verdicts are not influenced by their attitudes toward the death penalty. Zeisel's (1968) study of actual jurors, though lacking the control of the

Cowan et al. study, showed that the correlation between death penalty attitudes and guilty votes is not restricted to simulated juries. The fact that both studies reached the same result shows that this result could not be due to any "flaw" unique to either study. If 10 studies were done to test the effectiveness of a new drug, five on samples of women and five on samples of men, and all showed that the drug cured the disease, the logic of the *Lockhart* opinion would compel the conclusion that we have no information about the drug's effectiveness, since five of the studies should be dropped from consideration because they included no women, and the other five because they included no men, leaving not a single study. The lower court opinions in *Hovey* and in *Grigsby* contained extensive discussions of the principle of convergent validation and the necessity of viewing the studies "as a whole, not in isolation" (*Hovey,* 1980, p. 1343). The APA brief in *Lockhart* contained a clear account of the value of convergent validation, as did the dissenting opinion:

> The chief strength of respondent's evidence lies in the essential unanimity of the results obtained by researchers using diverse subjects and varied methodologies. Even the Court's haphazard jibes cannot obscure the power of the array. (*Lockhart,* 1986, Marshall, J., dissenting, p. 1773).

Nonetheless, the majority managed to miss the point.

2. *No bias exists because none of the jurors who tried McCree was biased.*

Having completed its excursion into the unfamiliar realm of social science criticism, the Court returned to its own turf—the close analysis of the individual case—and focused on McCree's particular jury. Since the 12 people who served on McCree's jury had all said they could judge the case impartially, the Court concluded that it was therefore a neutral jury. The social scientists argued that across many trials it could be demonstrated that juries comprised only of death-qualified jurors were not neutral, because the proportion of guilty verdicts would be higher than it would be in juries that included the whole spectrum of death penalty attitudes. The probability of guilty verdicts is affected by the group that is not there—just as it would be if Catholics (or atheists) were never allowed on juries in abortion cases. Social scientists are trained to think in terms of comparison. Death-qualified juries are not biased or unbiased in some absolute sense; rather they are biased toward guilty verdicts relative to the juries that try all other cases in American courts. Following the Court's reasoning, it would be constitutional to exclude all Republicans, or all people with a college education, or any other group, as long as 12 impartial jurors remained.

Although aggregate, comparative statistical reasoning is uncommon for courts, it is by no means beyond their capacity. In *Ballew v. Georgia* (1978) the Supreme Court considered a variety of empirical studies of jury size and concluded that juries composed of only five people were unconstitutional; the Court did not examine the competence of the particular group of five people who tried Ballew, but reached a general conclusion based on general data. More to the point, the Court in *Witherspoon* found that by excluding all opponents of the death penalty from the penalty decision, "the state crossed the line of neutrality. In its quest for a jury capable of imposing the death penalty, the state produced a jury uncommonly willing to condemn a man to die" (*Witherspoon,* 1968, p. 520-521). The fact that the 12 people who did try Witherspoon's case all said that they could be fair and impartial was irrelevant. The logic of the Court's decision on bias at the penalty phase of *Witherspoon* was exactly the same as the logic of the argument on bias at the guilt phase in McCree's case.

The *Lockhart* Court bolstered its faulty reasoning with two other spurious arguments. The majority opinion claimed that McCree was asking that every single jury be perfectly representative of the community, with "the proper number of Democrats and Republicans, young persons and old persons, white-collar executives and blue-collar laborers, and so on" (*Lockhart,* 1986, p. 1767). McCree's brief is quite explicit on this point, admitting that "no defendant can demand that all elements of the community be included on his or her jury," but arguing that no state has the "right to remove an entire class of jurors from every capital jury." (*McCree,* brief, p. 88). For example, if I were on trial, I could not claim unfairness if, by the luck of the draw, there were no female professors on my jury. But I could reasonably claim unfairness if, at the beginning of jury selection, the judge told all the female professors in the room that they were disqualified from serving in my case. The *Lockhart* Court confused these two very different positions.

Finally, the Court argued that there is no problem because McCree might have gotten the very same jury by chance, even if death qualification did not exist: "[I]t is hard for us to understand the logic of the argument that a given jury is unconstitutionally partial when it results from a state-ordained process, yet impartial when exactly the same jury results from mere chance" (*Lockhart,* 1986, p. 1767). Leaving aside the fact that the likelihood that McCree would have gotten "exactly the same jury" by chance is minuscule, the idea that any practice is constitutional as long as any particular consequence of that practice could have occurred by chance is astounding. All-white juries are possible by chance; therefore blacks may be banned from jury service. A defendant might have confessed to a crime inadvertently; therefore defendants may be forced to confess. Or Mr. McCree could argue that the woman he was accused of killing might by chance have been struck by lightning that day, so why was his act illegal?

Again, the lower court opinions avoided these mistakes, recognizing that it was necessary to compare one type of jury with the other, not simply to examine the 12 jurors in a particular case:

> The issue is not whether non-death-qualified jurors are acquittal prone or death-qualification jurors are conviction prone. The real issue is whether a death-qualified jury is more prone to convict than the juries used in non-capital criminal cases—juries which include the full spectrum of attitudes and perspectives regarding capital punishment [*Grigsby v. Mabry,* 1985, p. 241, note 31].

> It can be confidently asserted that, over time, some persons accused of capital crimes will be convicted of offenses—and to a higher degree—who would not be so convicted if the jury were more representative of the populace [*Hovey v. Superior Court,* 1980, p. 1314, note 57].

3. *The excluded jurors are not a distinctive group.* The majority opinion held that death-qualified jurors were not a "distinctive group" whose elimination would impair jury representativeness. From the perspective of social science, the excluded jurors are obviously a distinctive group. They can easily be distinguished from other jurors on the basis of their answers to a few simple questions asked during the voir dire and in study after study their attitudes and behavior have been significantly different from those of other jurors.

In this case the obvious social science argument is insufficient to answer the legal question. Most previous cases on jury representativeness had dealt with the exclusion of blacks, women, or Mexican Americans, groups that have enjoyed special constitutional protection in recent years. Although one of the justifications for including these groups on juries was that the absence of their distinctive attitudes and perspectives would result in a jury that did not reflect the common-sense judgment of the whole community, it was not the only justification. There was also the need to eliminate formal discrimination against these historically disadvantaged groups.

During oral argument in *Lockhart,* McCree's counsel was asked numerous questions about other attitudinal groups that might claim a constitutional right to representation on juries. Some Justices may have feared that the case could set a dangerous precedent. McCree's counsel argued first of all, that no other attitudinal group of fair and impartial jurors was automatically excluded from jury service, and second, that no other attitudes had been found to affect verdicts as powerfully as attitudes toward the death penalty. Judge Eisele, in the District Court opinion in *Grigsby v. Mabry* (1983) concluded that shared attitudes were an insufficient criterion to define a constitutionally "distinctive" group unless it could be shown that the presence or absence of those attitudes actually affected the functioning of the jury. He went on to conclude that the attitudinal exclusion created by death qualification had a substantial adverse effect on the functioning of the jury and thus was unconstitutional. He also pointed out that the representation of unimpeachably cognizable groups was impaired by the process of death qualification because blacks and women are more likely to be excluded are than white males.

Justice Rehnquist chose not to follow this reasoning, holding for the majority in *Lockhart* that a group defined solely in terms of shared attitudes is not a constitutionally distinctive group that needs to be considered in assessing jury representativeness. "Unlike blacks, women, and Mexican-Americans, '*Witherspoon*-excludables' are singled out for exclusion in capital cases on the basis of an attribute that is within the individual's control" (*Lockhart,* 1986, p. 1766). This analysis may also lead some observers to fear a dangerous precedent, suggesting that citizens may be banned from jury service on the basis of unpopular religious or other beliefs.

4. *The constitutional requirement of representativeness is satisfied if the jury pool is representative.* The majority opinion in *Lockhart* cited several precedents holding that the right to a representative jury did not mean that every single group of 12 citizens who sit as a jury must proportionally reproduce the characteristics of the population: "The point at which an accused is entitled to a fair cross-section of the community is when the names are put in the box from which the panels are drawn" (Justice Blackmun, *Pope v. United States* (1971), cited in

Lockhart, (1986, p. 1765). McCree, of course, was not arguing that his jury must include people adamantly opposed to the death penalty, but that such a person must have the same *chance* of inclusion as a death-qualified juror. To say that the fair cross-section requirement was met because the names of these people were put in the box from which the panels were drawn is a childish effort at sleight-of-hand. One doesn't have to have any statistical training to realize that in order to achieve representativeness, the names must not only be put in the box, they must still be in the box when the names of the actual panel members are drawn. True, the names of the death-penalty opponents are put in the box, but then they are all taken out again, and then the actual jury is drawn. Obviously, their chances of serving on a capital jury are exactly the same as if they had never had their names in the box at all: zero.

Again, the courts in *Hovey* and *Grigsby* avoided this error. The opinion in *Grigsby,* which was reversed by the *Lockhart* decision, explicitly stated:

[1] Any implication by the dissent suggesting the majority requires representation of all cognizable groups on each petit jury is misplaced. [cites omitted] Our holding simply forbids the systematic exclusion of any cognizable group from a petit jury" [*Grigsby v. Mabry,* (1985) p. 230, n. 6].

and

[2] There is no functional difference between excluding a particular group of eligible citizens from the "jury wheels, pools of names, panels or veniires from which juries are drawn" and systematically excluding them from sitting on a petit jury [cites omitted]. The result is the same in either case: a distinct group of the citizenry is prevented from being considered for service on petit juries [*Grigsby,* 1985, p. 230, n. 7].

5. *The state has a legitimate interest in a single jury to decide both guilt and penalty.* The *Witherspoon* opinion explicitly recognized that if future research established that death-qualified juries were

less than neutral with respect to *guilt* . . . the question would then arise whether the state's interest in submitting the penalty issue to a jury capable of imposing capital punishment may be vindicated at the expense of the defendant's interest in a completely fair

determination of guilt or innocence—given the possibility of
accommodating both interests by means of a bifurcated trial
[*Witherspoon*, 1968, p. 520, n. 18].

Justice Rehnquist did not admit that the bias of death-qualified juries
had been established, but he did go on to argue that the state had a
legitimate interest in "obtaining a single jury that could impartially
decide all of the issues in McCree's case" (*Lockhart,* 1986, p. 1768).
Neither the state's brief nor the opinion in *Lockhart* is very clear in
explaining why a single jury system serves an important state interest.

One argument that was repeatedly raised in the brief and at oral
argument was that the excluded jurors were people who would not
follow state law, and the state had a legitimate interest in keeping
lawbreakers off the jury. Since the excluded jurors were lawbreakers
only in the sense that they would not vote to execute anyone, this
argument simply restates the basic issue. The group in question included
only people who said they *could* follow state law in deciding guilt or
innocence, and they were asking only to be included in the guilt/inno-
cence stage of the trial. Thus the state's interest in a single jury is not
really addressed by this argument.

A second argument was that having two separate juries would be
costly and inefficient. The Court seemed to assume that the only remedy
would be to have two entirely different groups of jurors decide guilt and
penalty, although various other methods, less expensive and less
cumbersome, had been suggested in the lower court opinion (*Grigsby v.
Mabry*, 1985). In any case the cost/efficiency argument was never very
explicit, perhaps because it seemed tasteless to weigh such considerations
against the fairness of the trial.

Finally, the Court reiterated an argument that had first been made in
Smith v. Balkcom (1981) and had become standard in court decisions
that found that death qualification was constitutional. Even though a
juror is convinced beyond a reasonable doubt when he or she votes to
convict a defendant, there still may be some residual, "whimsical"
doubts about the evidence. These residual doubts might cause the juror
to hesitate to execute the defendant; thus it is in the *defendant's* best
interest to have the same jurors decide both guilt and penalty in order to
profit from the mercy associated with whimsical doubts.

Whether such residual doubts are common and whether they result in
a reluctance to vote for death are, of course, empirical questions, just as
surely as the conviction-proneness of death-qualified jurors is an

empirical question. The difference is that there is not a scrap of empirical evidence on the residual doubt question.[8] Yet the Court rejects the evidence on conviction-proneness because 14 of the 15 studies have some flaw, and endorses the residual doubt argument based on no evidence whatsoever. And of course the argument that a single jury increases one's chances for a sentence of life imprisonment rather than death is likely to seem cold comfort to a defendant who believes he was unfairly convicted in the first place. As Finch and Ferraro (1986) argue, "The trade-off suggested by the court—a more conviction-prone jury for a less death-prone jury—seems one that the accused is unlikely to make" (p. 69-70, n. 169).

6. *None of the research examined real jurors' decisions in real capital cases.* There is one criticism made by the majority in *Lockhart* that applies to all of the empirical research. The studies investigated the behavior of people "who were not actual jurors sworn under oath to apply the law to the facts of an actual case involving the fate of an actual capital defendant" (*Lockhart,* 1986, p. 1763). Zeisel's study had investigated the behavior of sworn jurors in actual felony cases, but they were not capital cases. Of course the very existence of the questionable practice makes it impossible to carry out the "perfect" research to condemn or exonerate the practice. If no *Witherspoon*-excludable citizens are allowed on the jury in any capital case, then it is impossible to discover how their behavior might differ from that of the death-qualified jurors, and the suggestion in *Witherspoon* that future research might establish a bias toward guilt in death-qualified juries becomes meaningless. The *Witherspoon* court assumed that the question could be answered empirically; the *Lockhart* decision seemed to assume that it can not, at least not in this world.

The decisions in *Hovey* and *Grigsby* recognized that the "perfect" experiment would have two juries hearing each of a large number of capital cases, one jury empaneled with the usual method of death qualification, the other questioned only about their ability to be fair and impartial in deciding guilt, each jury believing that it was responsible for the decision. The lower court decisions also recognized that "such an experiment is legally impossible." Thus, "the hypothesis must be tested indirectly" (*Hovey,* 1980, p. 1315). "[I]t is the courts who have often stood in the way of surveys involving real jurors and we should not now reject a study because of this deficiency" (*Grigsby,* 1985, p. 237).

In his dissenting opinion in *Lockhart,* Justice Marshall argued that the absence of the impossible "perfect" study is compensated by the convergence of findings in all the studies conducted: "Where studies have identified and corrected apparent flaws in prior investigations, the results of the subsequent work have only corroborated the conclusions drawn in the earlier efforts" (Marshall, J., dissenting *Lockhart,* 1986, p. 1773). When the bulk of the data (or in this case, all of the data) points to one conclusion across many settings the scientific "burden of proof" shifts to those who would discredit the data to propose some hypothesis to explain why the findings will not apply in a new setting—in this case, to explain why the excluded jurors would be expected to behave like the death-qualified jurors if they sat on a real capital case.

A more respectable version of the majority's concern is that the research can not predict the *magnitude* of the bias created by the practice of death qualification. How many cases would come out differently? The opinion quoted Finch and Ferraro, who attempted to estimate the size of the biasing effect of death qualification, and concluded that "no definite conclusions can be stated as to the frequency or magnitude of the effects of death qualification" (1986, p. 66). The opinion did not quote Finch and Ferraro's statement that "extant research findings may actually *understate* the magnitude of the problem raised by death qualification" (1986, p. 62). It is quite true that estimates of the magnitude of the bias are likely to be highly unreliable. It could be more serious or less serious than the studies suggest. There is no question, however, that there is a bias.

THE STANDARD OF REVIEW

Ordinarily, and especially recently, the Supreme Court has been reluctant to reconsider the factual conclusions of the lower courts, preferring to rely on the "traditional testing mechanisms of the adversary process" to reveal the facts most clearly to the judge who actually witnesses this testing. In this case, the court of appeals affirmed the district court's findings, and previous Supreme Court decisions had held that the Supreme Court "cannot undertake to review concurrent findings of fact by two courts below in the absence of a very obvious and exceptional showing of error" (*Graver Tank & Manufacturing Co. v. Linde,* 1949, at 275; see also *United States v. Doe,* 1984).[9] Given that the lower courts had dealt extensively with all of the considerations raised in the majority's analysis of the empirical research, where was the obvious error? The answer is that despite the Court's criticisms of the research, the quality of the research and the lower court's factual findings were not at issue, "[b]ecause we do not ultimately base our decision today on the invalidity of the lower courts' 'factual' findings." (*Lockhart* 1986, p. 1762, n. 3). The Court was unwilling to assert that the studies are invalid, but unwilling to admit that they are valid. With masterful condescension, the Court revealed that it was willing to set aside its better judgment and accept the empirical conclusions. Nevertheless, the practice of death qualification remains constitutional.

Having identified some of the more serious problems with McCree's studies, however, we will assume for purposes of this opinion that the studies are both methodologically valid and adequate to establish that "death-qualification" in fact produces juries somewhat more "conviction-prone" than "non-death-qualified" juries. We hold, nonetheless, that the Constitution does not prohibit the states from "death-qualifying" juries in capital cases [*Lockhart*, 1986, p. 1764].

Basically, the majority held that a jury of 12 impartial people was an impartial jury for constitutional purposes, as long as no traditionally protected group, such as blacks or women, is excluded.

It seems that the Court's only plausible course was to decide that the basic question was not an empirical question after all. Even if it were possible to demonstrate the biasing effects of death qualification on the outcome of real capital cases, it would make no difference. In capital cases it is constitutional to decide guilt or innocence with juries that are biased toward conviction. In other words, despite the explicit question raised in *Witherspoon,* death qualification is immune to empirical challenge.

CONCLUSION

In the 1980s the public strongly favors capital punishment. In most cases this attitude is based on very little information. The desire to acquire more information is negligible, and when new information contrary to one's attitude is learned, the attitude remains unchanged (Ellsworth and Ross, 1983). The Supreme Court and the public have something in common in this regard.

The majority of the Court has been ideologically committed to the constitutionality of capital punishment since 1976. In addition to the ideological commitment, there is the practical problem of the ever-increasing number of prisoners under sentence of death. If the death penalty, or some common feature of its administration such as racial bias or death qualification, were to be declared unconstitutional, hundreds of convicted murderers might have to be dealt with all over again. Since *Furman,* the Court's opinions on the death penalty have often been plurality opinions, confusing and contradictory. When a particular practice has been held unconstitutional, the decision has typically affected very few cases. As Gross and Mauro remarked, "*Furman* became the fountainhead of an expanding swamp of uncertain rules and confusing opinions" (1984).

In part, this messy line of constitutional doctrine is a function of the Court's attempts to circumvent the empirical data. Opponents of capital punishment, in particular the NAACP Legal Defense and Educational Fund, have relied heavily on empirical arguments in their challenges to the death penalty. Their use of data has been extraordinarily sophisticated, and their preparation of empirical challenges exceptionally thorough. Therefore the Court's evasion of the data is bound to blur the issues, and it makes the Court's handling of death penalty cases look less competent than its handling of other issues.

An alternative hypothesis worth considering is that the Court is *generally* reluctant to give serious consideration to social science data, and the recent history of opinions on capital punishment has more to do with the Court's attitude toward social science than with its position on the death penalty. Although it is true that the Court has been skeptical of data in other contexts (cf. Ellsworth and Getman, 1987), I do not think this general reluctance can explain the Court's response to data that challenge capital punishment or its administration. First, the Court has considered data on racial discrimination and jury composition in other contexts, and has ruled in accordance with weaker data than those presented in death cases (*Griggs v. Duke Power and Light Co.,* 1971; *Ballew v. Georgia,* 1978).

Second, the Court has cited empirical evidence when it supports the constitutionality of the death penalty. A good example is the use of public opinion data. The Eighth Amendment's prohibition of cruel and unusual punishment has been interpreted as a prohibition against punishments that are seen as excessive or barbaric in contemporary society. Thus punishments that were acceptable when the Constitution was written, such as mutilation, may be found to be cruel and unusual by later generations (*Weems v. United States,* 1910; *Trop v. Dulles,* 1958).

In the years just preceding *Furman,* public attitudes toward capital punishment were evenly split, and in some polls opponents outnumbered proponents. These polls were used by those who challenged capital punishment to argue that the death penalty was cruel and unusual by contemporary standards.

Since then, however, polls have shown increasing levels of support for the death penalty. Since 1976 the Court has often referred to evidence from opinion surveys and state referenda, new legislation, and jury verdicts—"objective indicia that reflect the public attitude" to support its conclusion that "a large proportion of American society continues to regard death as an appropriate and necessary criminal sanction" (*Gregg v. Georgia,* 1976, p. 878), and thus not cruel and unusual by contemporary standards. Likewise, in 1977, when the Supreme Court held that the death penalty for rape was disproportionate and excessive, and therefore unconstitutional, the opinion relied heavily on empirical data indicating that the public rejected the death penalty for rape (*Coker v. Georgia,* 1977).

The most telling evidence that the Court's opinions are a product of the Justices' attitudes toward capital punishment rather than their attitudes toward social science is the case of *Barefoot v. Estelle* (1983). In order to sentence a person to death in Texas, the jury must find that the convicted person is likely to be a continuing threat to society, that is, the jury must predict that he or she will commit dangerous acts in the future. There is substantial consensus among social scientists that the field has not advanced to the stage at which predictions of dangerousness can be made with any accuracy. In *Barefoot,* then, the American Psychiatric Association argued against the use of expert testimony on future dangerousness, because the data indicated that the predictions of experts are usually wrong. The Court, however, held that the Texas law was constitutional, and that experts should be allowed to testify about whether or not the defendant would pose a continuing threat to society. In Texas, the prediction of future dangerousness is usually the only issue the jury must decide in determining whether to execute a defendant. One would expect that the criteria for evaluating the psychiatric evidence would thus be particularly stringent. Instead, the majority found such evidence satisfactory because "Neither petitioner nor the [American Psychiatric] Association suggests that psychiatrists are always wrong with respect to future dangerousness, only most of the time" (*Barefoot v. Estelle* 1983, p. 901).

In *Barefoot* the Court accepted a form of social science "evidence" that was strongly repudiated by the scientific community in order to uphold the constitutionality of the administration of the death penalty in Texas. In *Lockhart* and in *McCleskey* the Court rejected empirical arguments that were strongly endorsed by the scientific community in order to uphold the constitutionality of the administration of the death penalty. The parsimonious explanation for the failure of social science data to influence the Court in death penalty cases seems to be that the outcome of these cases is frequently a foregone conclusion.

NOTES

1. These figures were derived from a computerized search of the LEXIS (Mead data) library.

2. An alternative argument in favor of deterrence is that by punishing certain crimes by death, a government communicates to its citizens that these crimes are completely intolerable. The existence of the punishment teaches the people that murder is evil. Opponents of the death penalty would argue that most people learn that murder is unacceptable whether or not their state or country executes murderers. Some opponents argue that capital punishment actually teaches people the opposite—that killing human beings is sometimes the right thing to do.

3. Of course there are many different ways of determining the proportion of cases in which defendants are sentenced to death because there are many different ways of defining the relevant universe of cases. The figure of 8 out of 10 was cited by the Court itself in the plurality opinions in *Gregg v. Georgia* and *Woodson v. North Carolina* handed down a year before *Coker*. It was cited in support of the propositions (a) that the public accepted capital punishment but felt that is was only appropriate for a few extreme cases, and (b) that the public would therefore reject mandatory death penalty laws. The figure of 8 out of 10 agrees fairly well with the 1983 findings of Baldus et al.

4. Justice Douglas, in his dissenting opinion in *Witherspoon v. Illinois* (1968) argued that the jury would not be truly representative of the conscience of the community unless all members of the community had a chance of serving at the penalty trial as well as the guilt/innocence trial.

5. The Court has been criticized for relying on bad research and for misinterpreting some of the social science evidence in the earlier jury cases. I do not claim that the Justices used the data well. My only point is that the Court has sought out social science research in Sixth Amendment cases, and has incorporated it into several major decisions.

6. Grigsby died in prison; McCree's case had been joined to his; thus the name change. Two lower courts had previously held that the factual evidence was immaterial to the constitutionality of death-qualified juries (*Smith v. Balckom*, 1982; *Keeten v. Garrison*, 1984), but the courts that actually considered the evidence had all concluded that death qualification biases juries against capital defendants on the issue of guilt (*Hovey, Grigsby* and *Keeten v. Garrison* (W.D.N.C. 1984).

7. The one possible alternative might have been to condemn the practice on the ground that excluding any group, however defined, violated the representativeness of the

jury. This was the position Justice Douglas took in his dissent in *Witherspoon.*

8. The opposite hypothesis, that a new set of jurors would be *less* convinced of the rightness of the guilty verdict than the jurors who were responsible for that verdict, seems at least as plausible.

9. Justice Rehnquist argued that the Court is not bound by lower court decisions with regard to this sort of legislative fact finding. However, the fact that they are not *bound* by the lower court's review hardly justifies the majority Justices' complete failure to *consider* the lower court analyses of exactly the same facts that were discussed—and misunderstood—in the Supreme Court opinion.

REFERENCES

BALDUS, D. C., C. A. PULASKI, and G. WOODWORTH. (1983) "Comparative review of death sentences: An empirical study of the Georgia experience." Journal of Criminal Law & Criminology 74: 661-753.

BLUMSTEIN, A., J. COHEN, and D. NAGIN [eds.] (1986) "Deterrence and incapacitation: Estimating the effects of criminal sanctions on crime rates." Panel on Research on Deterrent and Incapacitative Effects, Committee on Research on Law Enforcement and Criminal Justice, Assembly of Behavioral and Social Sciences, National Research Council. Washington, DC: National Academy of Sciences.

BOWERS, W. J. (1974) Executions in America. Lexington, MA: D. D. Heath.

BOWERS, W. J. (1984) Legal Homicide: Death as Punishment in America, 1864-1982. Boston: Northeastern University Press.

BOWERS, W. J. and G. L. PIERCE. (1980) "Arbitrariness and discrimination under post-*Furman* capital statutes." Crime and Delinquency 26: 563-635.

COWAN, C. L., W. C. THOMPSON, and P. C. ELLSWORTH. (1984) "The effects of death qualification on jurors' predisposition to convict and on the quality of deliberation." Law and Human Behavior 8: 53-79.

DANN, R. H. (1935) "The deterrent effect of capital punishment." Friends Social Series, 29: 1-20.

DIKE, S. T. (1982) Capital Punishment in the United States: A Consideration of the Evidence. New York: National Council on Crime and Delinquency.

EHRLICH, I. (1975) "The deterrent effect of capital punishment: A question of life and death." American Economic Review 65: 397-417.

ELLSWORTH, P. C. and J. G. GETMAN (1987) "The use of social science and legal decision making." In L. Lipson and S. Wheeler (eds.) Law and the Social Sciences. New York: Russell Sage.

ELLSWORTH, P. C. and L. D. ROSS. (1983) "Public opinion and the death penalty: A close examination of the views of abolitionists and retentionists." Crime and Delinquency (January): 116-169.

FINCH, M. and M. FERRARO (1986) "The empirical challenge to death-qualified juries: On further examination." Nebraska Law Review, 65: 21-74.

GROSS, S. R. (1984) "Determining the neutrality of death-qualified juries: Judicial appraisal of empirical data." Law and Human Behavior 8: 7-30.

GROSS, S. R. (1985) "Race and death: The judicial evaluation of evidence of discrimination in capital sentencing." U.C. Davis Law Review 18: 1275-1325.

GROSS, S. R. and R. MAURO. (1984) "Patterns of death: An analysis of racial disparities in capital sentencing and homicide victimization." Stanford Law Review 37: 27-153.

HANEY, C. (1984) "On the selection of capital juries: The biasing effects of the death-qualification process." Law and Human Behavior 8: 121-132.

HASTIE, R., S. D. PENROD, and N. PENNINGTON. (1983) Inside the Jury. Cambridge, MA: Harvard University Press.

JACOBY, J. E. and R. PATERNOSTER. (1982) "Sentencing disparity and jury packing: Further challenges to the death penalty." Journal of Criminal Law & Criminology 73: 379-387.

KADANE, J. B. (1984) "After *Hovey*: A note taking into account automatic death penalty jurors." Law and Human Behavior 8: 115-120.

KALVEN, H. and H. ZEISEL. (1966) The American Jury. Boston: Little, Brown.

LEMPERT, R. O. (1981) "Desert and deterrence: An assessment of the moral bases of the case for capital punishment." Michigan Law Review 79: 1177-1231.

Louis Harris & Associates, Inc. (1981) Study No. 814022.

OBERER, W. E. (1961) "Does disqualification of jurors for scruples against capital punishment constitute denial of fair trial on the issue of guilt?" University of Texas Law Review 39, 545-573.

RADELET, M. (1981) "Racial characteristics and the imposition of the death penalty." American Sociological Review 46: 918-927.

RADELET, M. and G. L. PIERCE. (1985) "Race and prosecutorial discretion in homicide cases." Law and Society Review 19: 587-621.

RIEDEL, M. (1976) "Death row 1975: A study of offenders sentenced under post-Furman statutes." Temple Law Quarterly 49: 261-290.

SELLIN, T. (1959) The Death Penalty. Philadelphia: American Law Institute.

SELLIN, T. (1980) The Penalty of Death. Beverly Hills, CA: Sage.

van den HAAG, E. (1975) Punishing Criminals: Concerning a Very Old and Painful Question. New York: Basic Books.

WOLFGANG, M. E. and M. RIEDEL. (1973) "Rape, judicial discretion, and the death penalty." Annals of the American Academy of Political and Social Science 407: 119-133.

ZEISEL, H. (1968) Some data on juror attitudes toward capital punishment. Monograph. Center for Studies in Criminal Justice, University of Chicago Law School.

ZEISEL, H. (1981) "Race bias in the administration of the death penalty: The Florida experience. Harvard Law Review 95: 456-468.

ZIMRING, F. E., J. EIGEN, AND S. O'MALLEY. (1976) "Punishing homicide in Philadelphia: Perspectives on the death penalty." University of Chicago Law Review 43: 227-252.

CASES

Ballew v. Georgia, 435 U.S. 223 (1978).

Barefoot v. Estelle, 463 U.S. 880 (1983).

Batson v. Kentucky, 467 U.S. 106 S. Ct. 1712 (1986).

Brown v. Board of Education of Topeka, 347 U.S. 483 (1954).

Coker v. Georgia, 433 U.S. 584 (1977).

Colgrove v. Battin, 413 U.S. 149 (1973).

Furman v. Georgia, 408 U.S. 238 (1972).

Graver Tank & Manufacturing Co. v. Linde, 336 U.S. 271 (1949).

Gregg v. Georgia, 428 U.S. 153 (1976).

Griggs v. Duke Power and Light Co., 401 U.S. 424 (1971).

Grigsby v. Mabry, 569 F. Supp. 1273 (E.D. Ark. 1983).

Grigsby v. Mabry, 758 F. 2d 226 (8th Cir. 1985).

Hovey v. Superior Court, 28 Cal. 3d 1 (1980).

Jurek v. Texas, 428 U.S. 262 (1976).

Keeten v. Garrison, 742 F. 2d 129 (4th Cir. 1984).

Keeten v. Garrison, 578 F. Supp. 1164 (W.D. N.C. 1984).

Lockhart v. McCree, 106 S. Ct. 1758 (1986).

Maxwell v. Bishop, 398 F. 2d (8th Cir. 1968), rev'd on other grounds, 398 U.S. 262 (1970).

McCleskey v. Kemp, 107 S. Ct. 1756 (1987).

People v. Moore, Alameda County Superior Court (California), No. 67113, August-September, 1979.

Pope v. United States, 372 F. 2d 710 (8th Cir. 1967) cert denied 401 U.S. 949 (1971).

Proffitt v. Florida, 428 U.S. 242 (1976).

Smith v. Balkcom, 651 F. 2d 858 (5th Cir. 1982).

Strauder v. West Virginia, 100 U.S. 303 (1880).

Trop v. Dulles, 356 U.S. 86 (1958).

United States v. Doe, 104 S. Ct. 1237 (1984).

Weems v. United States, 217 U.S. 349 (1910).

Williams v. Florida, 399 U.S. 510 (1968).

Witherspoon v. Illinois, 391 U.S. 510 (1968).

Woodson v. North Carolina, 428 U.S. 304 (1976).

Chapter 8

A CASE STUDY OF THE MISUSE OF SOCIAL SCIENCE IN CAPITAL PUNISHMENT CASES
The Massachusetts Supreme Judicial Court's Finding of Racial Discrimination in *Watson* (1980)

DENNIS D. DORIN

Death penalty cases at the appellate level progressively have become battlefields for rival social science hypotheses (Daniels, 1979: 336-337). The U.S. Supreme Court recently upheld Georgia's death penalty law despite strong statistical evidence demonstrating that blacks who kill whites are more likely to be sentenced to death than any other defendant/victim combination.[1] Nevertheless, abolitionists and retentionists will continue to press their social science arguments before state and federal judiciaries (Baldus et al., 1986: 135-145; Dorin, 1981: 1691-1692).

It is therefore not surprising that social scientists intimately concerned with the capital punishment question are writing works that they say are explicitly designed to provide jurists with advice on how they might effectively evaluate social science contentions (Baldus et al., 1986; Dorin, 1981).

This chapter fits within this trend. Its thesis is that courts may be able to protect themselves from at least serious social science errors if they

AUTHOR'S NOTE: *I wish to thank Mary Cornelia Porter, G. Alan Tarr, and, with special admiration, William J. Bowers, for their comments upon earlier drafts of this analysis.*

follow a few relatively simple procedures. It proposes, more or less, a judge's or justice's checklist. Such a listing cannot guarantee that members of the judiciary will not engage in substantial misapplications of social science. But it can make the occurrence of such mistakes less probable.

A WORST-CASE SCENARIO

One way to derive and demonstrate such a series of admonitions might be through a case study. At least three types are possible. We might focus upon a success story, a court's brilliant employment of social science theory and data. Or we might examine an average performance. A third approach, however, is suggested by a comment of U.S. Circuit Court of Appeals Judge John Wisdom concerning the notorious Footnote 11 to *Brown v. Board of Education* (1954). Despite Footnote 11's problematical recourse to social science, Wisdom concluded, it nevertheless had a "healthy" impact on subsequent courts' uses of social science analyses, because it acted as a foil, encouraging, "in a dialectical fashion," far better performances (Driessen, 1983: 479).

Our case may serve a similar purpose. The Massachusetts Supreme Judicial Court's racial discrimination ruling in *District Attorney for the Suffolk District v. Watson* (1980), we will argue, involved a gross misapplication of social science by a highly regarded state supreme court intent upon playing a major role in the development, not only of its state's, but of the nation's capital punishment policy. As such, the *Watson* case's chronicle would seem to be replete with warnings that went unheeded—ones that could easily lend themselves to becoming prescriptions for future courts confronting such cases.

Our account will develop in the following manner. First, we sketch the admonitions relating to the courts' uses of social science that were available to the Supreme Judicial Court as it focused upon the very important racial discrimination issue presented by *Watson*. Second, we describe and explain how the court ignored such signals and misused social science when it found racial discrimination in Massachusetts's procedures for imposing the death penalty. Third, we consider the price that court, and the law itself, paid for *Watson*'s misuse of social science. Finally, in the context of our checklist, we conclude that future *Watsons* are not inevitable. When playing the expansive social scientist role recently thrust upon them, our judges and justices are not preordained to failure.

WARNINGS

The Supreme Judicial Court confronting *Watson* could boast of being the oldest continuously sitting judicial body in the nation (*Encyclopedia Americana,* 1984: 465). During its 200 years as a state court, it had interpreted a constitution drafted largely by John Adams, one containing such experimental features in Adams's day, and even presently, as advisory opinions. And the Court itself had been regarded as an innovator (Caldeira, 1983: 89), a role that it hardly renounced in capital punishment litigation. Indeed, a number of its justices seemed to welcome the opportunity for it to seize the initiative in death cases—to serve as a pacesetter for their sister states' and federal judiciaries.[2]

How did this judiciary, one of the leading ones in the country (Caldeira, 1983: 89), grossly misapply social science in *Watson?* In a nutshell, the court, in the *Watson* case, became the nation's only appellate tribunal to hold that, for all intents and purposes, the infliction of capital punishment in the United States is inherently racially discriminatory. And it did so by presenting little more than raw statistics indicating that murderers with white victims were disproportionately represented on the post-1976 death rows of Florida, Georgia, Ohio, and Texas. Without considering whether these disparities resulted from such constitutionally permissible factors as the relevant homicides' aggravating and mitigating circumstances, the Court simply concluded that these statistics proved that Americans valued a white's life more than a black's when inflicting capital punishment.

Important studies with contrary conclusions were ignored.[3] And the Supreme Judicial Court went on to strike down Massachusetts's capital statute, with no one on that state's death row, on the basis of racial discrimination that it thought it saw in Florida, Georgia, Ohio, and Texas.

Such an analysis would not be likely to earn a passing grade in any undergraduate course on social science inquiry. No other court emulated it. It may well have come back to haunt the Court in its later conflicts with the Massachusetts legislature and electorate. It may, in the long run, have detracted from the Court's reputation and legitimacy. Had the Court received no warnings that such an undesirable outcome was possible? And, if there were such signals, how might their identification several years after *Watson* still prove useful?

Given the Supreme Judicial Court's sophistication and the seriousness of the racial discrimination issue it was considering, it is somewhat amazing that it did not take judicial notice of caveats available from at least two sources: (1) the general literature on the courts' use, misuse, or nonuse of social sciences, and (2) other appellate courts' responses to invitations to employ social science to resolve racial discrimination issues in capital punishment cases.

The Law and Social Science Literature

The Supreme Judicial Court was hardly treading upon virgin ground when it contemplated employing social science in *Watson*. *Muller v. Oregon* (1908) and its famous Brandeis brief had gone a long way toward inaugurating the modern debate over the use of social science in judicial decision making. And *Brown v. Board of Education*'s highly questionable infusion of social science greatly intensified this controversy, serving as a stimulus for what Stephan Michelson has described as "an explosion of literature." (Michelson, 1980: 7).

Running through this commentary, moreover, was a strong current of pessimism. Commentators like Donald Horowitz (1977) and Paul Rosen (1972), for example, detailed what they saw as the pitfalls of the courts' recourses to the social sciences. Their indictment was long. Relying upon writings from them that preceded *Watson*, Patrick Driessen found that their bill of particulars contained at least a dozen charges.

Jurists lacked the training to understand social science evidence, the Horowitzes and Rosens contended. Judges and justices were not versed in probabilistic thinking, or in the high degree of intolerance for inaccuracy, of the social scientist. They were too preoccupied with the minutia of individual cases to use social science appropriately. They could not easily reverse their decisions in the face of new scientific discoveries. They might well be overwhelmed by allegedly expert witnesses. Their hearsay rules prevented a full consideration of social science evidence. The vagaries of the judicial process frequently shielded them from the best social science analyses. Judiciaries might well be biased against certain social science theories and data. There was an excellent chance that social science, still largely in its infancy, would often have not evolved to the stage at which it could provide jurists with the information they were seeking. Social science was likely to come to judges and justices via advocates using it not to search for the truth, but to advance their clients' interests. The odds of the adversary system's distorting social science findings were high. Finally, communication could easily become dysfunctional when carried on between jurists engaged in normative-prescriptive patterns of thinking and social scientists at least attempting to reason in ways that were value free (Driessen, 1983: 480-491).

The courts, Horowitz thus contended three years before *Watson*, had been:

> Too slow to raise empirical questions and altogether too quick to answer them once raised. [Too often they had paid more heed to social science] than its reliability warranted. Too rarely [had the judiciary approached it with] the circumspection . . . merited by the partial, tentative character of most findings and by the imperfect fit between them and the legal questions to which [they might have had some relevance] (Horowitz, 1977: 283).

Such considerations—ones that had been broadly disseminated for many years—might surely have been expected to have put the Supreme Judicial Court on guard against what David O'Brien was to describe by the time of *Watson* as "the seductiveness of [a] reliance on social science information" in its decision making (O'Brien, 1980: 9).

But the literature was not without its optimism. Kenneth Karst, Daniel Patrick Moynihan, and others did conclude that jurists might, with substantial preparation and assistance, find their way through a number of the social science issues confronting them (Karst, 1960; Moynihan, 1979: 30). All of these commentators, though, also believed that judiciaries could no longer, in David Riesman's phrase, "play by ear" the role of social scientist (Dorin, 1981: 1674). They needed a minimum grounding in the scientific method and its ramifications. An education thus awaited many of them. Yet it was not generally beyond their capabilities. Their mastery of a few pointers would at least constitute an acceptable foundation (Abt, 1980: 69).

Despite such views, the pre-*Watson* Supreme Judicial Court would have had to have looked carefully for a codification of such commentators' prescriptions. With limited exceptions, their advice was to be found scattered throughout the many books and articles comprising the law and social science commentary.

If the court had diligently perused such works to take judicial notice of ways it might "incorporate good social science" into its policymaking (Michelson, 1980: 4), though, what might it have found? It might have concluded, as one possibility, that there were at least a dozen significant questions that it might ask itself when resolving the social science issues of capital punishment cases.

Half of these queries, for example, related to what might be called threshold concerns. They would involve its justices in calculating, however roughly, how high the stakes might be in their invocations of the social sciences. They concerned whether, generally, an issue before the court called for a primary, or merely a tangential, use of social science theory, methodology, or data.

The first of these required its justices to ask themselves whether they were contemplating using social science in a way that would be pivotal or decisive, or merely supplemental, to their holding. Were they about to employ it to undergird the creation of new precedents? Or simply to provide additional support for what was already an established body of law (Dorin, 1981: 1675-1676; Driessen, 1983: 477). If such analyses were being employed for the latter, their use might not have to meet such stringent standards. At the most, they would merely be illustrative materials. But if a transformation of the law were to be premised upon them, there would be a far greater need for them to prove valid and reliable. For they would be a crucial part of the court's rulings (Dorin, 1981: 1675-1676; Driessen, 1983: 477).

Second, and in a similar vein, the court would have to ponder whether it was relying upon social science to vindicate or proscribe a governmental action previously presumed to be constitutional. The Brandeis brief had often been "invoked to sustain legislative rationality, thereby combining with presumptive constitutionality as a potent force" (Driessen, 1983: 478). But if the court were to rely upon social science to vitiate such government actions, it would be carrying a far greater burden. Again, it would have to try very hard to present only those social science findings the validity and reliability of which could be strongly defended.

Third, the court would have to be aware of the pitfalls of mistakenly appearing to be decisively using social science. It would have to be cognizant that its employment of such analyses and data as supplementary material might well be interpreted, in the context of its opinion, as pivotal. A major part of the debate over *Brown*'s Footnote 11, for example, had centered upon precisely this issue. Chief Justice Warren had argued in his later years that the social science cited in that footnote did not play a significant part in resolving the *Brown* case's issues. But his critics had many times contended the contrary. Footnote 11's sources, they had maintained, had been legitimated as crucial evidence by Warren's invocation of them (Rosen, 1980: 9).

Fourth, the court would have to be vigilant against a justice's making the use of social science the price of his or her signing the opinion. Such an additional expression of support for the majority's or plurality's reasoning might be extremely important, especially in a close case. But the precedent that might be established relating to the use of such materials might well have an equal or superior importance. It could be a serious mistake, therefore, for the court to assume that a colleague proffering social science analyses had fully gauged their validity and reliability. One more signature on the court's holding might well not be worth a fallacious, or even a questionable, recourse to such sources.

Fifth, as at least one possible final threshold concern, the court might well have pondered whether the pattern of behavior before it could be sufficiently delineated through common sense, rather than social science, approaches. If it could, perhaps such invocations of social science might not be worth their drawbacks. Conversely, as merely tangential sources, they might not have to be as resistant to the criticisms of social scientists as studies central to its holding.

Having considered the general stakes of employing such evidence, and concluding that they were at least tentatively not prohibitive, the court would next have to consider what might be called seven operational concerns. What basic factors would it have to keep in mind as it sought to incorporate social science into its cases?

The slightest acquaintance with the literature, or even a superficial cognizance of the intense debate that followed the use of social science in *Brown*, might have suggested strongly to the Supreme Judicial Court that its employment of such sources should be taken very seriously. Hence, one of its major considerations in *Watson* might have been to maximize its ability to gauge the validity and reliability of the social science works with possible relevance to the racial discrimination issue.

One approach to this task—and perhaps the first of the court's operational concerns—might thus be to encourage the lower courts to serve as initial forums for the assessment of potentially relevant contentions. The chances of a high court employing such materials validly and reliably would be improved were it to receive them after they had been examined in some depth by the parties, amici, and judges at the trial and intermediate levels (Karst, 1960: 101; Canon and Baum, 1981: 981). Such a course would do more than bring more minds to bear on social science issues; it would permit more time for reflection at each level of the system. And the court could use such a procedure to augment the data it might receive through briefs and oral argument. Added to these data would be whatever insights were produced by the dialectic of the expert trial testimony (Karst, 1960: 101; Canon and Baum, 1981: 981).

The commentary on the interface between law and social science also suggested a number of ways that the justices could increase, at their own level, their input on potentially pivotal issues. As a second operational concern, they could resolve not to base a holding upon a particular social science analysis unless a fair opportunity to refute it were given to the party against whom it might prove dispositive (Driessen, 1983: 10; Maxwell, 1980: 32, 48). One way this might be accomplished would be through a carefully focused request for supplemental briefings. A Supreme Judicial Court focusing in upon a particular social science approach could, for example, call upon the parties to evaluate it through additional submittals.

Third, Donald Horowitz, among others, would warn the court not to rely upon secondhand accounts of social science studies (Channels, 1985: 24-25; Horowitz, 1980: 151, 280-281). Too much might be at stake in such situations for its justices not to assess alleged key research for themselves. It was too easy, Horowitz had observed several years before *Watson*, for commentators and advocates to report social science inaccurately. The court would consequently be on much firmer ground were it to examine such analyses personally (Channels, 1985: 24-25; Horowitz, 1980: 151, 280-281).

A number of writers on the relationship between law and social science would also have advised the court, as a fourth operational admonition, not to consider a potentially decisive social science analysis *in vacuo*. Any court considering the possibility of using such a study should determine how well it fitted into the overall research of its field. Was it a leading work? Was it controversial? The justices should be especially on guard against works that conveyed a false impression of a consensus within a discipline marked by disagreement (Driessen, 1983: 484; Abt, 1980: 67; Channels, 1985: 19, 26). Such inquiries might be pursued through the justices' taking judicial notice of a field's main studies. They might also be undertaken through queries posed to the parties and amici during oral arguments and briefing.

A fifth operational concern would place the court substantially into the role of social scientist. Relying upon all of the sources available to it, it would have to confront several major questions: Was the study in question's design valid—in its conceptualization, in its measurement techniques, and in the propositions it chose for analysis? What degree of statistical confidence could be placed in it? What, generally, was the extent of its explanatory power? Did it engage in a proper level of disaggregation? (Light, 1980: 63-67). How good were its controls? Had it tested for a significant number of variables? (Driessen, 1983: 481).

Sixth, even a perfectly valid and reliable social science analysis might fall short of the claim made for it by parties or amici. The court would thus have to be concerned with whether a study was being used by counsel, or the lower courts, to buttress a position that was really beyond its purview. The court would consequently want to know the researchers' explicit findings. It would then have to determine how close the patterns of behavior discerned by them were to the ones presently before it (Carlson, 1980: 70). Could it legitimately leap from one to the other?

Seventh, and as a possible safeguard relating to all of the other threshold and operational considerations, the court would surely need to avail itself of the experiences of federal and state judiciaries confronting similar questions. "Judicial federalism" had long entailed "a collaborative [informational] framework" among the state and national benches (Friedelbaum, 1982: 47). Drawing upon this communications network, the court should consequently seek illumination from its sister state and federal courts' cases.

Most, if not all, of the Supreme Judicial Court's members would not have thought of citing a precedent that either they or their law clerks had not examined carefully. For this reason, they may well have joined the great majority of justices who routinely "shepardized" all potentially applicable cases.[4] Case citations were too important to be added cavalierly. In much the same fashion, though, even a slight acquaintance with the law and social science literature might well have convinced the court, by the time of *Watson*, to take the same care when it approached social science issues. The odds of misapplying social science were simply too high for it not to have scrutinized the rulings of courts facing comparable challenges.

Perhaps the *Watson* Court could not have been expected to have been fully apprised of all 12 of these threshold and operational admonitions. Its time and docket pressures, not to mention its small staff, would not have been conducive to its developing substantial expertise on social science matters. But it would be most unlikely, given the massive body of commentary that followed *Brown*'s Footnote 11, that it would be wholly innocent of the kinds of pitfalls that could accompany its invocation of such social science materials.[5]

At the outset, it would have been difficult for its justices not to perceive that the issue of whether racial discrimination inhered in American capital sentencing entailed "legislative or social facts" that especially lent themselves to social science analyses. This question could not be approached adequately solely through a reliance upon their personal feelings and anecdotes. Its determination required a systematic and statistically demanding scrutiny of interactions among highly complex social phenomena. Such a task did, as the court concluded, call for the social scientist.

But before it went so far as to hold that racial discrimination was endemic in all state and federal impositions of the death penalty, it might well have been expected to have cast its net wide for relevant analyses and data. And at least one potentially far-reaching perspective on this task would have been available to it through its perusal, in accordance with its seventh operational consideration, of past cases. So, it would not at all have been unexpected for it, or any court in a comparable situation, to have conducted a careful examination of other courts' experiences with the issue of racial discrimination in capital punishment.

Lessons From the State
and Federal Judiciaries

The experience of other state judiciaries confronting claims of racial discrimination in death sentencing might well have suggested that the court move cautiously. No major exertion of judicial notice would have been required for it to discover that no state supreme court had ever invalidated the death penalty on racial discrimination grounds.

Repeated attempts by abolitionists to induce state courts to accept the racial discrimination argument had failed. Even the California Supreme Court, perhaps the leading state supreme court in the country (Caldeira, 1983: 89)—and certainly one of the most activist and most liberal—had rebuffed such contentions. Its path-breaking *Anderson* case, the only one before *Watson* in which another state supreme court had struck down its state's death penalty, had ignored the racial discrimination arguments (*People v. Anderson,* 1972).

Had the court pondered this development, it might have wondered whether the California Supreme Court's lack of receptivity to the racial discrimination argument in *Anderson* stemmed from that court's awareness of a *Stanford Law Review* study published two years previously (*Stanford Law Review*, 1969: 1297-1497). This analysis of California's imposition of death sentences for first-degree murder found no appreciable indication of racial discrimination. Cited approvingly by Justice Potter Stewart in a case repeatedly considered by the Supreme Judicial Court in *Watson, Furman v. Georgia* (1972), it might have conveyed an important warning. For it suggested that racial discrimination might not be a discernible factor in at least some states' death sentencing.

The federal courts' assessments of racial discrimination claims tended, when viewed in the long run, to be sensitive to many of the threshold and operational considerations of the law/social science literature. Social science studies of whether capital punishment was racially discriminatory were often treated as potentially pivotal to the creation of far-reaching new doctrines—especially since the federal courts regarded the states' death penalty statutes as presumptively constitutional. The federal courts thus showed a very strong tendency to protect themselves against mistakenly endorsing social science analyses and data. In the few years directly before *Watson*, for example, they attempted, with increasing frequency, to produce rigorous critiques of the social science presented to them.

This mode of decision making began a full two decades before the *Watson* case. And it initially focused upon federal case records that embodied far more powerful prima facie showings of racially discriminatory sentencing than *Watson's*. For the abolitionists' targets in these 1960s and 1970s cases were the capital rape statutes concentrated in the South and border regions.

Of all the inmates subsequently executed under these laws, 90% had been black; and a black's chance of meeting such a fate escalated radically when he was convicted of raping a white woman (Meltsner, 1973: 34). Yet, as Michael Meltsner, one of the main abolitionist attorneys of this period reports, the abolitionists never believed—even given the liberal optimism of the mid-1960s—that the federal judiciary would legitimate their racial discrimination argument on the basis of nothing more than raw statistics indicating the massive disproportion of black rapists of whites receiving the death penalty. "Southern prosecuting attorneys," Meltsner has recalled, "could claim that this result was the product of factors other than racial discrimination." (Meltsner, 1973: 34). They could argue, for example, that condemned blacks had had longer criminal records or had used more violence or employed more weapons against their victims.

And such explanations, Meltsner has observed, were not inconceivable. Indeed, sound social science called for the objective and careful testing of all "plausible nonracial" hypotheses (Meltsner, 1973: 34-35). For only when these were accounted for theoretically and statistically, could the researcher, and the federal court, be sure that they had actually discerned racially discriminatory patterns.

With such considerations in mind, the early 1960s abolitionists commissioned and invoked the most sophisticated social science study yet undertaken on possible racial discrimination in the infliction of capital rape sentencing.[6] And, after almost a decade and a half of research and argumentation, they saw the death sentence for rape fall in *Coker v. Georgia* (1977), via a U.S. States Supreme Court opinion that never even mentioned the possibility of that sanction's racially discriminatory infliction.

Coker thus symbolized the federal judiciary's substantial reluctance to accept such arguments. Federal judges frequently sidestepped or rejected them. Their very rigorous standards for social science argumentation were well established by the time of *Watson*. The burden of proof was clearly on the abolitionists to present a prima facie case of racial discrimination (Baldus and Cole, 1977: 57). They might do so by a showing, for example, that black murderers with white victims were radically overrepresented on a state's death row. But such a finding, in and of itself, would be insufficient. For the state would have an opportunity to suggest how such a pattern may have developed from nonracial, and hence constitutional, factors. Were it to do so, the abolitionists would then be called upon to attempt statistically to rebut the state's assertions. And, were they found not to have done so, the federal courts would not find racial discrimination (Baldus and Cole, 1977: 54 and 58; Berk and Oppenheim, 1979: 126).

Such cases tended to be fought out in the context of state-of-the-art social science. The studies presented in them were usually based upon data directly related to the statutes being contested. These requisites generally applied even if they led to federal jurists' plunging into such esoteric social science concerns as regression analysis and multicolinearity. Such litigation, moreover, was frequently developed through a complex record, with extensive testimony from the abolitionists' and states' social scientists at the trial level. And the federal district court judges' resolutions of such issues were to be examined in depth yet again by the U.S. Circuit Courts of Appeals before they could be brought before the U.S. Supreme Court's Justices.

The geographical focal point for such determinations also tended to be the specific jurisdiction in which the death row inmate had been tried, convicted, and sentenced. Statewide figures might, however, be entertained, but in no instances would national statistics, or those from sister states, be permissible indicators of a particular state's racially discriminatory sentencing.

The upshot of these policies was a climate hardly conducive to judicial findings of racial discrimination. But, whether or not they were too demanding, such standards of proof would be binding upon the Supreme Judicial Court to the extent that it was applying the U.S. Constitution. They would, however, be no more than admonitions if it invoked the Massachusetts Constitution. Yet, with the federal cases that delineated these criteria before it, via the briefs and oral arguments, as it considered *Watson*, the court could hardly have been unaware of them. It could, of course, decide to ignore some, most, or all of them if it based its determination of whether Massachusetts's death penalty was racially discriminatory on independent state grounds (Friedelbaum, 1982: 23-25). But it would do so at a risk to its reputation, influence, and legitimacy.

A WORST-CASE SCENARIO: THE SUPREME JUDICIAL COURT'S FINDING OF RACIAL DISCRIMINATION IN *WATSON*

The Holding

In *Watson,* the Supreme Judicial Court concluded that Massachusetts's capital punishment statute, Chapter 488 of the Massachusetts Criminal Code—a law patterned directly upon statutes found facially constitutional under the Federal Constitution by the U.S. Supreme Court—constituted cruel or unusual punishment in violation of Article 26 of the Massachusetts Constitution.[7] The court based this ruling on two grounds. First, Chapter 488 was unconstitutional because it offended Massachusetts society's "contemporary standards of decency." Second, Chapter 488's implementation would inevitably be attended by caprice and arbitrariness entailing racial discrimination.

Turning to the first ground, Chief Justice Edward Hennessey

conceded that Article 26, when originally incorporated into the Massachusetts Constitution, did not invalidate capital punishment. But Article 26, like the Eighth Amendment, he found, evolved. The court thus had to consider its present meaning.

Public opinion polls suggested, Hennessey observed, that support for the abolition of the death penalty was presently not unanimous. But, he argued, the court had to consider not so much what people said, as what they did. From this perspective, he noted, no one had been executed in Massachusetts from 1948 through 1972, when all executions at least temporarily ceased nationwide owing to the U.S. Supreme Court's provisional invalidation of every state death penalty in *Furman v. Georgia* (1972).

The death sentence violated Massachusetts's "contemporary standards of decency" for yet other reasons, Hennessey contended. Persons mistakenly executed could not be raised from the dead (411 N. E. 2nd 1274, 1282, 1980). An individual premeditatively killed by the state was utterly denied his or her humanity. And, perhaps most importantly, capital punishment, with its physical and mental horrors, had a "unique" and inherent capacity to inflict pain (p. 1283).

Hennessey might consequently have rested his decision upon this "contemporary standards of decency" presentation. Chapter 488 needed to be declared unconstitutional only once to be wholly invalid. But he proceeded to his second contention—that Chapter 488 would inescapably be administered in a capricious and arbitrary manner—and, in doing so, confronted the racial discrimination issue.

Given the thousands of murders committed annually, Hennessey noted, only a tiny number of their perpetrators would ever receive the death penalty. The infliction of capital punishment would thus remain "freakish." It mattered little whether Chapter 488 might be considered constitutional by the U.S. Supreme Court. Viewed from the vantage point of the Massachusetts Constitution, it was obvious that Chapter 488 would create a system rife with untrammeled discretion. Juries would still have to cope with the utterly elusive, and yet life-and-death, distinction between first- and second-degree murder. Police, prosecutors, defense attorneys, and judges would continue to make all sorts of crucial decisions that determined who would live and who would die, while largely "unguided and uncurbed by statutory standards." Public outcries over especially emotional cases, plea bargains, and other such influences would determine, to a degree wholly violative of Article 26, who would receive the ultimate sanction (pp. 1284-1285).

This argument—propounded by abolitionist commentators like law professor Charles Black; Watson and Real, two defendants facing prosecution under Chapter 488; and, as amicus curiae, the Massachusetts Association of Criminal Defense Lawyers, (Massachusetts Association of Criminal Defense Lawyers Brief in *Watson*, 1980, pp. 6-30)—intellectually, might have stood by itself as an a priori rationale for Chapter 488's invalidation. A showing of racial discrimination was hardly essential to a demonstration of capriciousness and arbitrariness.

But Hennessey elected to go beyond it; he would also find Chapter 488 to be racially discriminatory. Many commentators, including the President's Commission on Law Enforcement and the Administration of Justice of the late 1960s, he observed, had found the infliction of the death penalty to be permeated with racial discrimination. And the most recent "criminal homicide data"—those obtained since the U.S. Supreme Court approved certain kinds of capital statutes in 1976—showed that this condition continued.

Drawing upon statistics compiled by William J. Bowers and Glenn L. Pierce, Hennessey thus reported that in Florida:

> Of 286 blacks who killed whites, forty-eight (16.8%) were sentenced to death; of 111 whites who killed blacks, *none* were sentenced to death. In Georgia, of 258 blacks who killed whites, thirty-seven (14.3%) were sentenced to death; of seventy-one whites who killed blacks, two (2.8%) were sentenced to death. In Texas, of 344 blacks who killed whites, twenty-seven (7.8%) were sentenced to death; of 143 whites who killed blacks, *none* were sentenced to death [pp. 1285-1286].

The implications of such figures, according to Hennessey, were inescapable. As the noted abolitionist commentator, Hugo Bedau, had noted, "the death penalty is reserved for those who kill whites, because the criminal justice system in these states simply does not put the same value on the life of a black person as it does on the life of a white" (p. 1285).

But could Florida, Georgia, and Texas figures, assuming *arguendo* that they did demonstrate that, in some Southern states, Bedau's assertion was correct, possibly be decisive for a Massachusetts that presently had no one facing execution? For Hennessey, Bower's and Pierce's percentages showed that such racial discrimination was hardly confined to the South. Ohio's experience also demonstrated the following:

Of 173 black persons who killed white persons, thirty-seven of them (21.4%) were sentenced to death. Of forty-seven whites who killed blacks, *none* were sentenced to death (p. 1285).

Moreover, Hennessey argued, citing the two Massachusetts cases of *Commonwealth v. Soares* and *Commonwealth v. Franklin* (1978), "the existence of racial prejudice in some persons in the Commonwealth of Massachusetts is a fact of which we take notice" (p. 1285). Hence, he concluded, racial discrimination would "inevitably persist" in Chapter 488's implementation, and consequently, this was yet another reason for it to fall as an Article 26 violation.

Misapplying Social Science

Did this treatment by Hennessey of *Watson*'s racial discrimination issue entail a substantial misapplication of social science? We might best answer this question by making recourse to the 12 threshold and operational considerations that the law/social science literature suggests jurists should apply when considering social science issues. A failure to concern itself properly with one or a few of the lesser of these might not necessarily indicate that the Supreme Judicial Court misused social science. But its violation of the letter or spirit of a great majority would constitute a powerful case of such a misapplication.

Was the court's resort to social science pivotal in Watson? As noted earlier, despite other grounds for its holding, the court squarely addressed the racial discrimination issue in *Watson*. Moreover, it stated explicitly that it was basing its resolution of that question on social facts derived from applicable studies. Only two such sources were cited. One was the 1968 report of the President's Commission on Law Enforcement and the Administration of Justice. The other constituted the social science data produced by the Bowers and Pierce study.

The former, even assuming, *arguendo*, that its analysis was valid, was clearly obsolete. It was completed almost a decade before the appearance of the capital statutes modeled on the U. S. Supreme Court's opinion in *Gregg v. Georgia* (1976). Hence, it was of no use in determining whether these laws, among which was Chapter 488, were racially discriminatory. Indeed, they were supposedly designed to ameliorate the very kinds of inequities that the Commission, among other such bodies, had castigated (Dorin, 1981: 1684-1685).

So, the court's racial discrimination determination rested solely upon the Bowers and Pierce percentages. They *were* pivotal to it. The court might accordingly have been expected to take special care that they were valid and reliable.

Was the court employing social science to invalidate presumptively constitutional legislation? The kinds of policy concerns that usually supported a presumption of constitutionality might well have been at work in *Watson*. The Massachusetts legislature had gone out of its way to declare in Chapter 488 that legislatures were inherently better designed than courts to weigh the kinds of societal imperatives that were at stake in the development of defensible death penalties. And it added accurately that, in passing Chapter 488, it was responding to the wishes of a large number of Massachusetts's citizens.

Moreover, the state could draw upon almost a universal tradition of such acts being presumptively constitutional. They were so regarded by the federal judiciary. They had this stature in every other state that had passed death penalty statutes previous to *Watson*.[8] Their popularity nationally was underscored by the speed with which they reappeared on the books of 35 states and the United States following the *Furman* case's invalidation of all previous capital statutes.

These developments meant that the *Watson* Court was facing a direct clash with the Massachusetts legislature relating to an act well within an area where the legislative branch was usually assumed to have substantial discretion and expertise. In addition, a striking down of Chapter 488 could be expected to be highly unpopular. For these reasons, the court might not have been wrong to approach Chapter 488 as if it were presumptively constitutional. Had it done so, it might have required the abolitionists to present a prima facie case of racial discrimination—one that could be discounted were Massachusetts able to present an effective rebuttal.

But the court chose, instead, to leave the burden of proof ambiguous. And it also did not suggest that the delicacy of the situation might require it to give the Bowers and Pierce data a particularly rigorous assessment. Indeed, as argued subsequently, it appeared to give them no critical evaluation at all!

Might the readers of Watson *mistakenly see the Bowers and Pierce data as decisive?* It is highly plausible that the racial discrimination holding was not essential to Chapter 488's invalidation of *Watson*. Perhaps Hennessey's "contemporary standards of decency" argument alone might have garnered enough votes for the striking down of this legislation. Or maybe it plus the earlier stages of the capriciousness and arbitrariness contention could have carried the day.

In such a situation, the finding that Chapter 488 was racially discriminatory would have been gratuitous. At best, it might have been a mere additional piece of evidence pointing toward an Article 26 violation. If this were the case, the court's use of the Bowers and Pierce percentages would have been supplemental. As additional supportive material, these data might have been viewed as suggestive, rather than definitive.

But, if this had happened, the court had hardly taken the care to indicate it. The racial discrimination issue, on the contrary, was presented as a prominent part of its holding. The Bowers and Pierce statistics were not relegated to a footnote, but were a major segment of the text of the opinion (pp. 1285-1286). Thus, no matter how they ended up in the court's holding, it would be impossible for the rest of the bench, the bar, and the public to view them as merely ancillary. For the world outside the court, therefore, rigorous social science standards in the usage of such materials might well have been expected.

Had the Bowers-Pierce statistics been added through a compromise? As noted previously, the chance of a court's misusing social science analyses and data might be increased appreciably if they were added to its opinion as a result of a compromise. It is therefore at least conceivable that Hennessey might have given the Bowers-Pierce statistics less than adequate scrutiny if they came before him with the strong recommendation of one or more of his colleagues.

It is impossible at this time—without, for example, public access to the justices' working papers—to determine whether such a dynamic was at work in *Watson*'s policymaking. But a hypothesis concerning the role in the case's outcome of Justice Robert Braucher is at least suggestive. Justice Braucher had not joined Hennessey in the court's invalidation of capital statutes in earlier cases. Yet, he did in *Watson*.

Might the racial discrimination argument have made a difference? One of the attorneys who participated actively in the *Watson* case has contended that it played a major part in Braucher's joining the court's opinion (telephone interview, March 28, 1986). And this assertion is not, at least, wholly discounted by Braucher's concurrence in *Watson*.

Braucher's brief statement did not expressly mention the racial discrimination issue. And it seemed to place a substantial emphasis upon the argument that since post-*Gregg* executions had been very rare—and inflicted only after agonizingly long delays—they constituted a cruel or unusual punishment violative of Article 26. But Braucher also stated that he would not have signed the majority's holding "solely on (the) 'contemporary standards of decency'" ground (p. 1287). "In our criminal justice system," he maintained, the responsibility for determining who was to be executed was so "diffused," and such determinations were made in such diverse ways, that like cases were not treated alike and the death penalty was arbitrarily inflicted.

But whether or not the racial discrimination question, and, consequently, the Bowers-Pierce materials, found their way into Hennessey's ruling because of a Braucher-Hennessey compromise, the court may well have given far more attention to whether it was employing them properly.

Was the Bowers-Pierce material even necessary to Watson's *holding?* The last of these threshold considerations might have moved the court to ponder whether it even needed to risk the pitfalls of making recourse to a racial discrimination approach in *Watson.* Were its other arguments sufficient, in themselves, to justify Chapter 488's invalidation? Such a determination would have been suffused with subjectivity. Members of the court, appellate attorneys, and commentators might well have disagreed substantially concerning the level of argumentation that might have been necessary to buttress *Watson's* holding.

Yet, given, as we shall see, the substantial damage possibly done to the court and the law by Hennessey's invocation of the Bowers-Pierce figures, it would have been highly advisable for him to have brought his opinion to a close before he invoked them. His "contemporary standards of decency" approach was, concededly, hardly invulnerable. As noted previously, 35 states passed new death statutes in the wake of *Furman v. Georgia* (1972). National trends, which certainly reflected themselves within Massachusetts, were in the direction of increasingly higher levels of support for the death sentence (*Washington Post National Weekly Edition*, 1985: 38). The U.S. Supreme Court's *Gregg* decision, relying heavily upon the state legislatures to gauge such "contemporary standards of decency," had clearly rejected Hennessey's conclusions (p. 1300). But Massachusetts did have a long history of abolitionism. Its performance in recent presidential elections did suggest strongly that it was one of the most politically liberal states in the nation (Baum and Canon, 1982: 100). Hennessey's opinion had dramatized the mental torments of condemned inmates. Thus, intellectually, it would not have been impossible for him to have rested his ruling entirely upon his first proposition.

And his second reason for Chapter 488's invalidity—that it would entail capriciousness and arbitrariness in the infliction of the death penalty—might also have been based on contentions that excluded the racial discrimination issue. Charles Black, in particular, had vividly portrayed many ways in which the criminal justice system's opportunities for discretion might capriciously and arbitrarily lead to executions. And although racial discrimination provided the basis for one of Black's examples, it was hardly necessary to all of them (Black, 1981: 17-93).

But regardless of how much time and energy the court might have devoted to such threshold concerns, it did conclude in *Watson* that the risks entailed in using the Bowers-Pierce data seemed to be transcended by the contribution they would make to its opinion. With this decision, it assumed the role of social scientist. The law/ social science literature's seven operational considerations thus become operative.

Did the court encourage the development of an extensive lower-court record? Whether or not it perceived it, the court in *Watson* was, as noted earlier, about to rule that the death penalty could not be imposed in any state without racial discrimination. For if the racially discriminatory patterns that it thought it saw in Florida, Georgia, Ohio, and Texas were operative in Massachusetts, even before anyone appeared on that state's death row, they must have been inherent in the very nature of the death sentencing process. But, even if it failed to grasp this premise, the court had to be aware that it was about to make a fateful decision. For it had to know that no other court had found such a pattern of racial discrimination.

Facing such a far-reaching determination, the Court might well have been expected to have availed itself of the most thorough lower court record possible. But, in *Watson*, it chose to invoke social science analyses and data without making any use whatsoever of a trial or intermediate appellate court's assistance.

Watson, of course had the potential to travel up to the court through conventional trial and appellate court processes. But the *Watson* majority would not permit it to do so. The parties, as well as Massachusetts's entire criminal justice system, it argued, would profit from a foreclosure of delays at the system's lower levels. Therefore, it would permit Suffolk County District Attorney Newman Flanagan to test Chapter 488's constitutionality through a controversial declaratory relief action that would bypass all lower-level proceedings (pp. 1280-1281, 1287-1288).

Chapter 488 would accordingly be evaluated, as well as the Bowers-Pierce data, without any trial court testimony. Nor would the court receive any insights from Massachusetts's intermediate appellate judiciary. Indeed, it would determine whether Chapter 488 were racially discriminatory before a Watson, a Real, or any other defendant could even be tried, much less convicted and sentenced, under it.

Did the court provide an adequate opportunity for Massachusetts to critique the Bowers-Pierce findings? The court's unwillingness to look to the lower courts for guidance seemed to have an analogue in the way it approached the question of whether it should expand the scope of the materials directly submitted to it. The parties in *Watson* seemed, for the most part, to be focusing their arguments upon the possible application to *Watson*'s facts of doctrines that did not rest firmly on allegations of racial discrimination.[9]

Perhaps, for this reason, Watson's and Real's racial discrimination contention comprised only about a fifth of their brief, and may have been presented as a possible fall-back ground for a Chapter 488 invalidation. For it was the third of four arguments buttressing Watson's and Real's positions (Watson and Real Brief, 1980). And maybe this was why the briefs for the Suffolk County District Attorney and the Commonwealth of Massachusetts never challenged on social science grounds, the Bowers-Pierce statistics' validity, reliability, and applicability (Flanagan and Massachusetts Briefs, 1980).

Whatever the reason, though, *Watson* evidenced a particularly one-sided invocation of social science arguments. Watson and Real asserted that the substantial disproportions in black and white murderers and victims on Florida's, Georgia's, Ohio's, and Texas's death rows were enough, in and of themselves, to show racial discrimination in these states' impositions of their death penalties. And the state's responses failed utterly to inform or remind the court that, in accordance with social science's elementary requisites, the abolitionists still had to account for rival plausible hypotheses. Instead, the state merely admonished the court not to take "judicial notice of the statistical data and sociological opinion" that Watson and Real had presented. It would be inappropriate, it argued, from the perspective of the separation of powers, for the justices "to negate specific legislative findings in favor of 'so-called evidence' unable to be tested for trustworthiness." (*Massachusetts Brief*, 1980: 21) "[U]nable to be tested for trustworthiness. . . " There was much, in a different sense, in this statement. For, with no lower court record to rely upon, the court had made itself, as far as its formal input was concerned, totally dependent upon Watson's and Real's account of what Bowers's and Pierce's statistics indicated and whether they could appropriately be applied to *Watson*.

This development, however, had hardly been inevitable. Had a significant number of its members begun to regard the Bowers-Pierce research as potentially pivotal, they could have easily directed the counsel for the parties and amici to address it. All that would have been necessary would have been to invite them, via a supplemental briefing, to consider whether the Bowers-Pierce percentages could prove useful to *Watson*.

Did the Justices go beyond the briefs directly to review Bowers's and Pierce's study? It will be recalled that Donald Horowitz, among others, has criticized judges' and justices' tendencies to rely upon such secondary, and frequently biased, sources as investigatory commissions' reports and briefs when assessing potentially decisive social science studies. Did the court succumb to this temptation?

In the first place, the *Watson* Court was foreclosed from thoroughly examining Bowers's and Pierce's analysis because Bowers and Pierce had not yet published their findings. Their percentages had merely been made available to the abolitionists as preliminary data, fresh from the field and the computer (Addendum to Watson and Real Brief, 1980: 15-40). The court thus never gave itself the opportunity to assess them in the context of a fully developed study that might well have comprehensively canvassed the literature and flagged the study's strengths and weaknesses. Without such a presentation, it received the Bowers-Pierce materials bereft of customary social science conditionals.

Second, even in their use of these provisional figures, the justices bypassed some especially important evidence. The Bowers-Pierce data, for example, also indicated severe disparities, again relating to the races of the murderer and victim, in the specific category of felony-murders. This classification would encompass murders committed in the course of rapes or robberies—a type that might be expected to be a particularly good stimulus for the imposition of the death penalty. Hence, if the relationship between the race of the perpetrator and that of the victim continued into this area, it would be more difficult for Florida, Georgia, Ohio, and Texas to ascribe it to nonracial factors. For they would lose the argument that the overall pattern that Bowers and Pierce had discovered merely reflected, to a dramatic extent, a higher propensity of whites to be murdered while suffering other felonies (Addendum to Watson and Real Brief, 1980: 23-25).

Yet the court evidenced no interest in such variables. It was, on the contrary, apparently content to use nothing more than the initial raw statistics that the Watson and Real briefs reported. It thus seemed unwilling even to take a step toward subjecting them to the kind of analysis that might well be characteristic of a competent social scientist.

Did the court demonstrate a knowledge of the Bowers and Pierce materials' place within their field? Nowhere in Hennessey's opinion did he present an overview of the racial-discrimination-in-capital-punishment literature. Nor did he attempt to delineate the kinds of models and theoretical structures central to such inquiries. Similarly, he indicated no awareness of social science studies that had not found racially discriminatory patterns in states like California, even though such works had been expounded upon by federal jurists at least as far back as *Furman v. Georgia* (1972).

Had the court attempted to gauge whether Bowers's and Pierce's study was a leading piece of research? Had it determined whether the racial-discrimination-in-capital-punishment sentencing area was a settled field of inquiry? Did it try to find out whether Bowers's and Pierce's findings were representative of a consensus within their disciplines? Or had it merely dealt with the Bowers-Pierce figures *in vacuo?* There was nothing in Hennessey's opinion to suggest that the answer to the last question should not be in the affirmative.

Did the court show an awareness of how, as a social scientist, it might personally evaluate Watson's and Real's employment of the Bowers-Pierce statistics? Hennessey's exposition never indicated an interest in whether Bowers's and Pierce's specific conceptualizations, measurement techniques, and populations chosen for analysis were valid and reliable. It never discussed such a basic social science concern as the study's explanatory power. It likewise did not address the aggregation question. Indeed, as previously shown, it did not take advantage of an opportunity to disaggregate Bowers's and Pierce's overall percentages into perhaps the more significant ones that it could have presented relating to felony-murders. And, as also noted earlier, Hennessey, in a similar fashion, demonstrated no curiosity about such a crucial social science concern as whether Bowers and Pierce effectively controlled for other plausible variables.

Should the court have been aware of such factors? Given the law/social science commentary and the experiences of sister state and federal courts, it is somewhat remarkable that Hennessey did not examine them. Had he wished to, however, he would have found it impossible to do so, had he relied solely upon the submissions of the parties and amici. For the Watson and Real briefs, the court's sources of the Bowers and Pierce statistics, never attempted to indicate the kinds of issues that were central to this form of scholarship (Watson and Real Brief, 1980: 5870; Addendum to Watson and Real Brief, 1980: 15-40).

Could Florida, Georgia, Ohio, and Texas findings be transposed to Massachusetts? The most questionable part of all of Hennessey's racial discrimination analysis was probably when he took Florida, Georgia, Ohio, and Texas patterns of death sentencing and concluded, without a single inmate on Massachusetts's death row, that they also showed that the state's imposition of Chapter 488 would be racially discriminatory. It is, as argued previously, difficult to believe that any sociologist, any criminologist, or any graduate student would have written a paper taking such a position. Given all the social science inundating the state and federal courts, including material dealing with capital punishment and deterrence, the odds must have been exceedingly low that Hennessey was not aware that major demographic differences in states might well make such findings in four of them inapplicable to others.

But he was nevertheless willing to put his Court on record as concluding that the racially discriminatory patterns that it thought it discerned in three southern states and one midwestern state would inescapably be operative in a northeastern one like Massachusetts.

Constituting a major portion of Hennessey's rationale for doing so were, as observed earlier, the Court's holdings in *Commonwealth v. Soares* (1979) and *Commonwealth v. Franklin* (1978). These cases, Hennessey claimed, had indicated that Chapter 488's implementation would be as racially discriminatory as those of the capital statutes of Bowers's and Pierce's four states because *Soares* and *Franklin* revealed "the existence of racial prejudice in some persons in . . . Massachusetts." (p. 1286).

But who were these "persons" and how might they affect Chapter 488's imposition? *Soares* involved a black defendant's first-degree murder trial. But it was not a capital case, since Soares was facing a maximum sentence of life imprisonment if convicted of the highly publicized murder of a white Harvard football player. The court held in *Soares* that a prosecutor's dismissal, through the use of peremptory challenges, of 12 out of 13 prospective black jurors, constituted a prima facie violation of Soares's constitutionally protected right, under the Massachusetts Declaration of Rights, to a "jury fairly drawn from the community."

In *Franklin*, Franklin, a black convicted of firearms laws violations, contended that he had been the victim of racially discriminatory law enforcement. Franklin, the court concluded, had presented unrebutted evidence in the proceedings below that gangs of white youths, with seeming impunity, had stoned and firebombed blacks' homes in Franklin's neighborhood. Franklin was also able to make a prima facie case, it found, that racial discrimination had motivated at least some of the police officers and court officials dealing with these incidents. Hence, there was "a reasonable inference of selective prosecution" of Franklin, who argued that he had armed himself to repel the antiblack violence that had been permitted, if not sanctioned, by the authorities. At the very least, the court determined, the trial court should have afforded Franklin a full hearing on his assertion.

Hence, *Soares* and *Franklin* did suggest strongly that *some* Massachusetts law enforcement and judicial officials might, in certain instances, exercise their discretion in a racially discriminatory manner. But they hardly demonstrated that Chapter 488's implementation would inescapably entail racial discrimination. To reach such a conclusion required the court to engage in the most sweeping of speculations.

Possibly aware of the substantial pitfalls of transposing Florida, Georgia, Ohio, and Texas findings to Massachusetts, even the Watson and Real brief, in the heat of the adversary process, stated only that the Bowers-Pierce statistics made it "likely" that Chapter 488 would be imposed in a racially discriminatory manner. But Hennessey refused to proceed with such caution. For, with no additional data, he replaced their brief's "likely" with his "inevitably." He held that the Bowers-Pierce study showed that Chapter 488 would "inevitably" be administered with racial discrimination (p. 1286).

Had the court drawn heavily upon the experiences of other state and federal courts in its pivotal employment of Bowers's and Pierce's figures? The answer to this query, in light of so much that has already been noted, is an obvious "no." The *Watson* Court showed close to no inclination to review the work of the other state and federal judiciaries that had grappled with similar social science questions. It frequently made recourses to their cases for other purposes. It, for example, often employed quotations from *Gregg*'s *dissenters* to undergird its positions (pp. 1279-1283). But the court all but ignored the lessons stemming from other courts' confrontations with the racial issue.

That the overall result was unfortunate was demonstrated in two ways. First, as shown by the court's lack of concern with the letter and spirit of perhaps every one of the law/social science literature's 12 threshold and operational considerations, its racial discrimination ruling in *Watson* constituted a classic instance of a court's misuse of social science. Second, *Watson*'s aftermath indicated that the court, as well as the law, may have paid a high price for the court's substandard performance as a social scientist.

The Aftermath

Whatever the reasons for *Watson*'s racial discrimination holding, it was hardly a success from the perspective of the court's leading the way for other judiciaries. No state courts followed California and Massachusetts with per se invalidations of their states' capital statutes. Thus, it was not surprising that *Watson* was not cited approvingly by them. But, with the exception of Chief Justice Ray L. Brock of the Tennessee Supreme Court (*Tennessee v. Dicks,* 1981), even the dissenters on sister courts failed to refer to *Watson*'s racial discrimination analysis favorably. Moreover, the members of the federal judiciary, even those convinced that the infliction of capital punishment was racially discriminatory, did not avail themselves of *Watson*'s Bowers-Pierce argument. They were engaged in far more sophisticated and, in a number of instances, far more defensible, invocations of the social sciences.[10]

And the negative impact upon Massachusetts's own judicial policy-making was more severe. The Massachusetts legislature and electorate may well have not shared Hennessey's remarkable conclusion shortly after *Watson* that that case's racial discrimination finding was "indisputable" (Hennessey, C. J., dissenting in *Moe v. Secretary of Administration and Finance* (1981). For within two years of *Watson,* Massachusetts's voters approved an amendment of Article 26 that proclaimed that no provision of the Massachusetts Constitution was to be "construed as prohibiting the imposition of the punishment of death" (Article 116 of the Massachusetts Constitution, 1982).

It is highly probable, given the times and the attitudes unleashed by them, that even a brilliantly written *Watson* opinion would have been followed by a pro-capital punishment amendment. But the substantial controversiality of *Watson*'s racial discrimination determination, and the highly questionable social science basis on which it rested, might well have added fuel to the amending process fire.

Whatever caused the amendment's passage, at least some of its proponents argued that, in the wake of cases like *Watson*, it relieved the court of all future death penalty cases. The responsibility for determining the constitutionality of Massachusetts's impositions of capital punishment, so this argument went, had now been vested solely by Massachusetts's people in the United States Supreme Court as it interpreted the national constitution (Nolan, J., dissenting in *Commonwealth v. Colon-Cruz* 1984).

But the court had no intention of permitting the new amendment to extinguish its death penalty jurisdiction. In an opinion by Justice Paul Liacos, it consequently rejected such an approach to the amendment in *Commonwealth v. Colon-Cruz* (1984). The amending of Article 26 overruled *Watson*, Liacos observed, as he struck down Massachusetts's latest capital statute, Chapter 554 (1982). In its wake, the court could no longer contend that the death penalty constituted "cruel or unusual punishment." But the justices were still free, he found, to regulate the imposition of capital statutes, and in doing so to declare them null and void if they violated *other* provisions of the Massachusetts Constitution.

Yet, Liacos may well have ignored or sidestepped a serious implication of *Watson*'s racial discrimination analysis. Of course, the people of Massachusetts could demonstrate, by amending their constitution, that they believed the death sentence did not constitute "cruel or unusual punishment." But could they simply erase Hennessey's *social science* conclusions? Or did their assessment indicate that, despite their highest court's conclusion that, *inherently* and *inevitably*, capital punishment was racially discriminatory, they had opted for it anyway? Was this not the symbolic connotation of their action? Or did the amendment reflect their view that, from the perspective of social science, Hennessey's conclusions on the racial question had been unsound?

Both of these possibilities were distasteful. Massachusetts's citizens were either expressing their support for the killing of persons on a racially discriminatory basis; or they were, by mere votes, resolving questions that could be determined only through a proper invocation of the social sciences! Yet, Liacos's *Colon-Cruz* opinion failed to confront these possibilities. Unarticulated, therefore, were the disquieting residues of *Watson*'s racial discrimination determination.

CONCLUSIONS

In an increasing number of capital punishment cases, federal and state courts are being called upon to confront social science questions.

This development has placed them more and more in the position of social commentator, requiring them, to an ever greater extent, to legitimate or reject empirical interpretations of various social realities. The Massachusetts Supreme Judicial Court encountered one of these instances in *Watson*. In the *Watson* case, it chose to determine a social science issue of no small proportions. It found that Massachusetts could not separate racial discrimination from its imposition of the death penalty. Indeed, implicitly but obviously, the court concluded that no jurisdiction in the United States could employ a capital punishment statute in a way that would not be racially discriminatory.

Given the profundity of such a holding—and its relatively indelible and highly symbolic quality—the justices could have been expected to have carefully evaluated the relevant social science materials. But they failed effectively to avail themselves of a rich variety of approaches and sources, which, at a minimum, could have helped them to avoid a number of pitfalls.

Judiciaries at such junctures in the future may thus be able to profit substantially from the *Watson* experience—and lower substantially their odds of misapplying social science materials—if they consider very carefully a dozen or so threshold and operational questions. As approaches to the former, they might pose and answer for themselves the following:

Are we contemplating a use of social science that will be pivotal to our holding? Would our contemplated infusion of social science analysis tend to vindicate or proscribe governmental action previously presumed to be constitutional? Might our merely supplemental use of such materials be interpreted as a decisive one? Might social science sources find their way into our opinion without our studiously evaluating them, as a result of compromises among our justices? Could the patterns of behavior we wish to delineate be just as effectively demonstrated through common-sense presentations?

And as operational concerns, they might continue in similar self-questioning:

Have we made use of our state's trial and intermediate appellate courts to develop a record that will be insightful to us in our resolution of such social science questions? Have we made sure that the parties and amici have been able to rebut each other's positions on our possibly pivotal use of social science studies and data? Have we personally examined social science analyses that might be decisive to our holdings? Have we determined where such a study might fit into its field of inquiry? Have we applied elementary social science rules of thumb at least to begin an assessment of whether such an analysis is valid and reliable? Have we determined whether such materials really do apply to the specific issues before us? As a possible safeguard to all of the foregoing considerations, have we studied the experiences in similar situations of our colleagues on the state and federal benches?

With even a minimal level of care, the Supreme Judicial Court, or any comparable court, might have been expected to have asked itself at least some of these queries. There thus was little excuse for it to make the racial discrimination determination it made in *Watson*.[11]

But why should it, or any court for that matter, take such social science issues so seriously? Several reasons seem obvious. As Kenneth Karst (1960) predicted two decades ago, even to begin to grasp the facts of many of the complex new cases coming before them, our courts need, at a minimum, to become moderately capable social scientists. The accuracy of their decision making may simply depend upon their being able to do so. And there is far more. Their legitimacy as judicial institutions rests on more than their effectiveness in resolving legally articulated social problems. They must demonstrate that the reasoning of their opinions is not mere window-dressing for decisions determined by their biases (Porter, 1982: 9-17). They must show that they do not take their scholarship cavalierly—that, with a commitment to the highest intellectual standards, they seek a genuine understanding of social reality. They must be aware, to modify a phrase of the greatest jurist ever to sit on the Massachusetts Supreme Judicial Court, that poor social science makes for bad law (Holmes, J. in *Northern Securities Co. v. United States,* 1904).

NOTES

1. *McCleskey v. Kemp*, 107 S. Ct. 1756 (1987). For the federal courts' treatments of the *McCleskey* case at the district and circuit court of appeals levels, see *McCleskey v. Zant*, 580 F. Supp. 338 (1984) and *McCleskey v. Kemp*, 753 F. 2d 877 (1985) respectively.

2. See, for example, the comments of Chief Justice Joseph Tauro in *Commonwealth v. O'Neal*, 339 N. E. 2d 676, 690-691 (1975).

3. See, for example, *Stanford Law Review*, 1969: 1297-1497.

4. The lawyer's term, "shepardizing," of course, refers to the use of *Shepard's Citations* to research precedents. The *Shepard's* series is presently published in Colorado Springs, Colorado by McGraw-Hill.

5. Although a number of the sources cited in the preceding discussion of threshold and operational considerations have publication dates *after Watson*, these works, relying upon books and articles preceding the *Watson* case, largely summarized caveats that had long been disseminated in the law/social science field.

6. The fate of this study in the federal courts is chronicled in Dorin, 1981.

7. Article 26 of the Declaration of Rights of the Commonwealth of Massachusetts stated the following: "No magistrate, or court of law, shall demand excessive bail or sureties, impose excessive fines, or inflict cruel or unusual punishments."

8. By *Watson*, California had overturned the *Anderson* case through a constitutional amendment, which was acknowledged by the California Supreme Court in *People v. Frierson*, 599 P. 2d. 587 (1979).

9. Earlier capital punishment cases of the Supreme Judicial Court seemed to stress deterrence as the principal factor to be considered in such litigation. See, for example, *Commonwealth v. O'Neal*, 327 N. E. 2d. 662 (1975), *Commonwealth v. O'Neal*, 339 N. E. 2d. 676 (1975), *Opinion of the Justices to the House of Representatives*, 364 N. E. 184 (1977) and Dorin, 1986: 25-32.

10. See, as a contemporary example of such an invocation, U. S. Circuit Courts of Appeals Judge Frank Johnson's opinion in *McCleskey v. Kemp*, 753 F. 2d. 877, 907-927 (1985).

11. One of the attorneys in *Watson* has contended that its racial discrimination holding can best be explained by what this person characterizes as the majority's "sheer arrogance" (telephone interview, 1986). According to this individual, the court has become accustomed to using any rationale it finds convenient at any particular time. Whatever might be the basis for such a statement by a less than impartial participant, the court's performance in *Watson* does not discount it.

REFERENCES

ABT, C. (1980) "What judges and layers need to know about applied social research," pp. 67-69 in M. Saks and C. Baron (eds.) The Use/Nonuse/Misuse of Applied Social Research in the Courts. Cambridge, MA: Abt Books.

BALDUS, D. and J. COLE (1977) "Quantitative proof of intentional discrimination." Evaluation Quarterly 1: 53-86.

BALDUS, D., C. PULASKI and G. WOODWORTH (1986) "Arbitrariness and discrimination in the administration of the death penalty: A challenge to state supreme courts." Stetson Law Review 15: 133-261.

BAUM, L. and B. CANON (1982) "State supreme courts as activists: New doctrines in the law of torts," pp. 83-108 in C. Porter and G. Tarr (eds.) State Supreme Courts: Policymakers in the Federal System. Westport, CT: Greenwood.

BERK, R. and J. OPPENHEIM (1979) "Doing good well—the use of quantitative social science data in adversary proceedings." Law and Policy Quarterly 1: 123-146.

BLACK, C. (1981) Capital Punishment—The Inevitability of Caprice and Mistake (2nd ed.). New York: W. W. Norton.

Briefs of the parties and *amicus* in District Attorney for the Suffolk District v. Watson, 411 N. E. 2d 1274 (1980).

CALDEIRA, G. (1983) "On the reputation of state supreme courts." Political Behavior 5: 83-108.

CANON, B. and L. BAUM (1981) "Patterns of adoption of tort law innovations: An application of diffusion theory to judicial doctrines." American Political Science Review 75: 975-987.

CARLSON, K. (1980) "What judges and lawyers need to know about applied social research," pp. 69-71 in M. Saks and C. Baron (eds.) The Use/Nonuse/Misuse of Applied Social Research in the Courts. Cambridge, MA: Abt Books.

CHANNELS, N. (1985) Social Science Methods in the Legal Process. Totowa, NJ Rowman and Allanheld.

DANIELS, S. (1979) "Social science and death penalty cases." Law and Policy Quarterly: 336-372.

DORIN, D. (1981) "Two different worlds: Criminologists, justices, and racial discrimination in the imposition of capital punishment in rape cases." Journal of Criminal Law and Criminology 72: 1667-1698.

DORIN, D. (1986) "The Massachusetts Supreme Judicial Court's invalidation of Massachusetts's death penalty as racially discriminatory: A description, evaluation, and prescription," presented at the 38th Annual Meeting of the American Society of Criminology, Atlanta, Georgia, October 30, 1986.

DRIESSEN, P. (1983) "The wedding of social science and the courts." Social Science Quarterly 64: 476-493.

Encyclopedia Americana (1984) "Massachusetts" (pp. 448-473). Danbury, CT: Grolier.

FRIEDELBAUM, S. (1982) "Independent state grounds: Contemporary invitations to activism," pp. 23-53 in C. Porter and G. Tarr (eds.) State Supreme Courts: Policymakers in the Federal System. Westport, CT: Greenwood.

HOROWITZ, D. (1977) The Courts and Social Policy. Washington, DC: Brookings Institution.

HOROWITZ, D. (1980) "Overcoming barriers to the use of applied social research in the courts," pp. 149-154 in M. Saks and C. Baron (eds.) The Use/Nonuse/Misuse of Applied Social Research in the Courts. Cambridge, MA: Abt Books.

KARST, K. (1960) "Legislative facts in constitutional litigation." Supreme Court Review: 75-112.

LIGHT, R. (1980) "What judges and lawyers need to know about applied social research," pp. 63-67 in M. Saks and C. Baron (eds.) The Use/Nonuse/Misuse of Applied Social Research in the Courts. Cambridge, MA: Abt Books.

MAXWELL, T. (1980) "Misuses of applied social research," pp. 29-33 in M. Saks and C. Baron (eds.) The Use/Nonuse/Misuse of Applied Social Research in the Courts. Cambridge, MA: Abt Books.

MELTSNER, M. (1973) Cruel and Unusual—The Supreme Court and Capital Punishment. New York: Random House.

MICHELSON, S. (1980) "History and state of the art of applied social research in the courts," pp. 3-8 in M. Saks and C. Baron (eds.) The Use/Nonuse/Misuse of Applied Social Research in the Courts. Cambridge, MA: Abt Books.

MOYNIHAN, D. (1979) "Social science and the courts." Public Interest 54: 13-31.

O'BRIEN, D. (1980) "The seduction of the judiciary: Social science and the courts." Judicature 64: 8-21.

PORTER, M. (1982) "State supreme courts and the legacy of the Warren Court: Some old inquiries for a new situation," pp. 3-21 in C. Porter and G. Tarr (eds.) State Supreme Courts: Policymakers in the Federal System. Westport, CT: Greenwood.

ROSEN, P. (1972) The Supreme Court and Social Science. Urbana: University of Illinois Press.

ROSEN, P. (1982) "History and state of the art of applied social research in the courts," pp. 9-15 in M. Saks and C. Baron (eds.) The Use/Nonuse/Misuse of Applied Social Research in the Courts. Cambridge, MA: Abt Books.

Shepard's Citations (1970-1986) Colorado Springs, CO: McGraw-Hill.

Stanford Law Review (1969) "A study of the California penalty jury in first-degree murder cases: Standardless sentencing." Volume 21: 1297-1497.

Washington Post National Weekly Edition (1985) "Support for capital punishment increasing." March 18: 38.

CASES

Brown v. Board of Education, 347 U.S. 483, 494 (1954).

Coker v. Georgia, 433 U. S. 584 (1977).

Commonwealth v. Colon-Cruz, 470 N. E. 2d. 116, 120-123, 135 (1984).

Commonwealth v. Franklin, 385 N. E. 2d. 227 (1978).

Commonwealth v. O'Neal, 327 N. E. 2d. 662 (1975).

Commonwealth v. O'Neal, 339 N. E. 2d. 676 (1975).

Commonwealth v. Soares, 387 N. E. 2d. 499 (1979).

District Attorney for the Suffolk District v. Watson, 411 N. E. 2d. 1274 (1980).

Furman v. Georgia, 408 U. S. 238, 308-309 (1972).

Gregg v. Georgia, 428 U. S. 153 (1976).

McCleskey v. Kemp, 107 S. Ct. 1756 (1987).

McCleskey v. Kemp, 753 F. 2d. 877 (1985).

McCleskey v. Zant, 580 F. Supp. 338 (1984).

Moe v. Secretary of Administration and Finance, 417 N. E. 2d. 387, 406-407 (1981).

Muller v. Oregon, 208 U. S. 412 (1908).

Northern Securities Co. v. United States, 193 U. S. 197, 400-401 (1904).

Opinion of the Justices to the House of Representatives, 364 N. E. 2d. 184 (1977).

People v. Anderson, 493 P. 2d. 880 (1972).

People v. Frierson, 599 P. 2d. 587 (1979).

Tennessee v. Dicks, 615 S. W. 2d. 126, 134, 141 (1981).

Chapter 9

IMPOSING THE DEATH PENALTY ON CHILDREN

VICTOR L. STREIB

A quite rare but nonetheless shocking dimension of the death penalty in our criminal justice system is the imposition of that ultimate sanction upon our children. Offenders under the age of 18 at the time of their crimes, generally defined under American law as children or juveniles, have been executed in our past and 33 of their brothers and sisters are currently residing on the death rows of 15 states.

This chapter explores this complex issue from both legal and empirical viewpoints. First the legal environment is described in order to understand how some adolescents come to such an ignominious end. Then the past practice of actual executions for juvenile offenses is analyzed, focusing upon the executing jurisdictions, the crimes, the offenders, and the victims. Next the present practice is examined, including all juvenile death sentences imposed since 1982 and all persons currently under juvenile death sentences. A trend away from the death penalty for juveniles is identified, and the final section sketches seven key criteria to be addressed in such a trend.

LEGAL ENVIRONMENT

Juveniles in Criminal Court

Even when offenders are under the chronological age limit for juvenile court, several means exist by which their cases could be processed in adult criminal court rather than in juvenile court. The consequences of this change of court are enormous. Although juvenile court is limited to ordering probation or perhaps institutionalization until the child is age 21 (Davis, 1986), the criminal court typically has the full range of criminal sentences available even for young teenage offenders, including long terms in prison and even the death penalty (Zimring, 1982).

Three primary means are available for placing a juvenile offender's case in adult criminal court. Some states expressly exclude certain offenses from juvenile court jurisdiction and place all of these designated offenses within criminal court jurisdiction regardless of the age of the offender (Fox, 1984: 8). In these instances the case against the child is always filed directly in adult court and never goes through the juvenile court procedure.

A second method by which the case might be filed directly in adult criminal court is illustrated by those few states that give the prosecuting attorney the discretion to file cases either in juvenile court or in adult criminal court (Davis, 1986: 2-22). The third means by which a person under the juvenile court age could nonetheless end up in adult criminal court is for the juvenile court to waive its original jurisdiction over the case and transfer the case to the adult criminal court (*Kent v. United States,* 1966).

No matter how the child's case gets to adult criminal court, once there the case proceeds essentially as it would for any adult. The child receives all the rights and protections of adult criminal defendants but also faces all or most of the adult criminal sentences. For the most serious offenses, such sentences may include the death penalty.

U.S. Supreme Court Rulings

The Court's attention to death penalty issues during the past 15 years is well-known and widely reported (Bedau, 1982), making a detailed presentation unnecessary here. *Gregg v. Georgia* (1976) launched the current era, holding that the death penalty does not violate per se the eighth amendment. Although the issue was not specifically before the Court in *Gregg*, in passing the Court approved of Georgia requirements that the jury consider the youthfulness of the offender (*Gregg v. Georgia,* 1976: 197).

In a companion case to *Gregg*, the Court also approved of the Texas statute, which provided that the sentencing jury "could further look to the age of the defendant" (*Jurek v. Texas*, 1976: 273) in deciding between life imprisonment and the death sentence. In 1978 the Court's decision in *Lockett v. Ohio* held that unlimited consideration of mitigating factors was constitutionally required, in part because the Court thought it important that a defendant's youthful age be considered in the sentencing decision.

A few years later the Supreme Court agreed to decide the specific issue of the constitutionality of the death penalty for an offense committed when the defendant was only 16 years old. In its final holding, however, the Court in *Eddings v. Oklahoma* (1982) avoided that constitutionality issue, and instead sent the case back for resentencing after full consideration of all mitigating factors per the *Lockett* holding. On the issue of the offender's youth, however, the Court did hold that "the chronological age of a minor is itself a relevant mitigating factor of great weight" (*Eddings v. Oklahoma*, 1982: 116).

The Supreme Court has agreed again to consider the constitutionality issue, but as of this writing has not decided the case (*Thompson v. Oklahoma*, 1987). The determination of the legality of capital punishment for juveniles is thus left to each individual jurisdiction. The only constitutional mandate is that each jurisdiction must permit consideration of the youth of the offender as a mitigating factor of great weight by the sentencing jury or judge.

Specific Statutory Provisions

Within the 50 states and the District of Columbia the statutory law seems fairly well settled. Of these 51 jurisdictions, 15 have no valid death penalty statutes. These 15 jurisdictions don't execute anyone, including juveniles. The other 36 states have apparently valid death penalty statutes.

Table 9.1 arrays the 36 death penalty states according to their establishment, by whatever means, of the minimum age of the offender at the time of the offense for eligibility for the death penalty. No minimum age whatsoever is established in ten of these states.

Of the 26 states that do establish a minimum age, 10 states use age 18 directly in their death penalty statutes. Seven states have established age 14 as the minimum either as a result of their juvenile court waiver statutes or through their exclusive or concurrent jurisdiction provisions. Although this does operate to establish a minimum age for the death

TABLE 9.1

Minimum Age of Offender Required by
36 Death Penalty Jurisdictions

Age at Offense	Jurisdiction	Total
18	California, Colorado, Connecticut, Illinois, Nebraska, New Jersey, New Mexico, Ohio, Oregon, and Tennessee	10
17	Georgia, New Hampshire, and Texas	3
16	Nevada	1
15	Louisiana and Virginia	2
14	Alabama, Arkansas, Idaho, Kentucky, Missouri, North Carolina, Pennsylvania, and Utah	8
13	Mississippi	1
12	Montana	1
10	Indiana	1
No minimum	Arizona, Delaware, Florida, Maryland, Oklahoma, South Carolina, South Dakota, Washington, and Wyoming	9
Total		36

penalty, it is more precisely a minimum age for any criminal court jurisdiction. The rest of these 26 states have minimum ages scattered from 10 to 17.

Lower Court Cases

Eddings was decided by the U.S. Supreme Court on January 19, 1982, and has been relied upon by many lower courts since that time. As was discussed earlier, the Court in *Eddings* reaffirmed that youth of the offender is a mitigating factor of great weight that must be considered, but the Court avoided any direct holding on the constitutionality of the death penalty for juveniles. However, several lower courts have divined more from the *Eddings* holding than seems reasonable.

Cases such as *High v. Zant* (1983) and *State v. Battle* (1983) have cited *Eddings* as holding that the death penalty for juveniles is not unconstitutional. This proposition is, of course, precisely the issue presented to but not decided by the Supreme Court in *Eddings*. Most lower courts have agreed that *Eddings* did not settle the constitutionality issue but some then have gone on to decide that issue themselves. An illustrative case is *Trimble v. State* (1984) in which a Maryland court first noted that *Eddings* left the constitutionality question unanswered. Then the Maryland court went on to resolve the issue from reference to other Supreme Court cases. The *Trimble* court concluded that indicators of society's evolving standards of decency did not reject this punishment for Trimble and that it should take a case-by-case approach to future cases of the death penalty for juveniles.

A third approach to *Eddings* is exemplified by such cases as *Cannaday v. State* (1984). In *Cannaday*, the Mississippi Supreme Court noted that the U.S. Supreme Court had not found the death penalty for juveniles to be unconstitutional and so left the matter there without attempting its own constitutional analysis. The court reversed Attina Cannaday's death sentence on other grounds but expressly excluded the constitutionality issue as a basis for that reversal.

A final group of state court cases has placed strong emphasis upon the great mitigating weight to be given the defendant's youth, as is required by the *Eddings* case, and then found that mitigation to be so compelling that the death sentence must be reversed. A leading example is *State v. Valencia* (1982), in which the Arizona Supreme Court set aside the death penalty and ordered that 16-year-old Valencia be sentenced to life imprisonment. The *Valencia* court did not rule out the death penalty for all juveniles but left the clear impression that only the most extraordinary facts would justify a juvenile death penalty.

The lower court decisions, then, have gone in at least four directions. Some have erroneously assumed that *Eddings* decided the constitutionality issue for capital punishment of juveniles. Others have agreed that *Eddings* left that question undecided but then went on to decide the issue themselves, to the detriment of the young offenders before them. A third group has relegated the matter totally to their legislatures, finding no restrictions from *Eddings* or any other source. The last group has focussed upon the *Eddings* observation that youthfulness of the offender is to be given great weight as a mitigating factor and then usually have gone on to find that great weight to be a compelling reason in the case before them to reduce the juvenile's sentence from the death penalty to long-term imprisonment.

Questionable Constitutionality

Careful examination of the constitutional justifications for the death penalty for adults reveals their inapplicability to the death penalty for juveniles (Streib, 1986). The empirical evidence is overwhelming that the death penalty is not a greater general deterrent to murder than is long-term imprisonment (Bowers, 1984: 271-335) but some continue to cling to their intuitive belief that it is (*Gregg v. Georgia,* 1976: 185-186). Even if they were correct in the case of adults, it would not be correct for juveniles.

From what we know about adolescent psychology, teenagers have no meaningful concept of death and thus don't understand the threatened penalty (Corr and McNeil, 1986). To the degree to which they know that certain behavior could result in their death, they often seem attracted to it. Witness their persistent involvement in dangerous driving, ingestion of dangerous drugs, suicide attempts, and so on. It seems obvious that teenagers would be much more deterred by the threat of long-term imprisonment (no cars, no girlfriends, no parties) than by some fantasized perception of death.

The primary reason why our society strongly supports the death penalty in general is retribution, defined broadly as a sense of justice and the need for legal revenge against the offender (*Journal of Criminal Law and Criminology,* 1983). On this issue it seems generally agreed that "Crimes committed by youths may be just as harmful to victims as those committed by older persons, but they deserve less punishment because adolescents may have less capacity to control their conduct and to think in long-range terms than adults" (Twentieth Century Fund, 1978: 7).

The argument for the death penalty as the ultimate means of incapacitating juvenile offenders from committing future offenses asks for simply too much punishment for too little additional result. Juvenile murderers have one of the lowest recidivism rates of any type of offender and long-term imprisonment of them is more than adequate incapacitation (Vitello, 1976: 32-34).

The death penalty unequivocally rejects the alternative of rehabilitative efforts to reshape the offender into an acceptable member of society. This may be an acceptable decision when the offender is a 40-year-old, three-time loser who shows no desire or ability to change. However, the essential nature of teenagers is that they will grow and mature, almost always in directions more acceptable to society (*Workman v. Commonwealth,* 1968: 378). To unequivocally reject rehabilitation for teenagers is to deny the fundamental characteristics of that transitional stage of life.

As a result of increasing societal rejection of this penalty (Southern Coalition Report, 1986) and a general lack of justifications for it, the imposition of the death penalty upon juveniles is a prime example of an arbitrary, capricious, and freakish punishment. Juveniles commit about 1,500 intentional criminal homicides each year, about 9% of the total (Federal Bureau of Investigation, 1974-1984). Less than 0.5% of these juvenile homicides result in the juvenile death penalty being imposed. Of the approximately 300 total death sentences imposed each year (U.S. Department of Justice, 1986), juveniles receive only about five of them. Moreover, no rational basis can be discerned for why these three to six juveniles were sentenced to death and the hundreds of other juvenile murderers were not.

Perhaps the only question remaining is the specific age at which the line should be drawn for the death penalty. Age 18 seems by far to be the obvious choice. Eighteen is the juvenile court age for 38 states (Davis, 1986) and is the most common age for majority for noncriminal purposes (Zimring, 1982). Eighteen is the age used in international treaties and by almost all other countries (Amnesty International, 1979).

It seems clear that a firm line must be drawn and not simply be left to an after-the-fact deliberation concerning the maturity of a particular teenager. This is the approach used in comparable areas of law. Chronological age, not mental maturity, is the sole determinant for voting, drinking alcoholic beverages, getting married, buying a house, and scores of other adult rights and privileges (Zimring, 1982). To deny the offender under age 18 all of these adult rights and privileges but to impose the harshest of adult punishments raises the most serious questions of constitutionality, fundamental fairness and justice.

PAST PRACTICE

At least 15,000 legal, nonmilitary executions have occurred in the United States since colonial times. Executions for crimes committed by a person under age 18 have accounted for only 281 or less than 2% of these total executions. These relatively few juvenile executions occurred from 1642 through 1986 for a variety of crimes and in a variety of jurisdictions (Streib, 1987).

The first satisfactorily documented juvenile execution occurred in 1642. In that year, 16-year-old Thomas Graunger was executed in Roxbury, Massachusetts, for the crime of bestiality (Teeters and Hedblom, 1967: 111). The last juvenile execution occurred on May 15, 1986, when Texas executed Jay Kelly Pinkerton for a murder he committed at age 17 (*New York Times,* 1986).

Table 9.2 categorizes these juvenile executions by the decade in which they occurred, beginning with 1900. During the nineteenth century the numbers per decade had increased steadily, totaling 91 for the century. Executions of juveniles as well as adults reached maximum frequency in the twentieth century. The number of juvenile executions per decade increased steadily to an all-time high of 53 in the 1940s but dropped off dramatically after that decade. Juvenile executions ended temporarily in 1964 and did not reappear until 21 years later.

A total of 36 jurisdictions have executed persons for crimes committed while they were under age 18, including 35 states and the federal government. These 36 jurisdictions are listed in Table 9.3 in descending order of number of juvenile executions. Georgia is by far the leader with 41 juvenile executions, surprisingly over twice its nearest competitors. The second tier of states with a considerable number of juvenile executions includes not only the southern states of North Carolina, Texas and Virginia but also the northeastern industrial states of New York and Ohio. Florida and Texas, current leaders in adult executions in the 1980s (NAACP, 1987), historically are not among the top leaders in juvenile executions.

The heaviest concentrations are east of the Mississippi River, particularly along the eastern seaboard. The deep south states, except for Louisiana, are consistently heavy but so are such northeastern states as Massachusetts, New York and Ohio. Many midwestern states, from North Dakota down to Oklahoma, and back up to Idaho, have never executed any juveniles. The only western state with many such executions is California and its six juvenile executions is still only 1% of its over 500 executions in the past 100 years (Bowers, 1984: 407).

The southern region accounts for 65% (183/281) of the total juvenile executions. Almost two-thirds of these come from the south atlantic division of that region. The western region accounts for only 6% (18/281) of the total juvenile executions, the northeast region 14% and the north central region 11%. Federal jurisdictions account for 3% (8/281) of the juvenile executions but have not engaged in that practice for over a century

As mentioned earlier, 81% of these executions have been for crimes of murder and 15% for rape. Table 9.4 presents these data, along with those for all other crimes, according to time period. Note that the rape cases have been more of a modern phenomenon, with 84% (36 of 43) occurring since 1900.

TABLE 9.2

Total Executions and Juvenile Executions by Decade

Time Period	Total Executions	Juvenile Executions	Percentage
1900-1909	1,192	23	1.9
1910-1919	1,039	24	2.3
1920-1929	1,169	27	2.3
1930-1939	1,670	41	2.5
1940-1949	1,288	53	4.1
1950-1959	716	16	2.2
1960-1969	191	3	1.6
1970-1979	3	0	0
1980-present[a]	67	3	4.5
Total	7,335	190/c	2.6 (average)

SOURCE: For all executions: W. Bowers, *Legal Homicide: Death as Punishment in America, 1864-1982* (1984) and NAACP Legal Defense and Educational Fund, *Death Row, U.S.A.* (1987).
a. Current as of March 31, 1987.
*An additional 91 juvenile executions occurred prior to 1900.

TABLE 9.3

Total Juvenile Executions by Jurisdiction

State	Executions	State	Executions
Georgia	41	Missouri	6
North Carolina	19	New Jersey	5
Ohio	19	Pennsylvania	5
New York	18	Connecticut	3
Texas	18	Indiana	3
Virginia	18	Nevada	3
Florida	12	Washington	3
Alabama	11	Arizona	2
Kentucky	11	Delaware	2
South Carolina	11	Minnesota	2
Tennessee	11	Illinois	1
Louisiana	9	Iowa	1
Federal (various)	8	Montana	1
Massachusetts	8	New Mexico	1
Maryland	7	Oregon	1
Arkansas	6	Utah	1
California	6	Vermont	1
Mississippi	6	West Virginia	1
Total			281

TABLE 9.4
Juvenile Executions by Time Period
According to Offense

Offense	1642 to 1899		1900 to Present (percentages in parentheses)		Totals	
Arson	2	(2)	0	(0)	2	(1)
Assault & battery	1	(1)	0	(0)	1	(0)
Attempted rape	0	(0)	2	(1)	2	(1)
Buggery (animals)	2	(2)	0	(0)	2	(1)
Murder	76	(84)	150	(79)	226	(81)
Rape	7	(8)	36	(19)	43	(15)
Robbery	1	(1)	2	(1)	3	(1)
Spying	1	(1)	0	(0)	1	(0)
Totals	90	(100)	190	(100)	280	(100)
Unknown crime	1		0		1	
Grand totals	91		190		281	

Although murder cases constitute 81% of the total, the data categorization technique used in Table 9.4 may obscure other important information. Of these 226 murder cases, 19 were instances of rape or attempted rape in which the offender also killed his victim. This means that cases involving sexual assault total 64, or 23% of the total 280 cases for which the crime is known (43 rapes, 2 attempted rapes and 19 rape/murders). A total of 35% (80 of 226) of the murder cases involved a robbery or burglary that resulted in a murder.

The other crimes are few in number but nonetheless surprising in some ways. Perhaps one's view is clouded by a 1980s' perspective that limits the death penalty in essence to the worst forms of murder. It still seems odd that juveniles have been executed for crimes no more serious than arson, assault and battery, attempted rape, buggery, and robbery, none of which resulted in the taking of a human life or, in some of the cases, even any injury to any human being.

All 281 of these cases involved offenders who were less than 18 years old at the time of their crimes. The range of ages is somewhat surprising, running from a few days before the eighteenth birthday down to age 10. Table 9.5 presents the number of executions by age of the offender at time of the crime.

As Table 9.5 indicates, well over half of these 281 offenders were age 17 at the time of their crimes. A total of 82% were ages 16 or 17. Executions of persons under age 14 at the time of their crimes have been

TABLE 9.5
Juvenile Executions by Time Period
According to Age of Offender
at Time of the Crime

Age at Crime	1642 to 1899		1900 to Present (percentages in parentheses)		Totals	
10	2	(2)	0	(0)	2	(1)
11	0	(0)	0	(0)	0	(0)
12	5	(6)	0	(0)	5	(2)
13	4	(5)	1	(1)	5	(2)
14	6	(7)	4	(2)	10	(4)
15	13	(15)	16	(8)	29	(10)
16	25	(28)	49	(26)	74	(27)
17	34	(38)	120	(63)	154	(55)
Totals	89	(100)	190	(100)	279	(100)
Age unknown	2		0		2	
Grand totals	91		190		281	

quite rare with only 12 cases documented out of 15,000 executions in American history. Only one such case has occurred in this century. In fact, during this century 89% of all juvenile executions have been for crimes committed by persons age 16 or 17. Executions of younger juveniles was much more common prior to 1900 than in this century.

Of the 281 juveniles executed in American history, only nine have been females (Streib, 1985). The earliest case that could be documented occurred in 1786 (Sanders, 1970: 320) and execution of juvenile females ended in 1912 (Bowers, 1984: 515). However, two juvenile females are currently under a sentence of death, although they are appealing their cases.

Table 9.6 presents an overview of these 281 executions arrayed according to the race of the offender. The American experience with the death penalty has been one heavily infused with racial imbalance (Bowers, 1984: 67-102) and this truism seems to apply equally to the death penalty for juveniles. Executed white juveniles comprise only one-fourth of all executed juveniles.

Predictably, blacks constitute the overwhelming majority of these offenders, 69% of the total. And this is not simply an eighteenth and nineteenth century practice of executing slaves and poor blacks. The percentage of blacks has risen dramatically from 54% prior to 1900 to

TABLE 9.6
Juvenile Executions by Time Period
According to Race of Offender

Race of Offender	1642 to 1899		1900 to Present (percentages in parentheses)		Totals	
Black	47	(54)	139	(76)	186	(69)
Chinese	0	(0)	3	(2)	3	(1)
American Indian	7	(8)	1	(1)	3	(3)
Mexican-American	2	(2)	4	(2)	6	(2)
White	31	(36)	36	(20)	67	(25)
Totals	87	(100)	183	(100)	270	(100)
Race unknown	4		7		11	
Grand totals	91		190		281	

76% after 1900. The percentage of whites fell from 36% prior to 1900 to 20% after 1900.

The race of the victim has always had an impact in death penalty cases and is an issue of current importance in death penalty law (*McCleskey v. Kemp*, 1986). Table 9.7 provides an overview of the race of the victim in the 226 of these 281 cases in which that factor could be determined.

In striking contrast to the fact that 69% of the executed offenders have been black, Table 9.7 reveals that only 9% of their victims have been black. Overwhelmingly the victims have been white, 89% overall. For 90 cases the race of the victim could not be determined with satisfactory reliability but in most of those cases it seemed reasonable to assume that the victims were apparently white. Thus the 89% figure for white victims is somewhat conservative.

Considering all 276 victims for whom sex is known, 42% of the victims were female and 58% were male. The proportion of female victims has increased since 1900. Before then, only 35% of the victims were female. Since 1900 this proportion has increased to 46% female.

PRESENT PRACTICE

This 345-year experience of juvenile executions seems determined to continue for at least a little while longer. However, the practice is fading and may well disappear in the not-too-distant future.

TABLE 9.7
Juvenile Executions by Time Period
According to Race of Victim

Race of Victim	1642 to 1899		1900 to Present (percentages in parentheses)		Totals	
Black	13	(17)	6	(4)	19	(9)
Chinese	0	(0)	4	(3)	4	(2)
American-Indian	1	(1)	0	(0)	1	(0)
White	64	(82)	132	(93)	196	(89)
Totals	78	(100)	142	(100)	220	(100)
Race unknown	20		70		90	
Grand totals	98		212		310	

Juvenile Death Sentences, 1982 to 1987

In the time period from January 1, 1982, through March 31, 1987, 16 states actually imposed death sentences for crimes committed by persons under age 18. These juvenile death sentences were imposed in 38 separate instances upon a total of 34 different offenders. Four of these offenders received more than one death sentence for the same crime during this time period, an earlier death sentence having been reversed and then subsequently reimposed. Nevertheless, on 38 separate occasions a state trial court decided to sentence an offender to death for a crime he or she committed while under the age of 18.

As Table 9.8 indicates, the number of juvenile death sentences has declined significantly during this period. A total of 11 such sentences were imposed in 1982, 9 in 1983, 6 in 1984, 4 in 1985, 7 in 1986, and one during the first three months of 1987. Although the annual number of juvenile death sentences has fallen by at least 50%, the number of adult death sentences has remained fairly constant at a rate of 250 to 300 each year (U.S. Department of Justice, 1986).

During this five and one-quarter year time period, 36 states had apparently valid death penalty statutes. Of these states, 30 permitted imposition of the death penalty for crimes committed by persons under the age of 18. As Table 9.8 displays, only about half (16 states) actually imposed such a sentence. These 16 states represented a broad spectrum of the United States, ranging from New Jersey to Texas, and from Missouri to Florida.

TABLE 9.8

Thirty-Six Death Sentences for Juvenile Offenders,
January 1, 1982, to March 31, 1987

Year	Offender's Name	Age at Crime	Race	State	Current Status
1982	Barrow, Lee Roy	17	W	TX	reversed in 1985
	Cannon, Joseph J.	17	W	TX	now on death row
	Carter, Robert A.	17	B	TX	now on death row
	Garrett, Johnny F.	17	W	TX	now on death row
	Johnson, Lawrence	17	B	MD	reversed twice, but resentenced to death in 1983 and 1984
	Lashley, Frederick	17	B	MO	now on death row
	Legare, Andrew	17	W	GA	reversed in 1983; resentenced to death in 1984; reversed in 1986
	Stanford, Kevin	17	B	KY	now on death row
	Stokes, Freddie	17	B	NC	reversed in 1982; resentenced to death in 1983; reversed in 1987
	Thompson, Jay	17	W	IN	reversed in 1986
	Trimble, James	17	W	MD	now on death row
1983	Bey, Marko	17	B	NJ	now on death row
	Cannaday, Attina	16	W	MS	reversed in 1984
	Harris, Curtis P.	17	B	TX	now on death row
	Harvey, Frederick	16	B	NV	reversed in 1984
	Hughes, Kevin	16	B	PA	now on death row
	Johnson, Lawrence	17	B	MD	reversed in 1983 but resentenced to death in 1984
	Lynn, Frederick	16	B	AL	reversed in 1985 but resentenced to death in 1986
	Mhoon, James	16	B	MS	reversed in 1985
	Stokes, Freddie	17	B	NC	now on death row
1984	Aulisio, Joseph	15	W	PA	now on death row
	Brown, Leon	15	B	NC	now on death row
	Johnson, Lawrence	17	B	MD	now on death row
	Legare, Andrew	17	W	GA	reversed in 1986
	Thompson, Wayne	15	W	OK	now on death row

Continued

TABLE 9.8   Continued

Year	Offender's Name	Age at Crime	Race	State	Current Status
1985	Livingston, Jesse	17	B	FL	now on death row
	Morgan, James	16	W	FL	now on death row
	Ward, Ronald	15	B	AR	now on death row
1986	Comeaux, Adam	17	B	LA	now on death row
	Cooper, Paula	15	B	IN	now on death row
	LeCroy, Cleo	17	W	FL	now on death row
	Lynn, Frederick	16	B	AL	now on death row
	Sellers, Sean	16	W	OK	now on death row
	Wilkins, Heath	16	W	MO	now on death row
	Williams, Alexander	17	B	GA	now on death row
1987	None reported as of March 31, 1987.				

The states in the south region dominated this juvenile death-sentencing practice as they did in adult death sentencing. Almost three-quarters of the juvenile death sentences were imposed in the South, and 11 of the 16 states (69%) that imposed juvenile death sentences were in the south. Texas is the leader with five sentences but all five offenders were age 17 at the time of their crimes. Texas law establishes age 17 as the juvenile court cutoff (Texas Family Code, 1986) and as the minimum age at crime for the death penalty (Texas Penal Code, 1986). Other states with several juvenile death sentences are Florida and Maryland with four each.

Of the 38 juvenile death sentences imposed, five (13%) were for crimes committed while the offender was only age 15. These exceptionally youthful offenders were sentenced across the country including Arkansas, Indiana, North Carolina, Oklahoma, and Pennsylvania. Perhaps surprisingly, all of these death sentences for crimes committed at age 15 have been imposed in the past two years. Nine death sentences were imposed for crimes committed while the offender was age 16, but the majority (24/38 or 63%) were age 17 at the time of their crimes.

The race of the offenders is somewhat surprising, with 23 (61%) being black and 15 (39%) being white. The overrepresentation of blacks is not a result particularly of the sentences in the south, where a somewhat lower proportion (16/28 or 57%) were black. Outside of the south region, 70% (7/10) were black. Death sentences for female juvenile offenders were quite rare, comprising only two (5%) of the 38 sentences. They occurred in Indiana and Mississippi. The girls were ages 15 and 16, respectively, at the times of their crimes.

Table 9.9 presents the characteristics of the victims in these 38 juvenile death sentences. The total number of victims is 48 because some of the cases involved multiple victims. Three of the cases (Ward in Arkansas, Mhoon in Mississippi, and Sellers in Oklahoma) involved three victims each.

Overall, 82% (37/45) of the victims were white, excluding the three victims for whom race is unknown. All multiple victim cases involved only white victims. The region of the country involved does seem to be important as to race of victim. In the southern region, 89% (31/35) of the victims were white. For cases outside of the South, only 60% (6/10) of the victims were white. Even given this difference by region of the country, the nation-wide overrepresentation of whites among the victims cannot be ignored.

Analysis of the sex of the victims reveals another imbalance. For the 48 victims nationwide, 28 (58%) were female. Here the southern states are not particularly the cause of the imbalance, since the victims were female in only 21 of 36 (58%) instances. Outside of the south, 58% (7/12) of the victims were female.

In summary, the 38 juvenile death sentences during these five and one-quarter years fit a rough pattern. The sentences were imposed primarily in the earlier years but in a wide variety of states. The offenders were likely to have been black males who were age 17 at the time of their crimes. They almost always killed a single victim, typically a white female.

Juveniles on Death Row,
March 31, 1987

Of the 38 death sentences described in the preceding section, plus perhaps 50 or more imposed between 1972 and 1982, only 33 persons remain on death row for crimes committed while they were under age 18. Overall, 15 states are now holding such persons and apparently are ready, willing, and able to execute them.

During the time period from January 1, 1982, through March 31, 1987, the total death row population in the United States grew from 860 persons to 1,874 persons (NAACP, 1981, 1987). This is an increase of 118% in five and one quarter years, and 1,874 is the greatest number of persons on death row in U.S. history. During this same period the

TABLE 9.9

Characteristics of Victims in Death Sentences
for Juvenile Offenders,
January 1, 1982 to March 31, 1987

Region	Number of Sentences	Number of Victims	Race of Victim				Sex of Victim	
			B	H	W	?	M	F
Northeast	3	4	2	0	2	0	1	3
North Central	5	6	2	0	3	1	2	4
South	27	35	3	1	31	0	14	21
West	1	1	0	0	0	1	1	0
Totals	36	46	7	1	36	2	18	28

number of persons on death row for crimes committed while they were under age 18 remained essentially the same, ranging from the low to high 30s. Table 9.10 presents some basic information about the 33 persons under a juvenile death sentence as of March 31, 1987.

The original death sentencing date for these 33 persons ranges over more than 11 years, from March 19, 1975 for Larry Jones in Mississippi (*Jones v. Thigpen*, 1983) to February 25, 1987, for William Lamb in Florida (Johnson, 1987). Their ages as of March 31, 1987, range from 17 (Ronald Ward in Arkansas, Paula Cooper in Indiana, and Sean Sellers in Oklahoma) to 30 (Larry Jones in Mississippi). Most of these 33 persons have been sentenced to death only once for their crimes as juveniles. However, four of them have received two such death sentences, and two have received three such death sentences. All of the latter categories were instances of being sentenced to death originally, having that sentence reversed on appeal, and then being sentenced to death again at a subsequent trial court sentencing hearing.

Only two of these 33 persons is under a sentence of death for a murder unconnected to another major felony. The other 31 persons committed their homicides in connection with another crime. Most commonly the other crime was rape, involved in 15 of the cases. The other commonly connected crime was robbery, involved in 13 of the cases. In addition were two cases involving kidnapping and one case involving burglary. Overall, in 94% (31/33) of the cases the capital homicide was proven by the state through a felony-murder prosecution, involving proof of the seriousness of the homicide primarily through proof of its connection with another serious felony.

TABLE 9.10

Thirty-Seven Persons Under Juvenile
Death Sentences as of November 1, 1986

State	Name	Age at Crime	Race	Crime
Alabama	Davis, Timothy	17	white	rape/murder
	Jackson, Carnel	16	black	rape/murder
	Lynn, Frederick	16	black	burglary/murder
Arkansas	Ward, Ronald	15	black	rape/murder
Florida	LeCroy, Cleo	17	white	robbery/murder
	Livingston, Jesse	17	black	robbery/murder
	Magill, Paul	17	white	rape/murder
	Morgan, James	16	white	rape/murder
Georgia	Burger, Christopher	17	white	robbery/murder
	Buttrum, Janice	17	white	rape/murder
	Williams, Alexander	17	black	rape/murder
Indiana	Cooper, Paula	15	black	robbery/murder
	Patton, Keith	17	black	rape/murder
Kentucky	Stanford, Kevin	17	black	rape/murder
Louisiana	Comeaux, Adam	17	black	rape/murder
	Prejean, Dalton	17	black	murder
Maryland	Johnson, Lawrence	17	black	robbery/murder.
	Trimble, James	17	white	rape/murder
Mississippi	Jones, Larry	17	black	robbery/murder
	Tokman, George	17	white	robbery/murder
Missouri	Lashley, Frederick	17	black	robbery/murder
	Wilkins, Heath A.	16	white	robbery/murder
New Jersey	Bey, Marko	17	black	rape/murder
North Carolina	Brown, Leon	15	black	rape/murder
Oklahoma	Sellers, Sean	16	white	murder
	Thompson, Wayne	15	white	kidnap/murder
Pennsylvania	Aulisio, Joseph	15	white	kidnap/murder
	Hughes, Kevin	16	black	rape/murder
Texas	Cannon, Joseph	17	white	robbery/murder
	Carter, Robert	17	black	robbery/murder
	Garrett, Johnny	17	white	rape/murder
	Graham, Gary	17	black	robbery/murder

Overall, 26 (79%) of them received their death sentences from states in the southern region. However, a broad spectrum of jurisdictions currently have such persons on death row, ranging from the Northeast to the Midwest to the deep South. Florida with five and Texas with four have the greatest number, but three each are in Alabama and Georgia. In terms of proportion, Maryland is the leader with its two persons under a juvenile death sentence comprising 11% (2/18) of its total death row population (NAACP, 1987: 13). Although Florida has five persons under a juvenile death sentence, they represent only 2% (5/259) of the Florida death row population (NAACP, 1987: 8-10). Nationwide, persons under a juvenile death sentence account for less than 2% (33/1,874) of the total death row population (NAACP, 1987: 1).

The age of the offenders at time of crime ranges from 15 to 17. The 15-year-olds are only five in number, 15% of the total. They are under sentences of death in Arkansas, Indiana, North Carolina, Oklahoma and Pennsylvania. Six (18%) were 16 at the time of their crimes and the other 22 (67%) were 17.

Black offenders are 55% (18/33) of the total. Compare this to the total death row population, of which only 41% are black (NAACP, 1987: 1). This overrepresentation of blacks among those under juvenile death sentences seems distributed fairly evenly among the various regions of the country. The sex of these offenders is overwhelmingly male (31/33 or 94%). This overrepresentation of males, as with blacks, seems evenly distributed among the regions.

There were a total of 41 victims of these 33 offenders. Seven cases involved multiple victims, but 26 cases (78%) involved only one victim. The multiple-victim cases are spread out across the country, including Alabama, Arkansas, Florida, Indiana, Louisiana, and Pennsylvania. Of the 41 victims, 33 (80%) were white. The sex of the victims was female in 66% (27/41) of the cases overall.

In summary, the 33 persons now under a juvenile death sentence are alike in some ways but quite different in others. Although all were ages 15 to 17 at the time of their crimes, those crimes were committed from 1974 through 1986 and the ages of the offenders now range from 17 to 30. They have been under sentences of death from less than one year to over 12 years. The typical person now under a juvenile death sentence is a black male who was age 17 at the time of his crime. He was sentenced to death in the South for a murder connected to robbery or rape. He had only one victim, a white female. And, since he has been on death row over five years, his time is running out.

CRITERIA FOR CHANGE

Whether or not the death penalty for juveniles will be banned as unacceptable in our society is largely to be determined by appraisal of "the evolving standards of decency that mark the progress of a maturing society" (*Trop v. Dulles,* 1958: 101). Such progress is halting at best, and precision in determining the level of progress at any one time is extremely difficult. However, can it now be said that we have reached a maturation level at which we will reject the death penalty for juveniles?

During this accelerating change in societal acceptance of the juvenile death penalty, many individuals and groups are being asked to decide where they stand. Agencies as diverse as the U.S. Supreme Court, the Georgia State Legislature, leading political figures, and individual sentencing juries are considering making an exception for juveniles in their otherwise unwavering support for the death penalty. What are the key criteria that should be addressed in such considerations and decisions?

First, the choice of criminal punishment should be based both upon the harm inflicted and upon the criminal intent of the offender. It seems generally accepted that adolescents typically do not have an adult level of maturity and sophistication in their thought processes. Although they can intend behavior, it is unlikely they have thought about it deeply with insight and understanding. They fall short in the critical criterion of criminal intent and thus their punishment should be a little short of the punishment for a comparable adult's acts.

Second, retribution does not require the death penalty for juvenile crimes. Soaring anger at the misdeeds of children is always blunted somewhat, at least for reasonable persons, by the knowledge that children cannot be expected to behave as adults all of the time. The nonetheless strong if blunted need for retribution cannot be ignored but can be satisfied by long-term imprisonment. The death penalty is simply an excessive and overly emotional deference to this undeniable retributive feeling.

Third, deterrence is not enhanced by choosing the death penalty. The alternative sentence, long-term imprisonment, may be a punishment even more feared by adolescents. The only question left open in this regard is how long the imprisonment must be in order to provide satisfactory deterrence, a question answered in widely varying ways by different jurisdictions.

Fourth, it is unreasonable to totally disregard the goals of reform and rehabilitation for juvenile offenders. Behavior patterns change significantly as persons mature from adolescence to adulthood and into middle-age, usually to ways more acceptable to society. Imposing the death penalty for juvenile crimes completely disregards these universally accepted truisms about maturation. Long-term imprisonment holds out the possibility of such a destructive teenager becoming an acceptable adult at some time in the future.

Fifth, consider the message juveniles receive from juvenile death sentences. The crimes they have committed are almost always the killing of a person in order to solve some problem the juvenile perceives as otherwise unsolvable. Now they see the government struggling with a problem of its own, a person whose behavior is unacceptable to them. How does the government solve its problem? It kills the person who is causing the problem. It is most difficult to convince teenagers that they should not do something if they regularly see government officials doing it with the apparent blessings of adult society.

Sixth, abolition of the death penalty for juveniles is a common ground on which death penalty proponents and opponents can meet and agree. Opinion surveys have found that a majority would agree that at least this branch of the death penalty laws should be trimmed back (Southern Coalition, 1986). If everyone can reason together on this small issue, avenues of dialogue and understanding can be opened for more rational and constructive discussion of the death penalty for adults and for the appropriate application of criminal punishment in general.

Finally, if we discard the death penalty for juveniles what can be done about violent juvenile crime? For many, the willingness to acquiesce in the death penalty for juveniles stems from fear and outrage about violent juvenile crime. This fear and outrage is shared by all reasonable persons, whether for or against the death penalty. Two answers to this problem suggest themselves. The temporary solution is to impose long-term prison sentences on such violent juveniles. This will ensure that they are reasonably mature adults and have been subjected to whatever rehabilitative programs are available before they would ever again be free. And they would not be freed easily or by any means automatically even after many years in prison.

The long-term solution to violent juvenile crime cannot come from harsh criminal punishment, whether imprisonment or death. Our society must be willing to devote enormous resources to the search for causes and cures of violent juvenile crime, just as we have for the causes and cures of diseases such as cancer and polio. And, we must not demand a complete cure in a short time, since no one knows how long it will take.

Finally, we must beware of those who push for harsher punishment as the sole cure for violent crime. They are akin to the snake oil salesmen who loudly proclaim the curative effects of their foul tasting elixirs. Unfortunately, no one now has the cure for violent juvenile crime. However, it seems clear that the death penalty for juveniles has been given a long trial period and has been found wanting. Its societal costs are enormous, it tastes terribly foul, and it delays our search for a wise and just means of reducing violent juvenile crime.

REFERENCES

Amnesty International (1979) The Death Penalty. New York: Amnesty International.

BEDAU, H. A. [ed.] (1982) The Death Penalty in America. New York: Oxford University Press.

BOWERS, W. J. (1984) Legal Homicide: Death as Punishment in America, 1864-1982. Boston: Northeastern University Press.

CORR, C. A. and J. N. McNEIL [ed.] (1986) Adolescence and Death. New York: Springer.

DAVIS, S. M. (1986) The Rights of Juveniles (2nd ed.). New York: Clark Boardman.

Federal Bureau of Investigation (1975-1985) Uniform Crime Reports. Washington, DC: Government Printing Office.

FOX, S. J. (1984) The Law of Juvenile Courts in a Nutshell (3rd ed.). St. Paul, MN: West.

JOHNSON, P. (1987) "Convicted killer Lamb given the death penalty." Florida Today (Cocoa), Feb. 26, 1987, p. 1, col. 4.

Journal of Criminal Law and Criminology (1983) "Capital punishment for minors: An eighth amendment analysis." Volume 74, 4: 1471-1517.

NAACP Legal Defense and Educational Fund, Inc. (1981) Death Row, U.S.A. (December).

NAACP Legal Defense and Educational Fund, Inc. (1987) Death Row, U.S.A. (March).

New York Times (1986), May 16, p. 11, col. 1.

SANDERS, W. [ed.] (1970) Juvenile Offenders for a Thousand Years. Charlotte: University of North Carolina Press.

Southern Coalition Report on Jails and Prisons (1986) "SCJP poll results: Don't execute juveniles." Volume 13, 1 (Spring): 1.

STREIB, V. L. (1985) "Females executed for crimes committed while under age eighteen." (unpublished report available from author).

STREIB, V. L. (1986) "The eighth amendment and capital punishment of juveniles." Cleveland State Law Review 34, 3: 363-399.

STREIB, V. L. (1987) Death Penalty for Juveniles. Bloomington: Indiana University Press.

TEETERS, N. K. and J. H. HEDBLOM (1967) "... Hang By The Neck ...." Springfield, IL: Charles C Thomas.

Texas Family Code Annotated, section 54.02 (Vernon Supplement 1986).

Texas Penal Code Annotated, section 807 (d) (Vernon Supplement 1986).

Twentieth Century Fund Task Force on Sentencing Policy Toward Young Offenders (1978) Confronting Youth Crime.

U.S. Department of Justice (1986) Capital Punishment 1984. Washington, DC: Government Printing Office.

VITELLO, (1976) "Constitutional safeguards for juvenile transfer procedure: The ten years since Kent v. United States." DePaul Law Review 26: 23.

ZIMRING, F. E. (1982) The Changing Legal World of Adolescence. New York: Free Press.

CASES

Cannaday v. State (1984) 455 So. 2d 713 (Miss.)

Eddings v. Oklahoma (1982) 455 U.S. 104

Gregg v. Georgia (1976) 428 U.S. 153

High v. Zant (1983) 250 Ga. 693, 300 S. E. 2d 654, certorari denied (1984) 104 S. Ct. 2669

Jones v. Thigpen (1983) 555 F. Supp. 870 (S.D. Miss.), reversed (1984) 741 F. 2d 805 (5th Cir.), vacated (1986) 106 S. Ct. 1172

Jurek v. Texas (1976) 428 U.S. 262

Kent v. United States (1966) 383 U.S. 541

Lockett v. Ohio (1978) 438 U.S. 536

McCleskey v. Kemp (1987) 107 S. Ct. 1756

State v. Battle (1983) 661 S. W. 2d 487 (Mo.) (en banc), certiorari denied (1984) 104 S. Ct. 2325

State v. Valencia (1982) 132 Ariz. 248, 645 P. 2d 239

Thompson v. Oklahoma (1986) 724 P. 2d 780 (Okla. Cr. App.), certiorari granted (1987) 107 S. Ct. 1281

Trimble v. State (1984) 300 Md. 387, 478 A. 2d 1143, certiorari denied (1985) 105 S. Ct. 1231

Trop v. Dulles (1958) 356 U.S. 86

Workman v. Commonwealth (1968) 429 S. W. 2d 374 (Ky.)

Chapter 10

DEATH ROW
Hope for the Future

J O H N L. C A R R O L L

In December of 1975, I paid the first of my literally hundreds of visits to a death row. As I drove north from Baton Rouge and turned onto the narrow desolate country road that led to my destination, the Louisiana state penitentiary at Angola, my emotions were a curious mix of apprehension and curiosity. Before my trip to Angola, my sole exposure to the notion of a death row had been watching Edmund O'Brien minister to James Cagney before his movie execution. Now I was to see the real thing.

I arrived at the gate, my credentials were checked, and I was escorted to a large masonry prison building that housed the death row unit. My escort was a correctional officer in cowboy boots and a cowboy hat. We entered the prison building and proceeded through a series of locked steel doors, arriving eventually at the part of the prison housing death-sentenced inmates. I was then taken to the death row visiting area, a small metal enclosed area where I was to visit with my client. As I was entering the visiting area, I could see the death row cell block area, off to the left. It was simply a long hallway with standard metal cells along one side. I could also hear death row and felt assaulted by the cacophony coming from it. The television sets that were placed along the row were

AUTHOR'S NOTE: *The author wishes to thank Joel Berger for his assistance with this chapter. There is no lawyer in the country who has given more selflessly of his time to better the plight of death-sentenced inmates than Joel. His caring and his competence stand as examples of how a lawyer can be both a skillful advocate and a remarkable human being.*

turned up full volume. Added to that noxious noise were the shouts of inmates screaming to be heard over the television sets. I remember thinking to myself that no human being could maintain his sanity very long in that kind of environment.

After what seemed an interminable length of time, my client entered the visiting area. Because no contact visits were allowed, there was a thick wire screen separating us. We touched hands upon the screen in the customary greeting and proceeded about our business. In the course of our conversations, I was to find out that death row inmates in Louisiana at that time spent virtually all their time in their cells locked in the Dante's inferno of sound. I further learned that there was virtually no recreation or education going on on death row and that all there was to do was sit and think about dying. I knew from what was going on with our visit that inmates on death row could not have contact visits. I later learned that conditions on death row in Louisiana were typical of conditions elsewhere in the country.

My client and I concluded our visit by again touching hands through the screen. I then left the prison and drove back to Baton Rouge. On the long ride back, I thought constantly about what I had seen and heard. I remember being shocked by the inhumanity of the place.

My client is no longer on death row. In fact, he is a free man. His place has been taken by literally thousands of others. Our society is thus faced with a serious problem. What do we do with the men we have condemned to die while they await execution?[1] It is a problem that has moral, sociological and constitutional implications. This chapter will discuss how some states have addressed this problem in a way that offers hope for the future.[2]

THE PRESENT LEGAL SYSTEM
AND THE PROBLEMS IT CREATES

In 1972, in *Furman v. Georgia*[3] the U.S. Supreme Court determined that the capital punishment sentencing schemes then in use violated the Eighth Amendment to the Constitution of the United States. The decision came in the midst of a long moratorium on capital punishment that had begun in the mid-1960s. Though the court in *Furman* did not draw any bright constitutional lines, it did send a very clear practical message to the states—the death penalty was not unconstitutional per se and would be constitutionally acceptable if the procedures for its imposition were improved. Following the *Furman* decision, every state altered its procedures for imposing death sentences. Some states, Georgia, Florida, and Texas in particular, created so-called "guided discretion" statutes, which gave the sentencing authority statutorily enumerated factors to guide its sentencing decision. Other states, like North Carolina and Louisiana, created mandatory death penalty statutes, which removed all discretion from the sentencing authority. In 1976, in a series of five decisions handed down on July 2, 1976, the Supreme Court chose guided discretion over mandatoriness.[4] In so doing, it specifically approved the statutes of Texas, Georgia and Florida and specifically struck down the statutes of North Carolina and Louisiana. The 1976 Supreme Court opinions are extremely significant for two reasons. First, the opinions contained guidelines for states to follow in creating constitutionally permissible death sentencing systems.[5] Second and most important for purposes of this chapter, the court found that there was a need for more procedural protections in death penalty cases. As the court remarked,

> Death, in its finality, differs more from life imprisonment than a 100-year prison term differs from one of only a year or two. Because of that qualitative difference, there is a corresponding difference in the need for reliability in the determination that death is the appropriate punishment in a specific case.[6]

The notion that the punishment of death is different and that different procedural safeguards are required has become a central theme in the Supreme Court's jurisprudence about capital punishment. It is also a principle that has driven lawyers who represent death row inmates. The punishment of death is different and requires different treatment by the legal system.

The "death is different" approach is most obvious in the way that death penalty cases are handled in the postconviction stages. In nondeath cases, appeals are rarely prosecuted with the assistance of counsel beyond the state direct appeal process. Very few cases wherein the petitioner is represented by counsel enter the state postconviction stage and even fewer ever reach the federal habeas corpus process. The reason for the small numbers of noncapital lawyer-assisted post-conviction cases is obvious—inmates usually cannot pay for them and lawyers are extremely hesitant to do noncapital postconviction work without being paid. In addition, the Supreme Court has held that there is no constitutional right to appointment of counsel in postconviction relief cases.[7] Thus, inmates in noncapital cases usually represent themselves, a fact that seriously undermines the effectiveness of the litigation.

Death penalty cases, by contrast, always enter the postconviction stages following direct appeal. Although most death penalty defendants cannot afford any sort of legal representation, they are represented by volunteer lawyers who devote their time and use their own resources to ensure that a death row inmate makes use of every appeal avenue that is available. Thus every death row inmate usually follows the direct appeal process by entry into the state postconviction system and then follows that with a trip through federal habeas corpus. Although there is often intense pressure to speed death penalty cases through the system,[8] the normal death penalty case takes a significant amount of time to travel through the judicial system. In the 49 involuntary executions that occurred between May 25, 1979 and May 36, 1986, the average time between the date of the crime and the date of execution has been seven years and six months.[9] Although this average length of time will undoubtedly shrink in the future, death penalty cases will still spend a long time in the court system. It is simply impossible to review a death penalty case adequately in a short time.[10]

It is important for both the proponents and the opponents of capital punishment that death penalty cases proceed slowly through the courts. For the proponents, a lengthy review process creates an aura of reliability and counters arguments that the death penalty is being administered in an arbitrary and capricious manner. For opponents, the lengthy review process keeps the death row inmate alive and offers at least minimal hope that any errors that were committed in the process will be found. The slowness of the process, however, creates a serious problem for correctional administrators. They are required to maintain prisoners sentenced to death for a period of years rather than months.

DEATH ROW CONDITIONS—PRELITIGATION

As states passed new death penalty laws in the wake of *Furman v. Georgia,* the once empty death rows of America began to fill.[11] By 1983, there were well over a thousand prisoners housed in death rows throughout the country. The conditions in which they were housed in the years following *Furman* and then *Gregg* can only be described as horrible.[12] With few exceptions, death-sentenced inmates were housed in small cells, which became their world. They were fed in the cells, went to the bathroom in the cells, and read in their cells. They spent almost no time out of their cells. Their social contact with other human beings consisted of shouted conversations up and down the cell block tiers and brief encounters with guards who often taunted them. Social scientists describing death row in the late 1970s noted:

> Comparing the daily activities of DSI's (Death Sentence Inmates) with the general prison populations, the differences are distressing. Most DSI's cannot work at prison jobs, cannot attend education classes, clubs or religious services, have much less opportunity for exercise and recreation and much less adequate facilities and equipment. DSI's have little human contact. Most are confined to their cells over twenty-two hours a day. Most are shackled for trips within the prison. Most eat in their cells and are separated from visitors by barriers.[13]

Conditions like these were at least societally tolerable when execution followed swiftly after conviction. Under the present system, however, in which execution follows many years after conviction, the conditions plainly reached unconstitutionality. Not only were death-sentenced inmates condemned to die, they were condemned to suffer the period awaiting death in the most wretched and inhumane of conditions.

EARLY LITIGATION EFFORTS

In the late '70s, inmates concerned about conditions on death row turned to the courts for assistance. The first lawsuit dealing solely with conditions on death row was filed in Alabama in early 1978. The complaint in *Jacobs v. Locke*[14] sought changes in food services, health care, recreation and out-of-cell time, visitation and sanitation. The complaint alleged that the conditions on death row, taken in totality, violated the Eighth and Fourteenth Amendments to the U.S. Constitution.

Following an extensive discovery period the parties entered into a consent decree in February of 1980, which ended the litigation. The consent decree mandated significant improvement in visitation rights and in out-of-cell time. At the time the litigation began, death row inmates could visit on Saturday, and all visits were noncontact. Inmates were allowed only 30 minutes out of their cell per day for exercise. Following the settlement, death row inmates were allowed contact visitation for two hours or more at any time during the week. In addition, death row inmates were given a law library of their own and were allowed to use it in groups, thus significantly increasing the amount of out-of-cell time and opportunity for social contact.

The year 1980 also saw major improvements in the conditions of confinement for California's death-sentenced inmates as the result of litigation about the conditions of confinement on that state's death row. In *Thompson v. Enomoto*,[15] the court approved a consent decree under which death-sentenced prisoners classified as "Grade A" receive six hours out-of-cell time per day.[16] Under the decree the Grade A death row prisoners are also permitted to eat their noon meal at tables outside of their cells, attend religious services and receive contact visits. The decree also requires that even death row inmates who are classified below "Grade A" be given a minimum of 12 hours per week of outdoor exercise.

The successful completion of the litigation in California was followed by litigation concerning the conditions of confinement on Georgia's death row. That litigation, *Daniels v. Zant*[17] was successfully concluded by a consent decree that guaranteed all death row prisoners in Georgia a minimum of 32 hours per week out-of-cell time. That same decree also worked major changes in the areas of recreation and classification. Under it, prison authorities are required to provide at least six hours of outdoor recreation and such equipment as baseball gloves and basketball and volleyball nets and balls. Although out-of-cell time and recreation are not tied to classification status, the decree does require a classification system and links classification status to a variety of other activities, such as religious services and access to certain hobby materials.[18] During this period of time, conditions on Florida's death row were also improving as the result of litigation.[19]

The experiences in Alabama, California, Florida, and Georgia were encouraging on two fronts. First, they showed that litigation about the conditions of confinement for death-sentenced inmates could be successful, and second, they showed that correctional officials were willing to compromise to end litigation and to better the conditions on death row. These early successes were to be followed by two major litigational events—the settlement of the Texas death row conditions suit, *Ruiz v. McCaskle*[20] and the order of the U.S. District Court for the Middle District of Tennessee in *Groseclose v. Dutton*.[21]

RUIZ AND *GROSECLOSE*

Ruiz and *Groseclose* stand as landmarks in death row litigation efforts for different and independent reasons. *Ruiz* was the first settlement of a death row case that materially altered the way of doing business on death row. Although the earlier settlements were important and significant, none were as far reaching in their scope and approach. The settlements in Alabama, California, Georgia, and Florida made important changes. They made things better for death-sentenced inmates. They did not alter the basic correctional approach to management of those inmates. *Ruiz* did change that basic approach and much more.

Groseclose is important because it is the first instance of full judicial intervention on behalf of death-sentenced inmates. The successes for death-sentenced inmates that had been previously referenced came through the negotiation and settlement process. The court in *Groseclose* became the first to conclude that the conditions on a death row in the United States violated the Eighth Amendment to the Constitution of the United States and to issue an order requiring the state to remedy those conditions.

Ruiz

Ruiz v. Estelle[22] began as an across-the-board attack on the conditions of confinement in the Texas prison system and resulted in the implementation of a district court order creating major systemic changes. Part of that order required the defendants to file a plan providing for "increased and regular out-of-cell recreation opportunities for prisoners segregated on Death Row."[23] At the time the district court entered its order, the conditions on death row in Texas mirrored the conditions on death rows throughout the rest of the country. Death-sentenced inmates were allowed out of their cells for only three one-hour periods per week. At all other times, they were confined to their cells around the clock except for a brief shower period each day. The out-of-cell time was spent either in a day room or in a limited recreational environment.[24] The parties were unable to agree on a plan implementing the court-ordered relief and a hearing was set. Just prior to the hearing, the parties agreed on an experimental program to afford death row inmates more humane treatment and entered into a series of stipulations that were approved by the court.[25] The stipulations allowed Texas death row inmates to be classified as either "work capable" or "death row segregation." Inmates classified as "work capable" were assigned to jobs in the general population and given all the freedom, movement, and access rights as general population prisoners.[26]

The very forward-looking program created by the parties was successfully maintained even through a change of prison administrators in Texas.[27] The program was so successful in fact that it led to yet another agreement that was given final approval by the district court on January 3, 1986. That order and agreement embody a Death Row Activity Plan that continues the previous classification of death row inmates into "work capable" and "death row segregation" and establishes controlling criteria for those classifications. The plan calls for the assignment of all "work capable" inmates to a meaningful job. Many of those jobs will be in a garment factory that was built near death row for the specific purpose of providing death row inmates with a meaningful job. Paragraph two of the agreement contemplates that as many as 100 death row inmates may be classified into "work capable" status and requires adequate space for work and recreation of those inmates. It requires that space for these activities be designed to provide a reasonably balanced range of recreation, work, programming, and other out-of-cell activity simultaneously to at least 100 prisoners.[28]

The Death Row Activity Plan also requires that all "work capable" prisoners are to be allowed 14 hours per day of out-of-cell time between Monday and Friday and 10 hours per day of out-of-cell time on the weekends. At least four hours is to consist of outdoor recreation.[29]

The plan also greatly alters the treatment of inmates that are classified into death row segregation. Those inmates are allowed three hours of out-of-cell time five days a week. The inmates are also given access to religious and educational programs.[30]

The Texas death row experiment has been an overwhelming success. In the words of the lawyer who represented the inmates on death row in Texas:

> In summary, the [Death Row] Stipulation and Plan represent a remarkable relaxation of the cruel lock-in regimen to which all death-sentenced prisoners were subjected at time of the *Ruiz* trial. As many as 100 death-sentenced prisoners are accorded a minimum of 90 hours per week out-of-cell time, and participate in meaningful employment activity, and all other death-sentenced

prisoners are assured of at least fifteen hours per week out-of-cell time.[31]

Groseclose v. Dutton

Groseclose and *Ruiz* stand as opposites. The conditions on the Texas death row, as a result of the *Ruiz* stipulations and plans, are a monument to the success that can be attained when forward looking correctional officials and knowledgeable lawyers make intelligent and correctionally acceptable changes in the way death row inmates are treated. *Groseclose* stands as a symbol of the problems that inevitably result when correctional officials abdicate their responsibilities and require courts to intervene on behalf of inmates.

The litigation in *Groseclose* concerned the conditions of confinement on death row in Tennessee. At the time litigation commenced, the conditions on death row were terrible. Death-sentenced inmates spent more than 22 hours a day locked in their cells, which ranged in size from 35 to 44 square feet. The cells were alternatively hot and cold and were poorly lighted. The prison officials did not provide the death row inmates with any meaningful activities and the inmates themselves were powerless to relieve the tedium.

Dr. Seymour Halleck, a professor of psychiatry at the University of North Carolina Medical School, described the walks on death row as giving one a sense of being entombed. He also testified that of the death rows of which he was aware, it was the worst in the nation in terms of the deprivations, lack of exercise, and lack of human contact.[32] Dr. Dorothy O. Lewis, a professor of psychiatry at New York University, joined with Dr. Halleck in condemning the conditions on Tennessee's death row. Dr. Lewis testified that "based on her tours of death rows in several states, Tennessee had the worst death row that she had seen. She compared it to cages in a zoo."[33]

Faced with this type of testimony and other equally compelling evidence, the district court, applying a totality of the circumstances analysis, concluded that the conditions on Tennessee's death row violated the Eighth Amendment's prohibition against cruel and unusual punishment.[34]

The district court judge did not enter a comprehensive plan, preferring instead to allow the prison officials to do their job. The Sixth Circuit characterized his order as follows:

In ruling the totality of these conditions unconstitutional, the court found, among other things, that the cumulative effect of small, poorly lit, poorly ventilated and poorly heated/cooled cells, was constitutionally suspect in light of the time, twenty-three hours a day, inmates were confined to them. Furthermore and also related to the in-cell time was the court's concern that the inmates' emotional and psychological health was largely ignored. The court suggested that a classification system may help alleviate these concerns. In view of the deference due prison officials, the court refused to order the implementation of such a system and instead left to the defendants the solution of the problems caused by non-classification, i.e., automatic treatment of all death row inmates as high security risks with attendant limitations on inmates' activities (citations omitted).[35]

As of this writing, the litigation over the conditions on Tennessee's death row has still not ended. Though there has been some increase in the number of hours that inmates may spend out of their cells, the overall conditions have not improved greatly. An appeal filed by the State of Tennessee is currently pending before the U.S. Court of Appeals for the Sixth Circuit.

DEATH ROW CONDITIONS—1987

Some 10 years after the Supreme Court's decisions validating the use of capital punishment in this country, conditions on death row are a patchwork quilt. In some states, like Texas, conditions are decent and humane. In others, like Ohio, they are cruel, inhuman, and unnecessarily punitive. The purpose of this section of the chapter is to analyze the present conditions on death row as they relate to two important areas that are the key indicators in determining how humane a death row is—visitation and out-of-cell time.[36]

Because every death row is different in design, age, and cleanliness, comparisons on those grounds are difficult. One thing can be said without hesitation, however. No matter how clean death row is, and how large the cells are, no death row can be considered adequate unless there is meaningful opportunity for extensive out-of-cell time either for activities or visitation or both.

Visitation

For death row inmates, the only opportunity for human contact with the outside world comes through visitation with family and friends.

Though these visits may be infrequent, death row inmates view them as the most important things in their lives.[37]

> For those inmates who receive them, visits are the main link with the free world and the primary means through which social supports are maintained and the boredom of prison life is broken. It would be difficult to overestimate their significance. Visits give an inmate the opportunity to talk in confidence (the level of trust between inmates is generally not high), to enjoy a relatively decent meal from the prison canteen, to see women and children, and in general to be temporarily renewed.[38]

Given the importance of visitation, many states offer extensive death row visiting privileges.[39] Florida, for example, offers six hours per week on either Saturday or Sunday. Kentucky permits four hours per week on Saturday, Sunday, or holidays. Nevada and South Carolina offer three hours per week.[40]

Length of visitation, however, is not the only criterion by which visitation regulations should be measured. Unless the visit is a contact visit, it may be harmful rather than helpful to the inmate. Dr. Karl Menninger, the noted psychiatrist, described noncontact visits as "a violation of ordinary principles of humanity."[41] He has concluded that noncontact visits amount to "dangling a fragment of meat in front of a dog and jerking it away."[42] Dr. Menninger's comment is something we know to be intuitively correct. Noncontact visits are horrible. They simply exacerbate the feelings of rejection and abandonment that most death row inmates feel.[43]

The only possible argument that correctional administrators can give for having a no-contact visitation policy is security. The security argument is unsupportable given the contours of present day death-sentenced inmate management practices—of the states with the highest death row populations 80% permit contact visitation.[44] In fact, of the 25 death rows with the highest populations, 56% allow contact family visitation.[45] The fact that the majority of the large death rows in the country allow for contact visitation clearly indicates that whatever security concerns may exist can be overcome by forward-thinking correctional administrators.

Out-of-Cell Time[46]

The physical and mental well being of a death-sentenced inmate is directly proportional to the amount of out-of-cell time afforded him. If the inmate is allowed out of his cell for significant periods of time each day, then the rigors of confinement as a capital prisoner can be tolerated. If an inmate is locked down and his out-of-cell time limited, then the already present pressures of being on death row are exponentially magnified. Daily out-of-cell time is even more important than contact visitation to the death-sentenced inmate. Even a liberal visitation policy cannot make up for the psychological harm done by a limited out-of-cell time policy.

In non-death row settings, courts have been quick to recognize the importance of time spent out of a cell even in the case of inmates with serious disciplinary problems. They have particularly endorsed the idea of out-of-cell exercise. In *Ramos v. Lamm*,[47] for example, the court noted "while 'sophisticated' programs may not be required, the right to reasonable opportunity for exercise is fundamental. Especially [in administrative segregation], where life for most inmates is characterized by idleness and prolonged daily confinement in their cells, adequate exercise is critical."[48] Again our intuition tells us that the courts are right. It is unnecessary and unlawful to keep death-sentenced inmates confined to their cells for long periods of time. There are simply better ways of doing business on death row.

Many states have made significant progress in creating significant and meaningful out-of-cell time. In Texas, over 100 death row inmates are classified into "work eligible" programs in which they are out of their cells approximately 90 hours per week. They also have out-of-cell recreation for at least four hours a day and are allowed to eat out of their cells. Even Texas death row inmates who are not classified as work eligible are guaranteed three hours of outdoor group recreation five a days a week. In California, prisoners classified as grade A receive six hours of out-of-cell time seven days per week. They also eat their noon meal outside their cells. All death row inmates in California, regardless of their classification, receive 12 hours of outdoor exercise per week. Similar conditions exist in Georgia, Kentucky, and Virginia.[49]

Contrast the conditions in these states with those in Ohio, Arkansas, New Jersey, Mississippi, Louisiana, and Florida. In Ohio, death-sentenced inmates are allowed out of their cells for two hours per week for walks on the indoor tier catwalk and one hour per month for recreation. In Arkansas, death-sentenced inmates are allowed out of their cells for three hours per week. In New Jersey, it is seven hours per week for recreation, in Mississippi and Louisiana, it is five and in Florida, four.[50]

WHY THE DIFFERENCE?

As in many other areas of our legal system, where you are determines how you are treated. There is no national uniformity as to how death-sentenced inmates are treated. Maryland and Delaware, for example, refuse to create a death row. Death-sentenced inmates are housed in the general prison population and remain there until a "firm" execution date is set at which time the inmate is moved to a segregation unit.[51] Arkansas successfully maintained a similar practice in the late 1960s.[52]

What is striking about death rows is the wide divergence of treatment even within death rows themselves. Some death rows, like Florida's, have tremendously liberal visitation policies but very little out-of-cell time. Other death rows, like North Carolina's, have liberal out-of-cell time but poor visitation policies.

Of all of the death rows in the country, Texas's is clearly the best because of the extensive out-of-cell time afforded death-sentenced inmates.[53] Death-sentenced inmates in Texas who are classified as work eligible spend approximately 110 hours per week outside of their cells. Most of that out-of-cell time is spent in productive labor, which gives the inmate self-esteem and also benefits the state of Texas by creating additional revenues. Even inmates who do not work are permitted out of their cells and receive 15 hours a week out-of-cell time. A notch below Texas,[54] but certainly deserving of praise are the death rows of California, Georgia, Kentucky and Nebraska. All of those states permit contact visitation and all have liberal out-of-cell time policies. Death-sentenced inmates in California classified as Grade A are out of their cells for 42 hours per week. Those in Georgia, Kentucky, and Nebraska are out of their cells approximately 38 to 40 hours per week.[55] The death rows of North Carolina and Virginia are worth noting because both have liberal out-of-cell time policies. Death-sentenced inmates in both states spend most of the day outside of their cells in their own pods.[56]

There are some death rows, particularly those in Pennsylvania, Ohio, Louisiana, Mississippi, New Jersey, and Arkansas, however, which can only be classified as inhumane.[57] They share the common characteristic of denying contact visitation and almost totally curtailing out-of-cell time. The inmates housed on these death rows are condemned to a life of idleness, solitude, and psychological deterioration. They have no meaningful contact with outsiders or with each other. On these death rows, inmates become "human husks"; they are "dead as persons even as their bodies maintain physical life."[58] As an inmate on one of these death rows commented:

In general, an effort is made to place the inmate in an atmosphere that cultivates a loss of morale and self-esteem to deny dignity and place the inmate in a position of non-existence.[59]

On death rows like these, an inmate is sentenced to be slowly killed while he awaits execution and is likely to think of himself as already dead. In the words of one expert:

> Some death row inmates, attuned to the bitter irony of their predicament, characterize their existence as a living death and themselves as the living dead. They are speaking symbolically, of course; but their imagery is an appropriate description of the human experience in a world where life is so obviously ruled by death. It takes into account the condemned prisoners' massive deprivation of personal autonomy and command over resources critical to psychological survival; their suspension in a stark, empty tomblike setting marked by indifference to basic human needs and desires; and their enforced isolation from the living with the resulting emotional emptiness and death.[60]

What explains the vast differences in the way death-sentenced inmates are treated? Certainly geography offers no answer. There are good and bad death rows in every part of the country. Nor does the character of the death-sentenced inmate. Certainly the inmate under sentence of death in Texas is no better and no worse than his counterpart in Ohio. If the disparity can be explained at all, it can be explained by reference to one simple fact—the best death rows in the country are in states in which there has been litigation about the conditions of confinement of death-sentenced inmates.[61]

This is not to say that litigation is the answer. Litigation is expensive and time consuming. What litigation does, however, is focus needed attention on the conditions on death row and provide a process through which those problems can be illuminated, discussed, and solved. Unfortunately, it is generally true that without litigation very little gets done in any prison system. What litigation about prison conditions provides is an opportunity for data gathering and for assessment of a system by outside experts. That data gathering and assessment often inform state correctional officials about problems they did not fully appreciate. Those informed officials can then negotiate settlements that remedy the problems and yet save the state the embarrassing, expensive, and time consuming litigation. Information gained through litigation provides public officials with the data they need to improve the conditions on death row without antagonizing the general public.

If there were a systematic way to gather information about death rows and have it assessed by independent experts, there would be no need for litigation. Unfortunately, those mechanisms do not exist. It is only through litigation that there is a systematic and comprehensive gathering of information and assessment. Perhaps by the end of this decade, correctional administrators will stop needing the cattle prod of litigation to move them toward adopting a more sensible approach to the management of death-sentenced inmates. Until that time, litigation remains the best way for humanizing the conditions on death row.

THE FUTURE

Ten years ago, virtually all death rows were models of inhumanity. That situation has obviously changed for two main reasons: (1) The myth that all death row inmates are mindless killers has been destroyed; and (2) Correctional administrators have begun to recognize the importance of classification in the death row setting.

For many years, the prevailing correctional attitude was that death row inmates had to be locked down 24 hours a day because they had nothing to lose and would kill for the sheer joy of it. Present experience counsels otherwise. As previously noted, many systems allow extensive out-of-cell time without any increase in violence. That is because current death penalty litigation has resulted in an extremely high reversal rate. One study shows it to be as high as 79%.[62] Thus, many death row inmates have the very valid belief that their conviction will be reversed or their death sentence vacated. In that event, their prison record will be an important part of their new trial or sentencing hearing.[63] Thus death row inmates have a real incentive to avoid violent behavior in prison. Contrary to the old beliefs, death row inmates do have a great deal to lose if they engage in mindless acts of violence.

It goes without saying that there are some death row inmates who will present serious management problems who cannot be allowed extensive out-of-cell time. Those inmates can be easily identified through modern classification systems and can be treated accordingly. One of the real hallmarks of the Texas and California experiences is that death row inmates can be classified with confidence and that death-sentenced inmates not classified as security risks can be given great freedom. In fact, Texas and California treat death-sentenced inmates in their worst classifications better than states like Ohio, Pennsylvania, Louisiana, and Arkansas treat everyone.

Death rows do not have to be Russian gulags in order to protect inmates, guards, and the citizenry. In fact, those that remain that way are clearly out of step with developing correctional practices. If the trend continues, death rows of the future will be relatively decent. Those that are not will be unconstitutional.

NOTES

1. The problem is so serious, from a correctional management standpoint, that the American Correctional Association has begun an extensive study that will address the management of death row inmates. See, Nesbitt, Managing Death Row, *Corrections Today* at 90 (July 1986).

2. The primary focus of this chapter is not on the legal theories on which litigation about the conditions of death row confinement can be based. That subject has been adequately discussed elsewhere. See generally, Johnson and Carroll, "Litigating Death Row Conditions: The Case for Reform" *Prisoners and the Law* (Clark Boardman 1985); Comment, Death Row Conditions: Progression Towards Constitutional Protections, 19 *Akron L. Rev.* 293 (1985) (Hereinafter referred to as *Akron*).

3. 408 U.S. 238 (1972).

4. *Gregg v. Georgia*, 428 U.S. 153 (1976); *Proffitt v. Florida*, 428 U.S. 242 (1976); *Jurek v. Texas*, 428 U.S. 262 (1976); *Woodson v. North Carolina*, 428 U.S. 280 (1976); *Roberts (Stanislaus) v. Louisiana*, 428 U.S. 325 (1976).

5. Although stopping short of mandating a particular kind of statutory scheme, the Court made it clear that a constitutional death penalty sentencing system would have to bifurcate the guilt/innocence and sentencing decisions and would have to guide and channel the sentencing authority's discretion. As the Court remarked:

> In summary, the concerns expressed in *Furman* that the penalty of death not be imposed in an arbitrary or capricious manner can be met by a carefully drafted statute that ensures that the sentencing authority is given adequate information and guidance. As a general proposition, these concerns are best met by a system that provides a bifurcated proceeding at which the sentencing authority is apprised of the information relevant to the imposition of sentence and provided with standards to guide the use of the information.

Gregg v. Georgia, 428 U.S. 153, 195 (1976).

6. *Woodson v. North Carolina*, 428 U.S. 280, 305 (1976).

7. *Ross v. Moffitt*, 417 U.S. 600 (1974). Lawyers, of course, are sometimes appointed in habeas cases in which the court decides to hold an evidentiary hearing.

8. For an excellent discussion of this pressure see Winter, "Expediting Death Penalty Cases." *Litigation*, Vol. 12, No. 4 at 3 (1986).

9. The figures were compiled by Ed Carnes, who is an Alabama Assistant Attorney General, for presentation to a miniseminar of the Mississippi Bar Association. Other persons have reached similar conclusions. The District Court in *Groseclose v. Dutton,* 609 F. Supp. 1432, 1447 (M. D. Tenn. 1985) found that the "average death row inmate spends six to ten years pursuing appeals." A length of stay study done in *Ruiz v. Estelle* in 1983 revealed that 25% of the Texas death-sentenced inmates had been on death row five years or longer.

10. It is difficult to conceive of any system wherein the time from crime to execution would be less than five years. It is usually six months to a year before the case comes to trial. Preparation of the transcript and argument of the appeal takes another 18 months. Then four months, at least, is occupied by the petition for writ of certiorari in the U.S. Supreme Court. Thus the time from commission of crime through direct appeal is likely to take almost three years. Once the direct appeal process is complete, then the case is ready to enter the postconviction stage, which is likely to last just as long.

11. There was a temporary decrease in death row populations in 1976 when the Supreme Court emptied the death rows of Louisiana, North Carolina, and some other states through the decisions in *Woodson v. North Carolina* and *Roberts v. Louisiana.*

12. See generally, Johnson and Carroll, *supra* note 2.

13. Else, Kudsk and Meyer, "Living Conditions of Death Sentence Inmates in the U.S." 1 *Death Penalty Reporter* Vol. 11, p. 1 (July 1981).

14. No. 78-309-H (S.D. Ala. filed March 3, 1978).

15. No. 79-1630 (N.D. Cal.) (October 23, 1980).

16. *McDonald v. Armontrout,* No. 85-422-CV-C-5 (W.D. Mo. 1986) (Plaintiff's Trial Brief at 9).

17. CA No. 79-110-MAC (M.D. Ga. June 5, 1981).

18. *McDonald v. Armontrout* Plaintiff's Brief, *supra* note 16, at 9.

19. *Feamster v. Brierton,* No. 79-132-Civ.-J.C. (M.D. Fla. Sept. 25, 1979) (Restoring contact visitation for death row inmates after prison officials had eliminated it).

20. CA No. H-78-987 (S.D. Texas October 21, 1983).

21. 609 F. Supp. 1432 (M.D. Tenn. 1985) appeal dismissed 788 F.2d 356 (6th Cir. 1986).

22. 679 F.2d 1115 (5th Cir. 1982).

23. See *Ruiz v. Estelle,* 666 F.2d 854, 869 (5th Cir. 1982).

24. Brief for *Amicus Curiae* NAACP Legal Defense Fund, *Groseclose v. Dutton* No. 86-5448 (6th Cir. 1986) (Hereinafter referred to as *Amicus Curiae*) at 7. The inmates were allowed to play dominoes or exercise in a 12' x 15' yard.

25. The stipulations were approved on October 21, 1983 and February 18, 1984. They were reproduced as an appendix to Johnson and Carroll, *supra* note 2.

26. *Amicus Curiae* at 8.

27. On June 28, 1984, the district court issued an order approving the *Report of the Special Master Concerning the Fourteenth Monitor's Report of Factual Observations to the Special Master—Report on Stipulation and Order Regarding Death Row Conditions.*

In that order the court remarked that the parties to this case, the TDC employees involved in the experimental death row program and the Office of the Special Master, are each to be commended for the success of their cooperative efforts in this area. Both the smooth implementation of this innovative program design and the growth opportunities which it has offered to TDC prisoners under sentence of death constitute noteworthy achievements in the lengthy history of this complex case.

The findings of fact made by the Special Master in his Report reflect this success, and are supported by ample evidence.

28. *Amicus Curia, supra* note 24, at 11-12.
29. *Amicus Curiae* at 12.
30. *Id.*
31. *Amicus Curiae* at 14.
32. *Id.* at 1435.
33. *Id.*
34. *Groseclose v. Dutton, supra* note 9, at 1435-1438.
35. *Groseclose v. Dutton,* 788 F.2d 356, 360 (6th Cir. 1986).
36. See generally Johnson and Carroll, *supra* note 2, at 8-17 to 8-19.
37. In a study done of Florida death row inmates, the authors estimated

. . .[t]hat only about 15 of the 208 men (on death row) receive weekly visits, 60 others are visited about once a month and less than half receive a visit in any given year.

Radelet, Vandiver and Berardo, "Families, Prisons and Men with Death Sentences," *Journal of Family Issues,* 593, 603 (December 1983) (Hereinafter referred to as Radelet, Vandiver and Berardo).
38. Radelet, Vandiver and Berardo, *supra* note 37 at 603.
39. In some states with classification systems for death row inmates, death row inmates deemed to be a security risk will have less visitation time or have visitation time taken away from them.
40. Unless otherwise noted, information about conditions on death rows that is referenced in this chapter comes from an informal survey of death row conditions done by the author. The author prepared a short questionnaire, which was then distributed to attorneys who were representing death row inmates, to persons who were familiar with death row conditions and to some death row inmates. No attempt was made to solicit information from prison officials. Previous studies indicate that there will be some differences in the responses of inmates and prison officials. See generally, Elske, Kudsk and Meyer, *supra* note 13. The information contained in the surveys was then supplemented by calls to lawyers and on one occasion to prison officials who were familiar with the death rows in their states.
41. *Rhem v. Malcolm,* 371 F. Supp. 594, 602 (S.D.N.Y. 1974).
42. *Id.*
43. The sense of rejection and abandonment that death row inmates feel has been variously described.

". . . Death Row makes men feel trapped, suffocated and even entombed," Johnson, "Life under Sentence of Death," in *The Pains of Imprisonment* 129, 140 (R. Johnson & H. Toch, eds. 1982). "The death sentence is the ultimate rejection society can impose. No other status is so demeaning and damaging as that of being formally condemned as unfit to live." Radelet, Vandiver and Berardo, *supra* note 37 at 597.

44. As of March 1, 1988 the five largest death rows are found in Florida (278), Texas (260), Califorina (214), Georgia (108), and Illinois (107). Of those, only Texas does not permit contact visitation.

45. Florida, California, Georgia, Illinois, Alabama, Arizona, Tennessee, South Carolina, Missouri, Indiana, Nevada, Kentucky, Maryland, and Nebraska permit contact visitation. Texas, Idaho, Pennsylvania, Ohio, North Carolina, Oklahoma, Louisiana, Mississippi, Arkansas, Virginia, and New Jersey do not.

46. The term *out-of-cell time* as it is used in this chapter does not include time spent in visitation because for most death-sentenced inmates, visitation is rare. See Radelet, Vandiver and Berardo note 37, *supra.*

47. 485 F. Supp. 122 (D. Colo. 1979) *aff'd in pertinent part* 639 F.2d 559 (10th Cir. 1980) *cert. denied,* 450 U.S. 1041 (1981).

48. *Id.* at 158 (quoting *Laaman v. Helgemoe,* 437 F. Supp. 269, 309 (D.N.H. 1977) (citations omitted). See also, *Ruiz v. Estelle,* 679 F.2d 1115 (5th Cir. 1982), *modified* 688 F.2d 266, *cert. denied,* 408 U.S. 1042 (1983); *Spain v. Procunier,* 600 F.2d 189 (9th Cir. 1979).

49. In Georgia, death row inmates receive a minimum of 32 hours out-of-cell time, and are guaranteed at least six hours of outdoor recreation. In Kentucky, all death-sentenced inmates receive approximately 5 3/4 hours of out-of-cell time per day, seven days a week. They are allowed to eat in the main prison dining room and exercise in the prison gymnasium. In Virginia, all death-sentenced inmates are allowed out of their cells in groups of six or seven from 8 a.m. to 9 p.m. They eat meals outside of their cells and receive 10 hours a week of outdoor exercise.

50. There are other states with similarly little out-of-cell time—Pennsylvania (two hours per day of exercise, with the inmates exercising in separate kennels); Oklahoma (two hours of outdoor exercise per day).

51. Johnson and Carroll, *supra* note 2 at 8-16 to 8-17.

52. See Deposition of Robert Sarver, *Jacobs v. Locke, supra* note 14; Murton, "Treatment of Condemned Prisoners," 15 Crime & Delinquency 94 (1969).

53. The author has based this and the other assessments contained in this section on the examination of two critera—visitation conditions and out-of-cell time. In his experience, these are the best indicators of how humane a death row is. No attempt has been made to visit every death row or to survey inmates and staff as to their qualitative assessments of the conditions of confinement. This assessment is based on the author's previously stated conclusion that no death row that denies contact visitation and provides only limited out-of-cell time can be humane.

54. Texas is the only state where a serious attempt has been made to employ death row inmates in productive, revenue producing labor.

55. Missouri is currently operating under a consent decree that provides for 16 hours out-of-cell time per week. That figure is to increase to 24 hours per week on April 1, 1987 and to 32 hours per week on April 1, 1988. *McDonald v. Armontrout,* No. 85-422-CV-C-5 (W.D. Mo. January 7, 1987) (consent decree approved).

56. The death-sentenced inmates are housed in units within the prison called pods that are really separated housing units within the prison itself. In Virginia, for example, there are six to seven men housed in each pod.

57. In Pennsylvania, there is no contact visitation, and out-of-cell time is limited to two hours per day of exercise alone in separate kennels. In Ohio, there is no contact visitation, and out-of-cell time is limited to two one-hour walks per week and a one-hour

per month recreational period. In Louisiana, there is no contact visitation, and out-of-cell time is limited to one hour a day five days a week. In New Jersey, there is no contact visitation, and out-of-cell time is limited to one hour of recreation per day. In Arkansas, there is no contact visitation, and out-of-cell time is limited to three one-hour exercise periods per week.

58. Johnson and Carroll, *supra,* note 2. Although the comment was not directed at the death rows of the referenced states, the comment is certainly applicable.

59. Letter from an unnamed death-sentenced inmate on file with the author.

60. Johnson, *Condemned to Die* at 110 (Elsevier Press 1981).

61. In a previous part of this chapter the author identified four correctional systems that seemed to offer exceptionally humane treatment to their death-sentenced inmates. In three of them, Texas, California, and Georgia, there was litigation about death row. In Kentucky, litigation about general segregation conditions had a positive effect on death row. See, *Kendrick v. Bland,* 541 F. Supp. 21 (W.D. Ky. 1981). All of this litigation was "totality of circumstances" litigation that attacked the general conditions of confinement on death row rather than attacking a single issue such as visitation. The "totality of circumstances" approach offers the most hope for successful litigation of death row conditions. See Johnson and Carroll, *supra* note 2 and Akron, *supra* note 2.

62. The only exception is Pennsylvania where a suit is in progress, *Peterkin v. Thornburgh.* The case has been tried and is awaiting decision.

63. Greenberg, "Capital Punishment as a System," 91 *Yale L.J.* 908, 916 (1982).

CASE INDEX

SUBJECT INDEX

NAME INDEX

ABOUT THE AUTHORS

HUGO ADAM BEDAU is Austin Fletcher Professor of Philosophy at Tufts University. His Ph.D. is from Harvard University, where he was a Liberal Arts Fellow at the Law School; he has also been a Visiting Fellow at the Institute for Criminology, Cambridge University. His publications on the death penalty include *Death is Different: Studies in the Morality, Law, and Politics of Capital Punishment* (1987) and *The Death Penalty in America* (3rd ed., 1982).

WILLIAM J. BOWERS is Director of the Center for Applied Social Research at Northeastern University and author of two books on capital punishment: *Executions in America* (1974) and *Legal Homicide* (1984). His research on the death penalty examines both its arbitrary and discriminatory imposition and its deterrent or brutalizing effect on society. He has also studied the implementation and impact of gun control legislation, tort law decisions, and civil rights law.

JOHN L. CARROLL is presently a U. S. Magistrate for the Middle District of Alabama. In 1985-1986 he was a Professor of Law at Mercer University School of Law. He has also taught law at the University of Alabama and Georgia State University. Prior to entering the teaching profession, he was a practicing lawyer. He received his Juris Doctor (magna cum laude) from Samford University in 1974, and his Master's of Law from Harvard University in 1975. Recent publications include "The Defense Lawyer's Role in the Sentencing Process: You've Got to Accentuate the Positive and Eliminate the Negative" in the *Mercer Law Review* (1986); "Litigating Death Row Conditions: The Case for Reform," in *Prisoners and the Law* (edited by Ira P. Robbins, 1985); and *Post Conviction Remedies in Alabama* (1984).

DENNIS D. DORIN is Associate Professor of Political Science and Adjunct Professor of Criminal Justice at the University of North Carolina at Charlotte. He has written extensively about the decision making of Supreme Court Justice Tom C. Clark in publications such as *Judicature, Law and the Legal Process* (edited by Victoria L. Swigert (1982)) and *Harry S. Truman The Man From Independence* (edited by William F. Levantrosser, 1986). His major research interest is the U. S. Supreme Court's criminal justice policymaking, and he has published a number of works on this topic including "Two Different Worlds: Criminologists, Justices, and Racial Discrimination in the Imposition of Capital Punishment in Rape Cases," in the *Journal of Criminal Law and Criminology* (1981).

PHOEBE C. ELLSWORTH is Professor of Law and of Psychology at the University of Michigan. She completed her Ph.D. in social psychology at Stanford in 1970. She taught psychology at Yale from 1971-1981, and at Stanford from 1981-1987. She has published on various topics involving psychology and law, including jury decision making, criminal procedure, family law, and the use (and misuse) of social science evidence by legal decision makers.

KENNETH C. HAAS is an Associate Professor in the Division of Criminal Justice and the Department of Political Science at the University of Delaware where he has twice won the University's Excellence-in-Teaching Award. He specializes in criminal procedure and the law of corrections and postconviction remedies. His articles have appeared in both law reviews and social science journals, and he is coeditor of *The Dilemmas of Punishment* (1986) and *Crime and the Criminal Justice Process* (1978). His scholarly work has been cited in many law review articles and by the U.S. Supreme Court.

VALERIE P. HANS is Associate Professor of Criminal Justice and Psychology at the University of Delaware, where she specializes in the area of psychology and law. She received a Ph.D. in psychology from the University of Toronto in 1978. She has conducted research studies on factors influencing juries and on public attitudes toward the courts. Her coauthored book, *Judging the Jury,* was published in 1986. Funded by an NIMH fellowship in psychology and law, she spent the 1986-1987 academic year at Stanford University, teaching a course on jury decision making and attending law classes.

JAMES A. INCIARDI is Professor and Director of the Division of Criminal Justice at the University of Delaware. He received his Ph.D. in sociology at New York University, and has extensive research, teaching, field, and clinical experience in the areas of criminology, criminal justice, and substance abuse. He is a former editor of *Criminology: An Interdisciplinary Journal.* He has done extensive consulting work both nationally and internationally, and has published more than 100 articles, chapters, and books in the areas of criminology, criminal justice, law, history, folklore, substance abuse, and medicine.

ANNMARIE KAZYAKA is working toward her doctoral degree at the Institute of Criminal Justice and Criminology at the University of Maryland. Her research interest lies in the area of sentencing. Currently, she is examining the proportionality of capital sentencing in South Carolina and is doing research on the effects of judicial characteristics on the sentencing of felony offenders.

RAYMOND PATERNOSTER is an Associate Professor in the Institute of Criminal Justice and Criminology at the University of Maryland. He has published articles in the area of capital punishment and deterrence. Currently, he is examining the proportionality of capital sentencing in South Carolina and is doing research that attempts to integrate perceptual deterrence with social control theory.

MICHAEL L. RADELET is an Associate Professor in the Sociology Department at the University of Florida. His Ph.D. is from Purdue University, and his two major areas of interest are medical ethics and capital punishment. A frequent visitor to death row, he has published articles on such topics as race and capital punishment, the families of death row inmates, and the issue of mental competency to be executed.

JEFFREY REIMAN is Professor of Philosophy and Justice at the American University in Washington, D.C. He is the author of *In Defense of Political Philosophy* (1972), *The Rich Get Richer and the Poor Get Prison: Ideology, Class and Criminal Justice* (2nd ed., 1984), and numerous articles in scholarly journals on moral issues in criminal justice, including "Justice, Civilization, and the Death Penalty" in *Philosophy and Public Affairs* (1985) and "The Marxian Critique of Criminal Justice" in *Criminal Justice Ethics* (1987).

VICTOR L. STREIB is Professor of Law at Cleveland State University. As a researcher, he has written over 100 papers, articles, chapters, and books on juvenile and criminal justice. As a lawyer, he has served both as a juvenile court prosecutor and as a defense attorney and now is cocounsel in a juvenile death penalty case before the U.S. Supreme Court. His decade of research on the juvenile death penalty is reported in detail in his latest book, *Death Penalty for Juveniles* (1987).

NOTES

NOTES